Rural Living in *France*

A Survival Handbook

by

J.C. Jeremy Hobson

SURVIVAL BOOKS • LONDON • ENGLAND

First Edition 2006

Survival Books Limited
26 York Street, London W1U 6PZ, United Kingdom
☎ +44 (0)20-7788 7644, ▤ +44 (0)870-762 3212
✉ info@survivalbooks.net
💻 www.survivalbooks.net

To order books, please refer to page 287.

British Library Cataloguing in Publication Data.
A CIP record for this book is available from the British Library.
ISBN 1 901130 99 1

Printed and bound in Italy by Legoprint spa.

ACKNOWLEDGEMENTS

There are so many people to thank for their help in compiling *Rural Living in France*: in particular the many readers of my 'Rural Riddles' column in *French Property News*, whose questions and comments have, whether they realise it or not, contributed greatly to my decisions as to what information is most likely to be of assistance to those planning to live in rural France. Very special thanks must go to Phil Rant – both he and I know why! Others to whom I am sincerely indebted include Melinda Hobson for her computer expertise, Roger Morris for research on my behalf, Phil Pembroke for help with the fishing section and permission to use some of his previously published work, Laurence Huber of the European Mediation Centre, Karen Tait (Editor of *French Property News*) and Liz Wright (Editor of *Smallholding*).

I would also like to thank Sue Coleman and Phil Stevens for their invaluable help and willingness to share their knowledge of rural living in France and their permission to use emails and website information, which I found invaluable in the writing of **Chapter 8**, 'Other Livestock'. Thanks also to Bob Batty, David Bland, Steven and Lynn Cluer, Sandy and Eric Compton, Bob Dalton, Carole Deedman, John Maslin and Steve Midgley. My thanks are also due to Joe Laredo for editing the text, Alex Browning and David Hampshire for proofreading, Kerry Laredo for the layout and Jim Watson for the amusing cartoons, cover and colour pages. Finally, I must thank Joe Laredo and Peter Read for suggesting that I write this book in the first place.

What Readers & Reviewers

When you buy a model plane for your child, a video recorder, or some new computer gizmo, you get with it a leaflet or booklet pleading 'Read Me First', or bearing large friendly letters or bold type saying 'IMPORTANT – follow the instructions carefully'. This book should be similarly supplied to all those entering France with anything more durable than a 5-day return ticket. It is worth reading even if you are just visiting briefly, or if you have lived here for years and feel totally knowledgeable and secure. But if you need to find out how France works then it is indispensable. Native French people probably have a less thorough understanding of how their country functions. – Where it is most essential, the book is most up to the minute.

Living France

Rarely has a 'survival guide' contained such useful advice. This book dispels doubts for first-time travellers, yet is also useful for seasoned globetrotters – In a word, if you're planning to move to the USA or go there for a long-term stay, then buy this book both for general reading and as a ready-reference.

American Citizens Abroad

It is everything you always wanted to ask but didn't for fear of the contemptuous put down – The best English-language guide – Its pages are stuffed with practical information on everyday subjects and are designed to complement the traditional guidebook.

Swiss News

A complete revelation to me – I found it both enlightening and interesting, not to mention amusing.

Carole Clark

Let's say it at once. David Hampshire's ***Living and Working in France*** is the best handbook ever produced for visitors and foreign residents in this country; indeed, my discussion with locals showed that it has much to teach even those born and bred in l'Hexagone. – It is Hampshire's meticulous detail which lifts his work way beyond the range of other books with similar titles. Often you think of a supplementary question and search for the answer in vain. With Hampshire this is rarely the case. – He writes with great clarity (and gives French equivalents of all key terms), a touch of humour and a ready eye for the odd (and often illuminating) fact. – This book is absolutely indispensable.

The Riviera Reporter

A mine of information – I may have avoided some embarrassments and frights if I had read it prior to my first Swiss encounters – Deserves an honoured place on any newcomer's bookshelf.

English Teachers Association, Switzerland

Have Said About Survival Books

What a great work, wealth of useful information, well-balanced wording and accuracy in details. My compliments!

Thomas Müller

This handbook has all the practical information one needs to set up home in the UK – The sheer volume of information is almost daunting – Highly recommended for anyone moving to the UK.

American Citizens Abroad

A very good book which has answered so many questions and even some I hadn't thought of – I would certainly recommend it.

Brian Fairman

We would like to congratulate you on this work: it is really super! We hand it out to our expatriates and they read it with great interest and pleasure.

ICI (Switzerland) AG

Covers just about all the things you want to know on the subject – In answer to the desert island question about the one how-to book on France, this book would be it – Almost 500 pages of solid accurate reading – This book is about enjoyment as much as survival.

The Recorder

It's so funny – I love it and definitely need a copy of my own – Thanks very much for having written such a humorous and helpful book.

Heidi Guiliani

A must for all foreigners coming to Switzerland.

Antoinette O'Donoghue

A comprehensive guide to all things French, written in a highly readable and amusing style, for anyone planning to live, work or retire in France.

The Times

A concise, thorough account of the DOs and DON'Ts for a foreigner in Switzerland – Crammed with useful information and lightened with humorous quips which make the facts more readable.

American Citizens Abroad

Covers every conceivable question that may be asked concerning everyday life – I know of no other book that could take the place of this one.

France in Print

Hats off to ***Living and Working in Switzerland***!

Ronnie Almeida

THE AUTHOR

Jeremy Hobson is a freelance writer living in France and a member of the Association of Freelance Journalists. In 1974, he gained a Distinction in Game & Estate Management and was employed in shooting management for over 30 years. Since 1983, he has written regularly for all of the UK's country-orientated magazines and has had numerous books published. In addition, Jeremy has been involved with script writing for BBC2 television and BBC Radio 4. Unsurprisingly, his interests include all country sports, farming, gardening and poultry. He has exhibited bantams at some of the UK's most prestigious poultry shows and has judged beagles at hound shows.

Order forms are on page 287.

Contents

RURAL
LIFE

IMPORTANT NOTE

France is a large country with myriad faces and many ethnic groups, religions and customs. Although ostensibly the same throughout the country, rules and regulations tend to be open to local interpretation and are sometimes even formulated on the spot. **I cannot recommend too strongly that you check with an official and reliable source (not always the same) before making major decisions or undertaking an irreversible course of action. Don't believe everything you're told or read – even, dare I say it, herein!**

To help you obtain further information and verify data with official sources, useful addresses, references and websites have been included in most chapters and in **Appendices A, B** and **C**. Important points have been emphasised throughout the book **in bold print**, some of which it would be expensive or even dangerous to disregard. **Ignore them at your cost or peril.**

Unless specifically stated, the reference to any company, organisation, product or publication in this book doesn't constitute an endorsement or recommendation.

AUTHOR'S NOTES

- Where it may be useful, flora and fauna mentioned are identified by their Latin *genus* (the name for a group of closely-related organisms) and *species* (a unique name for each type of organism), in accordance with the Linnaeus System of nomenclature devised by Carl von Linné (*Linnaeus Carolus*, 1707-78), the Swedish-born founder of taxonomic botany. Also, when helpful, common French botanical names have been included. When attempting to find the French name of a plant or animal, check the Latin equivalent of the name you know and then compare it by looking up the French. For example, the bird known in English as the hooded crow = *Corvus cornix* = *la corneille mantelée*.
- Times are shown using the 24-hour clock, which is the usual way of expressing the time in France.
- Prices quoted should be taken only as estimates, although they were correct when going to print and usually don't change greatly overnight. Prices are quoted inclusive of tax (which is the method generally used in France) unless otherwise stated.
- His/he/him/man/men (etc.) also mean her/she/her/woman/ women. This is done simply to make life easier for the reader and, in particular, the author, and isn't intended to be sexist.
- British English is used throughout. French equivalents are given (usually in the singular) where appropriate. A glossary of useful terms can be found in **Appendix F**.
- Warnings and important points are shown in **bold** type.
- The following symbols are used in this book: ☎ (telephone), 📠 (fax), 💻 (internet) and ✉ (email).
- For those who are unfamiliar with metric weights and measures, conversion tables are included in **Appendix D**.
- A map showing the regions and *départements* of France can be found in **Appendix E**.

INTRODUCTION

Many people dream of moving to rural France – somewhere warm and sunny where days can be spent *al fresco* basking in the shade of a tree. In their mind's eye they see themselves relaxing over a leisurely lunch of newly-baked *baguettes* from the village *boulangerie*, fresh produce from the garden, mouth-watering cheeses and *charcuterie* from the local market, and a few bottles of chilled wine from a local vineyard. In the background, chickens wander from barn to garden scratching in the earth, geese graze happily in the orchard and the family pets gambol in the sun. In the winter, a plentiful supply of logs is stacked in the outhouse, while indoors a blazing fire reflects patterns on the tiled floors and the dreamers sip their *apéritifs* and bask in their good fortune . . .

It's good to dream, but what is the reality of life in rural France? ***Rural Living in France*** has been written in answer to this question. Unfortunately, the weather can be cold and wet, even on the Côte d'Azur, market produce can be expensive, livestock can contract diseases, and winters can be long and lonely – and you cannot live on panoramic views alone.

Loneliness, isolation and boredom are common experiences in rural France and have been cited by many expatriates as the reasons they returned home, especially those with little or no understanding of the language. Rural living is very different from town dwelling – no matter what country you come from. Villages can be insular and the neighbours daunting. Most rural properties require much more improvement than is realised, and, if you aren't prepared to carry out such work, you might be better off considering a more urban and modern home elsewhere. It may not be possible to find a job if money runs low as, understandably, the French look after their own before worrying about the needs of foreigners. Employment in the countryside is spasmodic, seasonal and likely to be of a casual nature.

The attractions of moving to rural France are well-documented: in the UK and elsewhere the high-income, high-outgoings treadmill of life can be stressful. French properties are still cheap by many countries' standards, although prices have been steadily rising due in no small part to the influence of TV 'lifestyle' programmes. Nevertheless, in many areas it's still possible to buy an adequate smallholding (*fermette*) for the price of a one-bedroom flat or cottage in the UK and some other countries. Mortgages, loans and other expenses can become a thing of the past by retiring early or downsizing to rural France – provided children are of an age when they can readily adapt to the language and village school life. Selling a property in a country where prices are high and ditching the mortgage while releasing enough equity to buy a house outright in France is a tempting proposition, as are growing your own vegetables, raising your own livestock and reducing your outgoings by adopting a more frugal (and satisfying) lifestyle.

In order to ensure that you're looking objectively at life in rural France, however, it's as well to face up to the realities before making any irrevocable decisions. (If you've never lived in the country, it's prudent to rent a property in rural France before burning your bridges.) ***Rural Living in France*** points out the pitfalls as well as the pleasures to those considering a lifestyle change and provides in-depth practical advice to those who've already taken the plunge. Within these pages, guidance is given on a wide range of topics as well as a wealth of references to further sources of information.

We trust this book will help you overcome or alleviate the potential problems of rural living in France and smooth your way to a happy and rewarding future in your new home.

Bon courage!

J.C. Jeremy Hobson
April 2006

1.

The Realities of Rural Life

The attractions of life in rural France are plentiful and the majority of expatriate residents cite similar reasons for moving to rural France. Generally, the climate is better than in the UK, Belgium, Germany and the Netherlands (where the majority of expatriate residents come from); the cost of living is lower; people are more willing to pass the time of day and to include you in their lives, especially if they see that you're making an effort with the language and participating in local activities. The countryside is outstanding, hugely varied and often unique – and access is easy as French landowners and farmers are generally unconcerned about visitors straying from public rights of way (see **Rambling & Hiking** on page 211).

There's peace and tranquillity in most rural regions and at night it's possible to see the constellations clearly. The huge skies make certain areas popular with painters and the clean fresh air is much appreciated – many newcomers are initially surprised at how healthily-tired they feel after a day spent in the countryside. Many expatriates insist, not in a negative way, that moving to rural France is like going back 50 years, to a time when there was less haste and aggression, and more peace and personal satisfaction. They love the courtesy of the French and their sense of family values. Young families have the opportunity of good schooling for their children, who often attain a higher academic level than they might in some other countries.

Nevertheless, the dangers of looking at life in rural France through rose-tinted spectacles are obvious and it's just as easy to have a holiday romance with an area, place or architecture as it is with a person – often with similar long-term consequences! You're likely to visit France in summer, when everywhere is active, but winters can be very quiet. The rural French make their own amusement. Cinemas and theatres, for example, may be a long way away and you obviously need to be fairly fluent in French to understand films and plays, although some cinemas in larger towns occasionally show films in their original language (*version originale* or *VO*). Bars are small, brightly lit, and sometimes uncomfortable and smoky, often closing as soon as the attached restaurants begin serving food. There are few 'take-aways' in rural areas, although mobile pizza vans visit some villages one evening a week.

Small villages and their inhabitants can be insular and you may be the source of gossip, which isn't always friendly. Without knowing it, you can find yourself alienated by choosing the wrong locals to be friendly with. There are plenty of petty rivalries, jealousies and even feuds amongst local families and if you offer a drink to the first person who tries to strike up a conversation with you in the local *bar/tabac*, you could be ignored by your more immediate neighbours or people you would rather mix with (see also **Meeting the Neighbours** on page 54).

Families arriving in France with children of school age can experience other problems. Generally, youngsters of primary school age fit easily into the local school, but teenagers will probably resent leaving their friends in their home country and may well experience considerable difficulty integrating into the French school system, which is pitched at a higher curriculum level than the British system, for example (it can be as much as two years ahead of what is being taught in UK schools at the same age). Teenagers used to walking down the street or catching a bus to meet their friends will – when they make new friends in France – find a huge difference, as in rural areas it can be difficult to get anywhere out of school hours. A regular bus service is unlikely and parents usually end up running a taxi service until children can drive – or accept the risk of their riding a moped. And the French language as it's taught in British schools won't help them much when all their school friends are conversing in slang or the local patois.

Although there are plenty of local workmen and *artisans*, they won't be much use to you if you cannot communicate with them in order to make them understand what you want them to do – always assuming that you can get them to come to see you in the first place. The pace of life is very slow and, although you may get a plumber to commit himself to coming on Tuesday, it's a very different matter pinning him down to a particular Tuesday! And when he does come, it's a pretty safe bet that he will arrive late, take himself off for a two-hour lunch break and depart early, often leaving a job half finished.

Rural communities are more likely to experience power cuts due to trees falling on overhead cables (see **Electricity** on page 47) and, like broadband, underground cables may be of low priority when there are more densely populated urban areas to be connected.

Like it or not, shooting and hunting (*la chasse*) are an integral part of French rural life and you may find your peaceful Sunday mornings disturbed by members of the local *commune* firing shotguns in the proximity of your boundary, and their dogs rushing through your open kitchen door and polishing off the food you'd left out for the cats (see **Hunting, Shooting & Fishing** on page 202).

Treat every small success as a triumph and be ready and waiting for the first hurdle – it's bound to arrive within days – but never give up; otherwise you might as well stay ensconced in your old life.

GENERAL CONSIDERATIONS

If you dream of peace and tranquillity, an abundance of flora and fauna, contact with neighbours and village life, the idea of living in rural France must appeal. Before proceeding further, however, it's important to draw up a list of 'fors' and 'againsts', as well as asking yourself some soul-searching questions, including the following:

- Why exactly do you want to live in France? Is it because you want to live a less stressful life in a sunny location – or is it because you know France well, can speak the language and all the sums add up?
- In what part of the country do you want to live? Are you open-minded, provided it's somewhere picturesque and the village is a pretty place to show off to visitors – or are you set on a particular region or department in an area close to an airport, port or shopping centre?
- Have you worked out where the money to live on is going to come from? Are you full of vague ideas and think you can easily convert part of your rural property into B&B or *gîte* accommodation and turn it into a money-making success once you're established or have you carefully researched the local economy and likely sources of income? If you're retired, have you calculated that your pension, less tax, will cover all your expenses? If you need to work, have you established contacts with employment agencies and found out what qualifications you might require?
- How 'rural' is rural in your eyes? Is it kilometres away from your nearest neighbour because you love the idea of sitting in your own woodland drinking a glass of locally-produced wine and admiring the river that runs through your property – or is it on the outskirts of a village so as to be close to shops and a primary school?
- If you have children, are you assuming they will adapt to a change of language, culture and school system – or have you investigated the schooling options available, the likely problems they will encounter and possible solutions?
- Have you experienced isolation and hard work before, in both winter and summer, when logs need chopping and fetching or animals/gardens need watering – or will a few months of cold, dark nights be a small price to pay for an idyllic summer lifestyle (and you never venture out much at night anyway)?
- What do you plan to do about medical cover? Are you going to worry about that when you get there and rely on your European health insurance card until you need to make other arrangements – or have you

investigated making social security contributions in France and how much this will cost?

- Having decided to move to rural France, are you crossing your fingers and hoping it will all turn out as you've imagined – or have you read all you can on the subject (you can do no better than read Survival Books' other books on France – see page 287) and opened a bank account in order to transfer money for the purchase of a property?

If you can identify with the first part of the above questions more than the second part, there's a good chance that you aren't yet facing up to realities of French rural living and need to clarify your objectives and narrow your options before taking the plunge. The following points may help you clarify your thoughts.

CLIMATE

The opportunity to get away from cold and wet weather is often one of the major attractions of moving to *la France profonde*, but it's necessary to research all the areas you think might be suitable. If you're looking primarily for a change in climate, you will probably eliminate the northern parts of the country and begin your search somewhere south of the Loire. But what about the extremes of temperature and excessive wind, rain, frost and snow that some regions experience? France is such a huge country that many areas are excessively hot in summer and below freezing in winter. If you're a keen gardener or want to become self-sufficient, you need to know which areas of France are likely to produce the best results for the plants you want to grow and the animals you want to keep.

It might seem a little thing, but can you cope with mud? The sun doesn't shine every day, even in the south of France, and there's a good chance that whilst maintaining your land or renovating your property in the winter months, you won't be able to avoid bringing mud into the house. Therefore you will have to decide early on whether to spend your life cleaning it up or simply learn to live with it.

FINANCIAL CONSIDERATIONS

Just because the cost of living in France is lower than in your home country, you shouldn't be tempted into thinking that you can live on virtually nothing. Even if you've disposed of a mortgage and have a few thousand euros in the bank, French rural properties are notorious for their ability to eat away at your savings, especially if there's major renovation work to be done. Do you have enough money to convert not only the house, but also any outbuildings – or at least make them safe? For example, will the house need re-wiring, necessitating the hire of a generator whilst the work is being carried out? What about the cost of installing a new septic tank, bearing in mind the demands of the new legislation (see **Sewerage** on page 36)? A new one can easily cost around €5,000. It's common for people to underestimate the cost of renovation and restoration by at least 50 per cent.

If you plan to start a smallholding there's likely to be the expense of purchasing wire netting and fence posts. If you've never owned property with a large amount of land before coming to France, it's unlikely that you will possess the tools and specialised equipment necessary for its management (see **Chapter 9**) and their purchase will obviously add to your costs. If you want to exploit your land (see **Chapter 4**), you will have to pay out money long before you have any hope of seeing a return, if indeed you're ever in that fortunate position. Being self-sufficient is possible, but there's the initial expense of buying livestock, seedlings and plants, and even if you eventually succeed you must face the fact that you're never going to sell enough surplus produce to pay for things such as petrol, fuel and property tax. **One of the reasons people fail to realise their dream of a rural lifestyle is that they under-estimate the amount of money they can live on.** A good rule of thumb is to reckon on needing at least a third of your previous income, even if you have no mortgage to repay.

Even searching for your ideal home can cost much more than you think. You will be lucky if you find it on your first trip and, even if you do, there are the costs of returning to sign various forms, when you may need overnight accommodation. Ferry crossings and flights (which may be at peak times) soon add up, as do petrol bills and hire cars.

If you're considering obtaining a French mortgage, it's important to remember that if your income is from a non-euro country such as the UK, an adverse change in the exchange rate could leave you struggling. For more details of the financial implications of purchasing property in France, read *Buying a Home in France* (Survival Books – see page 287).

ACCESSIBILITY

Rural doesn't necessarily mean remote. You can be in or on the outskirts of a village of 1,000 or 2,000 inhabitants and enjoy a rural existence while benefiting from easy access to shops, schools and other essential services.

In remote districts, on the other hand, you will have to use transport (invariably a car, as public transport will be severely limited or non-existent) every time you want a loaf of bread, and the nearest 'nightlife' may be at least a half hour's drive away – and probably no more than the local *bar/tabac*. If you have a strong interest in a particular sport or hobby, the distance you have to travel to engage in it may be prohibitive.

If you have friends and family members in another country, you will probably want to see them periodically and, with your idyllic rural property and the opportunity of cheap holidays, they will definitely want to come and see you! Bearing this in mind, how far from the nearest ferry port or airport do you want to be? Do the cheap airlines fly to your nearest airport or is it serviced by only the more expensive ones?

PLANTS & ANIMALS

If you have dreams of self-sufficiency, the weather is obviously important, but of more concern is how much land is attached to the property you eventually buy or rent. You obviously need to have some idea as to your intentions so that you don't commit yourself to too much or too little land: a huge vegetable plot to sustain you and your family may seem desirable, but can you manage it on your own? If, on your *fermette*, you intend to keep animals, are the soil conditions suitable to allow a small flock of sheep to over-winter without turning the fields into a quagmire? When you want to return 'home' for family occasions, will there be anyone to look after the livestock? Any animal, even the family pet, is a daily commitment, and it may not be easy to make alternative arrangements in a foreign country where the nearest neighbours live a kilometre or more away.

INTEGRATION

You must choose where you want to live very carefully, not only in terms of business opportunities, but also with regard to your social life – in particular whether you wish to be in an area where there are lots of your fellow countrymen or in one where there are only French people. In either case, be prepared to immerse yourself in French life as a means of being accepted and don't cling onto expatriate neighbours just because they speak your language; ask yourself whether you'd have chosen them as friends at home. No matter how poor your French, always try to use it when talking to neighbours, shop assistants and officials, and never be arrogant enough to presume that they should understand English. The reality is that if you speak little or no French when you arrive, you might struggle for years to enjoy a proper friendship with your French neighbours and will be at a huge disadvantage at any social gathering, being able to understand only half (or less) of what is said, let alone managing adequately to express your thoughts and feelings. The French might appear arrogant, but that's how they've managed to preserve their culture and lifestyle, which presumably you're moving to France to enjoy – and anyway, they're the natives and you're the foreigner!

With very few exceptions, French rural dwellers are welcoming and polite. Things might be different in Paris and other large cities, but in sequestered villages you're invariably greeted with a handshake and a comment as to the weather or your health. Much of the charm of living in France lies in observing local customs as you go about your daily business. In few other countries can you sit in a bar and be acknowledged by every person who enters. Quite often each new customer will go around the tables shaking hands before settling down for a drink. Where else can you sit in a restaurant and be wished "*Bon appétit*" as fellow diners take their seats around you? Not only are you wished it, but it always sounds sincere. Even youngsters aren't exempt from the conventions and greet each other and their elders without embarrassment. For the rural French, the weekly market (see **Markets** on page 243) is an opportunity to meet friends and acquaintances and catch up with local gossip; if you're noticed there by a neighbour, you will be introduced and included in the conversation – leaving you with a strange sense of pride at being accepted.

THE SYSTEM

It's essential that you realise the importance of belonging to the French 'system' – you will endear yourself to no one if you take from it and give nothing back. The French population might have made a national pastime of 'playing the system', but you as an outsider shouldn't even contemplate it. A *carte de séjour* is no longer essential, but is available if you ask and will show that you respect the formalities of becoming a resident. You should register at your local *mairie*, even if only as a matter of courtesy, and if you're planning to live in the country full-time you will need to apply for a *carte vitale* and consider taking out complementary medical insurance (see **Health Insurance** on page 46).

Your local tax office (*hôtel des impôts*) will be keen to get its hands on your money via the annual *taxes d'habitation* and *foncière*, and various organisations with mysterious acronyms will demand hefty *contributions sociales*. Therefore you should apply for the various forms and get yourself into the system as soon as possible after arrival – the *administration* will catch up with you sooner or later if you don't. As with all aspects of French bureaucracy, there's a lot of form filling to be done when you arrive, but generally each step will be explained as you go along. It's worthwhile taking as many documents as possible with you when visiting any official office, as you're sure to be asked for some form of identification and proof of address. Passport, birth certificate, papers confirming your marital status, a copy of your house purchase contract, utility bills (electricity, water, etc.) and your French bank account details will all prove to be essential requirements when you begin playing the snakes and ladders game of 'living in rural France'.

The *Maire* & *Notaire*

It's important that you get on well with the local *maire* and the *notaire* handling your home purchase. The latter you will meet when signing the agreements relating to the purchase and again whenever you need a document witnessed or when you want to prepare a French will. The *notaire* definitely makes a better friend than an enemy and a good one is to be looked after at all costs – a bottle of quality (single-malt, not blended) whisky offered at Christmas can result in minor fees being waived for the rest of the year!

A similar gift left with the *maire* (the *maire* is the person, the *mairie* his office) is also a wise investment and, if your *mairie* is a small one, a pot plant, bunch of flowers or bottle of good wine given to the *réceptionniste* will ensure that any future requests for an appointment or simply for general information are promptly granted. If you're having a party at which guests are expected to wander and mingle rather than a more intimate sit-down affair, extend an invitation to the *maire* and his partner; nine times out of ten they will be delighted to come and it might be the ideal opportunity to outline any plans you have for the property whilst they're on site and in a receptive mood!

Neighbours

Most inhabitants of rural France care for their family, friends and neighbours. An offer to help is often made without any ulterior motive or expectation of reciprocation or reward. National politeness ensures that you're never left standing on the doorstep when you have cause to visit a neighbour, but it's still an honour to be invited into someone's home for dinner or *l'apéritif*, even if such an invitation arouses as much anxiety as pleasure (see **Meeting the**

Neighbours on page 54). In most countries, a bottle of wine or a bunch of flowers is the usual gift to take for the host and hostess, but you can easily insult French neighbours by offering them a mediocre bottle (especially if they're wine-makers themselves!).

A stunning display of chrysanthemums, which would be greeted with delight in the UK, is bad luck in France, where they're only ever placed on the graves of dead relatives on 1st November, All Saints' Day (see **Beliefs & Superstitions** on page 239). A box of eggs from your own chickens is a better bet, although in a farming community this may be the equivalent of 'coals to Newcastle'. Play safe and take something home-made or a product only available in your home country. A *faux pas* will never be pointed out to you, however; whatever the present, it will be received with gratitude and is almost certain to be repaid by perhaps a box of vegetables left on your doorstep a few days later.

As with any country or group of people, there are exceptions to every rule and it's possible to encounter unhelpful and surly neighbours in France just as it is anywhere else. In some areas, they may resent newcomers, either because they're unused to them or, as in the highly publicised cases in Brittany in 2005, because they object to expatriates 'colonising' their villages (see **Choosing a Property** on page 31). Occasionally, for no apparent reason at all, they're downright hostile to foreigners and in many cases, irritatingly ignorant and condescending. Don't always take this hostility at face value, however, as once you've persevered with building up a relationship you often find that the individuals concerned appreciate your efforts and become good friends. Also, an attitude that might originally be seen as patronising may in fact be an example of the French sense of humour, which can at first be difficult to grasp and a little daunting.

Good neighbours can help in the most unexpected ways, but there's no limit to the trouble you can encounter from bad ones (see **Bonfires & Noise** on page 240).

FOR SALE
€20,000
OR NEAR OFFER
20 HECTARES

2.

Buying Rural Property

When it comes to choosing your property, location is of prime importance. If all you know is that you want to live in rural France but have no particular knowledge of an area, there are more scientific ways of coming to a decision than by closing your eyes and sticking a pin in a map!

CHOOSING AN AREA

There are many considerations when it comes to choosing a particular area in which to put down roots. The climate is an important factor for most (see page 21), especially if you're a gardening enthusiast or sun-worshipper, but important though it is, it's just one of the many deciding factors. Never lose sight of the fact that France is the largest country in Europe (it's more than twice the size of the UK) and certain parts are not easily accessible. If you have family abroad and it's important for you to be able to visit them easily, it's essential that your chosen area has reasonable access to motorways, airports or ferry ports, as appropriate (see **Accessibility** on page 22).

As a newcomer to the world of smallholdings, you will need to ensure that a certain location ticks all the boxes when it comes to good grassland and a climate in which your livestock isn't going to scorch in summer and freeze in winter (see **Plants & Animals** on page 23) and that, should you wish to sell your produce, there's a likely market for it locally (see **Selling Products & Produce** on page 192). If you're against the principle of shooting animals, don't consider an area in which it's a way of life for local *commune* members.

In addition to all this, there's the proximity of other expatriates to consider. Do you want to be in an area well populated by other foreigners or would you rather 'go it alone' and adopt a truly French lifestyle – and, if so, can you cope with the lifestyle and language, including the local patois?

Availability of the type of property you're looking for also needs to be considered and comparisons made between the price of similar houses in different parts of the country.

If you have no idea where you want to live, buy yourself a large road map that covers the whole of France and begin your search by identifying the forested areas, the fertile farming regions and the more mountainous parts, all of which should be obvious from the colour variations. When you've narrowed your choice, it's worth buying local maps and checking whether any particular features such as railway stations, quarry workings, waterways and woodland might be important factors in your eventual decision. The large scale *Carte Bleue* series is most likely to include the necessary information and can be bought from supermarkets, bookshops and some *bar/tabacs*.

Once you've found an area that interests you, you will need to carry out a great deal of research. Start by finding out all you can about the region and whether there will enough activity there to keep you happy. It's all very well whiling away the summer evenings in the garden, but it's a very different matter in the winter when you're faced with a choice between the TV and the radio, when you really want to go to the theatre or attend an evening class. For detailed information on each area of France, refer to ***The Best Places to Buy a Home in France*** (Survival Books – see page 287).

During the above process you will begin to see more clearly what it is you expect from your rural home. Everyone's hopes and expectations are different, ranging from a vegetable garden to a view. List your own priorities, which may include location, house size, family requirements, budget available, any financial expectations of the property or land, making a living, pursuing a hobby and, perhaps most importantly, your own and your partner's capabilities and health. This will help you to narrow your search and focus your mind on what's most important to you and your family.

CHOOSING A PROPERTY

Your next move must be to spend some time in each of the candidate areas, seeing what you get for your money and comparing property prices. It isn't enough to simply instruct an agent from the UK or elsewhere and, in any case, you won't find many specialising in property with land attached. It's far better – and more fun – to look in the *immobliers*' windows in the hope of finding something that catches your eye.

In France, most estate agents expect you to make an appointment as if you were going to the doctor, although it's always worth popping in on the off chance. You need to have a clear idea of what you're looking for – e.g. how many rooms, size of plot, number of outbuildings and the condition of the property; you cannot expect an estate agent to know the picture you have in your head, and many become frustrated after showing prospective clients houses which from the vague outline given they thought might be suitable, only to find after several hours touring the area that it's another sort of home altogether that you're after.

When considering old properties that might be suitable, do your own investigations and don't rely entirely on the information provided by an estate agent or vendor. French estate agents are no different from those found anywhere else and often exaggerate a property's attractions and underplay its faults: '*habitable*' can mean virtually derelict, while '*à rénover*' implies that major construction is likely! Bear in mind that some rural properties lack basic services such as electricity, water and sanitation (see **Checks** on page 33).

Take advice from any English-speaking people already living in the area. If you don't know anybody personally, go to the *mairie*, explain what and why you want to know, and ask whether they can give you the names and addresses of any English-speakers in the *commune* – which is also a good way of finding out what local attitudes are towards foreigners buying property in the area. You can also access property offers by logging onto the Société d'Aménagement Foncier et d'Etablissement Rural (SAFER)'s rural property offers website (💻 www.frenchland.com) and the SAFER website itself (💻 www.safer-fr.com – click on '*propriétés*').

Finally, bear in mind that, unless you're very fortunate, you will inevitably have to make some compromises on your original ideal.

SURVIVAL TIP

One very important point to remember is that whilst it's relatively easy to change a house and buildings to suit your needs, it's virtually impossible to change the character of land.

Size of Property

Hectares (ha) are the usual measure of land in France. If you're accustomed to thinking in acres, it's therefore useful to know a few rough conversions. There are 2.471 acres in a hectare, so you won't be far out if you multiply by 2.5 to convert hectares to acres. Thus, 4ha is approximately 10 acres – a lot of land! There are 10,000 square metres (*mètre carré* – written as *m. ca.* or m^2) in a hectare, which means that an acre is almost exactly 4,000m^2; so a 2,000m^2 plot is equivalent to half an acre. (An *are* is an archaic measurement equal to 100th of a hectare or 100m^2, and on some property deeds you will see '*Ca*', which indicates 100th of an *are* or 1m^2.)

It's possible to be reasonably self-sufficient on around 2ha of land but many rural properties are sold with more than that. You should beware, however, of buying too much land, thinking it to be an offer too good to turn down. Although it might seem like a good investment, bear in mind that, should you ever wish to sell, buyers may be reluctant to take on the responsibility of using or maintaining the land. On a large acreage, you might also be subject to the extra complication of requiring SAFER approval to sell (see below). Also, the more land you have, the higher the taxes you're likely to pay!

On the other hand, if you buy a farmhouse on just a few hectares, you should note that the land may not be of high quality. Unfortunately, most farm buildings were located near to roads or tracks for accessibility or on high ground, often consisting of clay or rock, for good drainage. The better quality land is often at some distance from the farm buildings but in many cases has been sold to farming neighbours. When a farmer owning several hectares of land dies and his children decide to sell the property, they or their solicitor (*notaire*) must inform SAFER, which in turn advertises that the land for sale, and anyone currently involved in agriculture has first refusal – the idea being to safeguard agricultural land and prevent it from being developed for industrial or residential use. Where this has happened in the past and neighbouring farmers have exercised their right to purchase (*loi de pré-emption*), the result is often that the farmhouse has been left surrounded by uneconomically viable land. Nevertheless, although perhaps not ideal for commercial farming, it could be ideal for a smallholding, where the demands from the soil aren't as high.

SAFER must give permission for the sale of farmland, but this is usually a formality with property consisting of only a couple of hectares.

CHECKS

It's essential to know about the actual and potential idiosyncrasies of an old rural property before agreeing to a purchase. Your tumbledown cottage or farmhouse might look quirky, picturesque and romantic, but what about the practicalities? Visit a prospective property on as many occasions as is practicable and possible before finally committing yourself. Plan your visits for different days of the week and at varying times of the day (and even in different seasons) to confirm your first impressions. Take a note of such things as where water lies and where the dry areas are after heavy rain, and which are the warmest spots in a cold north-easterly wind.

Land & Outbuildings

One of the first points to check when considering buying a house in rural France that has land attached is whether the neighbouring land is agricultural and, if so, whether there any plans for its re-designation. It's possible that the owners have applied to the Direction Départementale de l'Équipement (DDE) for the land to be 'upgraded' from agricultural to constructible use so that they can sell it (its value will double). In this case, you might discover that a piece of land on which cattle have been grazing for years has been turned into a building plot within a few months and part or all of the view from your property is blocked.

It's easy to look at buildings – either the house you hope to renovate or the cow byre in which you hope to set up a particular project – without considering the cost of any work, but you must have some idea how much renovations will cost relative to the purchase price. A typical DIY job (carried out over several years) could cost on average around one-tenth of the purchase price, whereas to convert a derelict shell professionally and quickly into a habitable home could cost as much as ten times the purchase price! It's therefore imperative to draw up a **detailed renovation plan** – perhaps with the aid of a professional – and obtain **detailed quotes** from local artisans before you commit yourself to buying a property (see **Improvements** on page 55).

With older dwellings it's impossible to see exactly how much work is likely to be involved until a start is made and this often leads to 'hidden extras', which will obviously add to the overall cost. Budget for an additional 50 per cent on any figures you might be given. Also, don't underestimate the length of time the work will take; many people think they can renovate a place in two or three years and are still struggling to complete it 10 or even 15 years later, by which time the original improvements may well need further attention!

Boundaries & Responsibilities

You will be shown the perimeters of your land on the legal paperwork required before drawing up a purchase contract, but boundaries may need defining by a fence line in order to prevent future disputes with neighbours. Make sure that this is sorted out before signing any paperwork and certainly before moving in. In many other countries, it's your responsibility to defend your land from other people's animals and not the neighbours' responsibility to ensure that your precious acres don't suffer from unwelcome visits by their sheep and cattle. In France, on the other hand, a boundary barrier belongs to one or other property owner and it's his responsibility to keep it livestock-proof. Note that a hedge must be at least a metre away from the boundary line (see **Hedges** on page 66).

The outbuildings of a potential neighbour may cause you problems – and not only in the most obvious ways. A barn that borders your land and has no guttering can leave you wondering whether the neighbour has a duty to dispose of his roof water or whether you will be required to dig ditches to channel it away from your property. In fact, French law stipulates that the neighbour is obliged to recover his own rainwater by a method of his choice and at his own cost but, if he is reluctant to do so, will you be able to come to an amicable agreement?

If the same barn has been neglected and stones have fallen onto your land, the neighbour would again be responsible for making good. If the wall were to collapse completely, you could insist that he pay for any damage to your property and, had you been walking under the wall at the time it fell, would (if you were able!) have cause to sue for personal injury. In addition, he would have to clear up the mess of stones.

Although you have the law on your side, confrontations with neighbours aren't the best ways of starting a new life and so it's as well to envisage the possible scenarios as you inspect a property.

SURVIVAL TIP

If you have cause to complain to a neighbour, it's advisable to use an intermediary who speaks fluent French and knows how to broach the subject without antagonising him.

Water

Mains water isn't always available in rural properties and so it's important that you check the cost of connection before going ahead and signing the *compromis de vente*. If water comes from a well or a spring, ownership of the source should be confirmed and you should try and establish the reliability the 'supply' – wells can run dry in a drought or if the underground watercourse changes direction. If the vendor assures you that well water is reliable all the year round, it's a good idea to make independent enquiries at the *mairie*. Unless a guaranteed water supply was included in the special clauses (*conditions suspensives*) of the *compromis de vente*, you will have no redress under French law.

Even if a supply of well water is guaranteed, it could still be unfit for drinking and you will have to have a mains water supply connected to the house or buy bottled water. When a well is the only source of water, it's advisable to have an annual check carried out, as the quality of underground watercourses can change as a result of building work, climate change or flooding. High levels of limestone can damage boilers, water heaters and washing machines. There are several ways of getting water quality checked. You can simply take a sample bottle to your local Laboratoire Municipal et Régional d'Analyses for testing or even do it yourself. Water analysis kits are widely available and give an indication of the levels of nitrates, copper, iron, chlorine, pesticides, ph levels and 'hardness'. Kits include litmus papers, which change colour when dipped in water and are then compared with a chart showing recommended levels.

If you'd like a private water source and the land doesn't contain a well or spring, it might be possible to have a borehole drilled. However, be sure to obtain an **accurate** estimate of the costs **before** signing the property purchase contract.

Sewerage

There's a lot of waste domestic water polluting the water courses and consequently the farmland of rural France, and new laws have been implemented to ensure that inadequate private systems for treating sewerage and waste water are no longer allowed to empty into rivers, lakes, ditches or roadside culverts. All properties not connected to mains drainage (which is the great majority in rural France) are currently being inspected and, whenever a house is sold, the *notaire* must ensure that the vendor provides an official report (*rapport de contrôle*) on the status of the waste water system. The law doesn't, as yet, require a *certificat de conformité* stating that the system meets all current standards, but since the beginning of 2006 no house can be sold as '*habitable*' if the *fosse septique* doesn't comply with at least some of the new regulations currently being implemented. If the system is causing pollution and the property owner doesn't take remedial action, he can be made to do so by law.

The most common sewage and waste water treatment system is a septic tank (*fosse septique*), but there are alternatives. Reed beds may comply if they're correctly installed and maintained, but a standard 'all-water' system (*fosse toutes eaux*) is generally the most cost-effective solution and the most likely to be accepted by the relevant authorities.

Only installations by qualified professionals are accepted and, if you're intending to put in a new system yourself or replace an existing one, you cannot do so without obtaining permission, which will dictate the size of tank, position and land preparation required.

Electricity

The majority of France's electricity is generated by nuclear power and is inexpensive compared to electricity in other EU countries. Nevertheless, if you intend using electricity to heat a house over 300m², it can work out very expensive. The cost of the supply is also worth bearing in mind if you intend heating greenhouses or using electricity in outbuildings.

In any case, you should check the power rating of a property, particularly an old property, as it may be inadequate to run several high-consumption applicances, such as a washing machine, dishwasher and tumble dryer, simultaneously and expensive to uprate. Older buildings may still have 110/120volt supplies, although these have been converted to 220/240 in most areas. Ask an electrician to test the power supply before signing the *compromis de vente*.

Heating

Your house must have efficient heating; there's nothing romantic about sitting huddled around a smouldering fire and sucking humbugs in an effort to keep warm during the winter months! Traditional stone houses have thick walls and flagstone floors, which take a long time to heat through, although conversely they retain heat well. Most rural homes have a fireplace or wood-burning stove, which provides an immediate heat source, but it's a sensible precaution to have more than one heating system – whether central heating or individual electric, gas or paraffin heaters.

Firewood is a natural and, if you have an adequate supply (see **Creating Woodland** on page 64), sustainable fuel, but it's a back-breaking job cutting, chopping and carrying it and it isn't a particularly efficient source of heat.

You can hire a huge propane tank from any of several gas companies and use it to run central heating, but a property must be accessible to the lorries necessary for installing and filling the tank. Having a gas tank (*citerne*) may increase your insurance premiums and they can be unsightly (they must be sited at least 3m from the house). If you take over a property with a gas tank, you will be responsible for paying the rental charge and must also pay for a full tank of gas, irrespective of how much was left in it!

Domestic heating oil (*fioul/gasoil domestique*) is probably the cheapest source of heating next to a log burner and, depending on its size, the tank can be sited in the basement, underground on your land or in an outbuilding. By law, an oil heating system must be cleaned and checked annually, and to do so will cost you around €130. As with gas, if you're considering this option you must check that the property is accessible to delivery tankers.

Insulation is obviously important, as it will reduce fuel bills considerably, so you should check whether your intended rural property has been insulated. If not, it will add considerably to the expense of making it habitable, although it may be possible to apply for a tax credit, which the

French government is currently providing for the installation of heating systems run on renewable fuel.

Further information on heat sources can be found in ***Renovating and Maintaining Your French Home*** (Survival Books – see page 287).

MAKING THE PURCHASE

The procedure for purchasing rural property is the same as for any other kind of property in France and is comprehensively covered in ***Buying a Home in France*** (Survival Books – see page 287); a summary of the main points is given below.

Once you've found a suitable property, you enter into an initial agreement with the seller. This is called the *compromis de vente* or *promesse de vente* and, after a seven-day cooling-off period, is a legally binding contract. This preliminary contract includes a full description of the property, the latest date by which completion must take place, the price, any escape clauses and the identity of both parties.

It might be possible to negotiate the estate agent's fee and the price of the house you're buying, but *notaires*' fees are set by law and cannot be negotiated. The same *notaire* usually acts for both the vendor and the purchaser, but this isn't obligatory and you can appoint your own if you wish. You should be aware that the *notaire*'s job is simply to make a legally binding agreement between the two parties and he won't necessarily advise or warn you of any inadequacies in it. Make sure that you itemise anything you want checking in the *compromis de vente* using clauses known as *conditions suspensives*.

Although it isn't a requirement to have a survey done in France, it might be worthwhile for your peace of mind. If work needs doing, obtain several quotes and use them to negotiate with the vendor before agreeing to anything that's legally binding. Once you've accepted a quote, decide on a deadline for the completion of work, after the date for completion of the property purchase has been agreed. Building in a penalty clause if work goes over a given time is a good way of tying French builders to the project.

Completion is when the final deed of sale is signed and also the point at which any outstanding money must be paid for the property purchase. This, and the signing of the *acte de vente*, is always carried out at the *notaire*'s office, usually in the presence of all interested parties (it isn't unknown for every member of the French family selling a property to turn out for the occasion!). Both the buyer and seller initial each page and are required to sign the final page after writing '*bon pour accord*', signifying that both have understood and accepted the terms. If your command of French isn't up to understanding the legal jargon (and not many foreigners' is!), *notaires* should arrange for an English-speaking translator to be present.

There are no title deeds in France and proof of ownership is provided and guaranteed by registration of the property by the Land Registry. Your certified copy of the transaction should be ready for collection from the *notaire* around two months after completion. It's a legal requirement that properties be insured against third-party risks on completion: your *notaire* will inform you of this and ensure that it's done.

REMOVALS

3.

Moving In

Moving in to your new home in France is an exciting prospect, but it can be a traumatic experience if you don't plan the move carefully and prepare for the worst. After the obvious technicalities and legalities involved with moving anywhere – change of address, form signing and transferring money – the priority for many embarking on a life in rural France will be arranging for pets, and possibly other animals, to be included in the move. There are a number of points regarding your arrival in your new home that require early consideration if you're to avoid unpleasant surprises just when you most want everything to go swimmingly.

REMOVALS

There are many specialised removal firms that run regularly to and from France, particularly from the UK. Their charges vary according to the volume of goods to be moved and whether a shipment is individual or shared. Ease of access at delivery/collection points and the type of items to be moved also have a bearing on cost. Most companies will consider a part load delivery, but you're more likely to have to wait for a convenient date – depending on the size of the firm and how many deliveries they make per week – although you shouldn't have to wait more than 14 days. There's a lorry ban on Sundays and bank holidays in France and this may affect your possible dates.

You will normally be given a choice of packing your belongings yourself or letting the removal company take charge of everything. If you choose to do it yourself, ask the company if they can lend you cardboard boxes and wrapping paper or cardboard (there may be a fee or deposit). Some companies provide portable 'wardrobes', which allow clothes to hang whilst in transit.

It's important that you take out adequate insurance – not necessarily with the removal company you're using. Most removal companies offer indemnity insurance and some provide 'new-for-old' cover. The biggest difference between the two is that under new-for-old cover, if an item is damaged beyond repair, it will be replaced, whereas with indemnity insurance only the value of the item immediately before the damage occurred will be reimbursed. Insurance premiums vary considerably; some insurers charging a percentage of the total value and others a percentage of the total removal cost. Many companies have an 'excess' charge of around 1 per cent of the shipment value, which would mean that you cannot claim for items worth less than this amount (e.g. £50 on a £5,000 shipment). **Always read the insurance proposal carefully before committing yourself.**

Rural properties are often difficult for removal lorries to access and it may be impossible for a large vehicle to park right outside your home (the ground must also be firm enough to support a large truck!). You should inform the company of any potential difficulties well ahead of your intended moving date so that they can, for example, arrange for a smaller vehicle to ferry your belongings from the lorry to your house (which will increase the cost).

Alternatively, with not much to move, you can hire a small van and do it yourself, the only problem being to get the van back to the point from where it was collected. Not many hire companies will let you leave vans anywhere other than where you collected them, even if they have offices in France.

ANIMALS

If you're planning to take animals with you, it's important to talk to your vet and your chosen ferry or airline company as soon as you've decided on a moving date. For some birds and animals, the legalities aren't too complicated but vaccinations may be needed several months in advance.

It's unlikely that many people moving to France will consider taking much more in the way of animals than household pets. Some people contemplate taking chickens or even a goat with them, but with the ever-increasing threat of avian influenza (see page 137) and EU regulations regarding cloven-footed animals (see **Chapter 8**), it's more practical to dispose of livestock before making the move. It may also be a kindness to have an aged animal or bird put down rather than subject it to the stress of transportation – and possibly quarantine on arrival – to a new home several hundred miles away.

Quarantine regulations apply to all animals belonging to any rabies-susceptible species that don't qualify for the PETS scheme (see below), which include most farm livestock and horses. Animals that fail a PETS check may also have to be quarantined, although they may not have to complete the usual six month period if the failure can be rectified. For further information on exporting animals from the UK, see the Department for the Environment, Food & Rural Affairs' website (💻 www.defra.gov.uk/animalh/rabies/default.htm).

Dogs & Cats

All a dog needs to travel to France is a microchip and the standard inoculations required in most western countries. Your vet can arrange this under the Pet Travel Scheme (PETS), which involves his checking your dog's general health. Make sure your vet has recorded all the following details on your dog's vaccination record and passport:

- Date of birth/age.
- Microchip number, date of insertion.
- Date of vaccination.
- Vaccine product name.
- Batch number.
- Date booster vaccination is due. (Boosters must be given by the 'Valid until' date in section IV of the pet passport.)

Rabies is present in certain parts of France (mainly, according to the authorities, as a result of dogs brought in illegally from other European countries) and it isn't unknown for 'rabies danger zones' to be declared.

In some situations, unless owners can prove that their dog has been vaccinated against rabies, it will have to be put down.

A rabies vaccination can be administered once an animal is three months old. (It used to be necessary in France to have a dog or cat tattooed before it could be micro-chipped and vaccinated, but this is no longer the case.) A blood sample is required to prove that the inoculation has been successful; this is taken a month after vaccination and sent off for laboratory examination. You will then receive conformation of the success of the injection but still have to wait a further six months before you're allowed to take the animal abroad.

To take a dog from France to the UK, you must have it vaccinated against rabies. This means that, if you're taking a dog from the UK to France, it's as well to have it vaccinated beforehand. Even if you aren't intending to return with your pet, you never know what emergencies may occur in the future, necessitating a rapid and unexpected trip back to the UK – when you won't be able to wait six months for a rabies jab to become valid.

If you want to bring a dog back to the UK, you must also take it to a French vet between 48 and 24 hours before your intended departure to be checked for ticks (European ticks carry more serious diseases than those found in the UK and you're recommended to use a preventive treatment such as Frontline or an anti-parasite collar, e.g. Scalibor) and tapeworms. The PETS information on the DEFRA website (🖳 www.defra.gov/animalh/quarantine/pets/contacts.htm) contains all the necessary information, or you can request a printed copy by email (🖂 pets.helpline@defra.gsi.gov.uk), giving your postal address and daytime telephone number.

Currently, only 'assistance' dogs such as 'hearing dogs' or guide dogs for the blind are allowed to travel on Eurostar passenger trains, but most pets are allowed on Eurotunnel shuttle trains between Folkestone and Calais. All passenger ferries will transport dogs, provided they remain in a car or van, but some limit the number allowed on each sailing.

Ferrets & Rodents

To travel from the UK to another EU country, a ferret must also be microchipped, vaccinated against rabies and issued with a pet passport. To take it back to the UK you must conform to the same rules as for dogs and cats (see above).

Currently, there are no restrictions on the movement of rabbits and other rodents between EU countries but conditions may be imposed on these animals. You should check with your vet before travelling and with the ferry or Tunnel operator, who will usually (with certain exceptions such as the one cited below) permit your pet to travel for a small additional fee.

Even though DEFRA and your veterinary surgeon may have approved your animals for transit, individual ferry companies may not. If, for example, you're planning to take a rabbit, check whether or not your chosen ferry company will carry it. Strange as it may sound, for over 400 years French sailors have been convinced that rabbits bring bad luck if allowed on a ship (apparently, several centuries ago, a cargo of rabbits gnawed through the hull of a French boat, sinking it and drowning the sailors – and presumably themselves also) and some French ferry companies apply this somewhat archaic ban even today. They may even forbid the use of the word 'rabbit' (like actors who refuse to give Shakespeare's play 'Macbeth' its proper name, preferring to call it "the Scottish Play"), referring to seaborne rabbits as the animals with long ears".

Travelling with Your Pet

Preparing your pet for its journey to France is largely a matter of common sense. Try to remain calm; if you're anxious on behalf of your pet this may unsettle the animal. Most vets don't recommend the use of a sedative, as the effect is unpredictable. If you decide to use one, make sure you have a record of what has been administered. Your pet will travel better on an empty stomach but water should be made available whenever it's practicable to do so. If it's an animal that needs to be in a carrier, make sure that it's large enough for it to stand, lie down in a natural position and turn around. Don't forget to include suitable bedding.

During the journey you should ensure that there's plenty of ventilation, as heat and moisture can rapidly build up in still air, and bear in mind that ferry port car parks and waiting areas offer little or no shade. **Animals should never be left in vehicles in direct sunshine, as it's difficult to ensure sufficient ventilation. Even a few minutes exposed to these conditions can cause overheating and distress.** (The temperature inside a vehicle standing in full sun on a hot day can be double that outside.) Where a dog or cat is carried loose, make sure it isn't able to escape through any windows left open for ventilation.

It's best to arrive at a port early so that loading staff can position your vehicle near an access door. Although access to the car decks isn't normally permitted once the ship is at sea, if the crossing is a long one it should be possible to make arrangements to visit your pet during the journey. This can usually be arranged at the on-board information desk.

HEALTH INSURANCE

A European health insurance card (EHIC), which superseded the E111 form at the end of 2005, entitles you to benefit from reciprocal health insurance arrangements between EU countries (including the UK and France). This cover is valid only for one year, however. If you're planning to live permanently in France, you should apply for French health insurance before leaving your home country.

When moving from the UK, this is best done via the Department of Work and Pensions (DWP) at Newcastle (☎ 0191-218 7777), which will issue you with form E106 or E121 (for pensioners) and send copies to the French authorities; they will (eventually) accept your transfer from the UK National Health system and issue you with a French medical card (*carte vitale*). If you're initially issued with an E106, it will need renewing.

If you aren't eligible for an E121, you may be entitled to *couverture maladie universelle* (*CMU*). Once you've been in the country for 90 days, go to your local Caisse Primaire d'Assurance Maladie (CPAM) office with proof of a permanent address in France and you will be issued with an *attestation provisoire*. Full *CMU* is available only to those below a certain income level, depending on the number of people in a household. If your income is above this level, you will have to pay a percentage of your medical costs.

It's important to realise, however, that no matter what your circumstances, the French health authorities will only ever reimburse around 70 per cent of any medical costs and it's therefore advisable to take out 'top-up' insurance (*complémentaire* or *mutuelle*) to cover the potential shortfall. Exclusive Healthcare gives more details on its website (💻 www.exclusive healthcare.com – go to 'Who are you?'/'The Fallback option'). ***Buying a Home in France*** (Survival Books – see page 287) also has more information on this subject.

FENCING

The French have an unusual habit of taking everything but the kitchen sink when they move house. This can include fencing, which is why it's essential – especially if you have a dog or other livestock that needs confining immediately on your arrival – to establish your property boundaries and ensure that there are no 'grey' areas regarding where they are, what they consist of and whose responsibility they are (see **Land & Outbuildings** on page 33 and **Fencing** on page 72) before signing the purchase contract (see **Making the Purchase** on page 38).

If you haven't done so, don't be surprised to find that fencing which was in situ when you viewed the property has disappeared by the time you move in. It's unlikely that the fence line will have been obliterated, but any wire netting or chain link that you fondly hoped would keep your dog from roaming may have been (legally) removed by the vendors unless you've made prior arrangements for it to remain.

SERVICES

Below is a summary of the action to be taken to connect or transfer to your name the essential services to the house; further information is contained in ***Buying a Home in France*** (Survival Books – see page 287).

Electricity

You might find that the previous occupiers have taken not only light bulbs, but also bulb holders, flex and even ceiling roses, so make that sure you have a supply of these handy – especially if you're due to arrive in the dark!

(Obviously, it's advisable to check the state of a property after buying it to ascertain exactly what you will need to make it habitable.)

Most people advise Electricité de France (EDF) a few days before leaving a property (so that they don't continue to receive bills!) and EDF normally assumes that someone else is taking it over. Nevertheless, you must usually go to the local EDF office (listed in yellow pages and searchable on 💻 http://particuliers.edf.fr – enter the name of your *commune* in the box at the top right of the screen) to have your electricity connected and to sign a contract specifying the power supply and tariff. It might be necessary to prove your identity and that you're the new owner of the property, so it's as well to take your passport and an *attestation d'acquisition*, obtained from the *notaire* handling the sale. If the supply is still connected, make sure that you have the meter read before you move in to ensure that you aren't paying for someone else's electricity.

Electricity supplies can be spasmodic in certain parts of France, due in part to the huge number of overhead rather than underground cables. Power surges and power cuts aren't unknown – especially in winter, when you need it most! Power cuts of several minutes (or hours!) are fairly frequent in some areas, especially during thunderstorms; in some departments, there's a high risk of lightning strikesl In many rural areas, the lights often flicker and come back on almost immediately – but just long enough to crash a computer. It's therefore advisable to connect vulnerable equipment to a power surge protector and a battery back-up, which allows you time to save all your work in the event of a power failure. If you're worried about lightning strikes, you can install an anti-lightning device (*parafoudre*) in your fuse box.

If the power keeps tripping, it probably means that the supply to your intended home is too low. If this is the case, you will need to ask EDF to upgrade the power supply. If you have any questions regarding your electricity supply, contact your local EDF office. Information can also be obtained via a local rate telephone line (☎ 08 10 12 61 26). Details of tariffs are given in ***Living and Working in France*** (Survival Books – see page 287).

Gas

Mains gas isn't generally available in rural areas of France, but most rural homes have cookers and some also water heaters that use bottled gas; some homes have large gas tanks which supply a central heating system. Before arrival, check your gas supply.

Gas bottles can be bought at most supermarkets, garages and village shops, but you should always return your empty one; otherwise it's much more expensive. An exchange bottle costs around €19. If you need to buy new bottles, you will be asked to register and pay a deposit (e.g. €40 per bottle) although it's worth checking local *foires à tout* or *vide-greniers*, as gas bottles are often sold at such events for as little as €5. Be aware, however, that there are several different types of bottle and that the supplier of one type won't accept an empty bottle of another type. Propane can withstand more extreme temperatures than butane and must legally be stored outside, whereas butane is for internal use only.

You can hire propane gas tanks from a number of gas companies, but your property must obviously be accessible to the delivery lorry. If you take over a property which already has a gas tank (*citerne*), you will be responsible for paying the rental charge and will also have to pay for a full tank of gas, irrespective of how much was left by the previous owners.

Mains Water

The water supply infrastructure is owned and managed by France's 36,000 *communes*, and rates vary across the country. If your property is supplied with mains water, you will need to register your ownership with the local supplier and enter into a contract specifying how much water you expect to use. Most properties are metered, so that you pay only for the water you use and are charged per cubic metre (1,000 litres). If you need to have a water meter installed, there's a small charge. Your meter is read every six months and you can opt to pay by direct debit; if your water consumption exceeds the agreed amount, an adjustment is made for the second half of the year. Ask the local water company to read the meter **before** you move in.

If your property isn't connected to the mains (see **Water** on page 35) but is near a village, you can usually be connected, although this can be quite expensive as you will be required to pay for any trench digging necessary for the installation of underground pipes. Expect the connection to cost at least €800 but **make sure that you obtain a written estimate before signing the contract**.

Telephones & Internet Connection

If your property is without an existing telephone line, it may be expensive to have one installed, as you must pay for the line to the property. Contact France Télécom (FT) for an estimate. Underground and/or overhead installations are possible. Overhead is obviously the cheaper alternative and it may be possible to run a wire directly from the nearest pylon, but there's the ever-present risk of being cut off if a tree falls on the line. You must have trenches dug for telephone cables if you want a below ground connection. This work can be carried out by FT, but their charges are high and it's possible to do it yourself, although you must observe certain standards. The cost of installing a new line (*frais forfaitaire d'accès au réseau*) is normally €104.

To make arrangements for the installation or connection of telephone lines, you must visit your nearest FT office (which you will find listed under *Télécommunications: service* in the yellow pages), taking with you the same documentation as is necessary for electricity connections (see above).

When moving into a house that has an existing line you won't normally be allowed to retain the existing telephone number and must have the account transferred and a new number issued. To do this, you can ring 1014 or go to the FT website (🖳 www.francetelecom.com) and follow the links to '*l'agence sur le net*'. Alternatively, visit your nearest FT office, where staff can usually sort things out immediately or, at the very most, within two days.

Problems can arise if you've purchased a property from a family in which the person in whose name the account was opened has died. In extreme cases you will need to obtain a death certificate (from either the family or the local *mairie*) to prove to France Télécom that this person is no longer among the living! If you're moving into a house where the telephone line hasn't been disconnected before you want to transfer the account into your name, it's essential that you obtain a special reading (*relevé spécial*).

Although you have no alternative but to have your line connected and serviced by FT and pay its quarterly line charges, there are several companies that offer much cheaper calls. Line rental costs are similar to those in the UK.

The number of French directory enquiries (12) was replaced in November 2005 by a range of six-digit numbers beginning 118 run by various operators. These have also superseded the mobile phone directory enquiry numbers of 222, 612 and 712.

In France, each emergency service has its own number. As soon as you settle in, keep a note of them by the telephone. The SAMU services for medical emergencies can be contacted by ringing 15, the fire brigade 18 (or 31' if calling from a mobile phone) and the police (*police* or *gendarmes*) 17. (See also **Crime** on page 241 and ***Sapeurs-pompiers*** on page 247.)

While you're organising your phone line, you may wish to ask if ADSLs (asymmetric digital subscriber lines) are available in your area. FT is committed to extending the availability of ADSLs, but it isn't yet available in all areas. If it is, you can ask the assistant to open an account with an internet service provider; the procedure is straightforward and, if you provide French bank account details, direct debit payment can be arranged.

REGISTRATION

It's important to register your arrival in France in several official quarters. Although it's no longer necessary to register for a *carte de séjour*, you might find it useful to visit the *mairie* or *préfecture* (don't forget to take the usual means of identification, together with some proof of address) and ask them for a *certificate de vie commune*, which, although not obligatory, can be helpful in situations where you need to prove that you're an inhabitant of a particular *commune*.

Doctor

It's important that you remember to register your existence not just with the relevant CPAM office (see **Health Insurance** on page 46), but also with a doctor who will be your regular health contact (*médecin traitant*). Your doctor is responsible for computerising your medical information and keeping your records up to date. All practitioners or medical establishments to whom you're referred are required to send him a report following a consultation or treatment. If you haven't registered with a doctor or go to a specialist without a referral, practitioners may charge you higher rates and your social security reimbursements will be reduced.

You're free to select your doctor, but the location of his clinic and his ability to speak your language may be important considerations. When you've made your choice, you should report it to the local CPAM office and complete form S3704 (*déclaration de choix du médecin traitant*), which you and your doctor must sign. You're also at liberty to change your doctor whenever you like, but you must give reasonable notice and complete another S3704.

For more information on this subject visit the French government website (💻 www.ameli.fr).

Car

If you're planning to bring a car to France from another country, you must re-register it within six months. To do so, go to your local *préfecture* and present the registration certificate, a certificate from the tax office to prove that VAT has been paid (if applicable) and an export certificate from the relevant licensing authority, e.g. the DVLA in the UK. The car must pass a French technical inspection (*contrôle technique*), for which modifications – such as new headlamps for right-hand-drive cars (which will cost around €350) – may be required. The *contrôle technique* itself costs €56 and the registration certificate (*carte grise*) costs €35 per horsepower (for cars over ten years old, the *carte grise* is half-price). A change of number plates is likely to add another €35.

Under Article R222-2 of the *Code de la Route*, it's possible for anyone who previously lived in an EU country to apply for a French driving licence, so there shouldn't be any problem for anyone wishing to exchange their foreign licence for a French one – although, as with any administrative procedure in France, it's seldom as easy as it ought to be. If you're found guilty of a motoring offence, such as speeding, you may be obliged to exchange your foreign driving licence for a French one anyway. Should you wish to enquire about changing your licence, go to your *préfecture* quoting the article number above and ask for form 11247, on which an exchange application is made. You will have to present a copy of your current licence, a copy of your identity documents and a self-addressed stamped envelope. The new licence is issued free of charge, but it's advisable to keep a copy of your original documentation as the French licence won't show how many years you'd been driving before its issue.

Tax

Wherever you are, it's a good idea to register with your tax office before they find you – and France is no exception! The tax office (*hôtel des impôts*) is responsible for collecting both *taxe d'habitation* and *taxe foncière*, which are the two types of property tax payable in France. It's sometimes thought that if you aren't permanently resident in France, you may be eligible for a reduction in *taxe d'habitation*, but in fact the tax must be paid in full no matter how much time you spend at the address in question. *Taxe d'habitation* is the responsibility of whoever occupies the premises on 1st January of the current year.

In France, the tax year runs from 1st January to 31st December and tax returns are submitted in arrears. Normally, returns must be completed by the end of March or the beginning of April (the exact date can vary from year to year). The onus is on you to apply for and complete an initial form and only after this are you sent forms automatically each year. It's possible to pay your *taxe d'habitation* in monthly instalments, but from June 2006 it will no longer be possible to pay *taxe foncière* in the same way.

TV Licence

French law dictates that if you buy a television from a shop, the retailer must inform the relevant authorities of the fact and you will subsequently receive a bill for *taxe d'habitation* which includes your annual television licence fee (*redevance audiovisuelle*) of €116. Until recently, it was up to residents with a TV to make a declaration; now it's assumed that everyone has a television and it's up to you to declare that you **don't** have a TV by ticking the relevant box on the first page of your tax return. **Even if you just use your TV for watching videos or never plug it in, you must have a licence.**

Electoral Roll

As a tax-paying resident, you have a right to vote, but only in local and EU elections. Doing so shows that you're interested in local affairs and keen to integrate into the community. The procedure is simple, necessitating only a visit to the *mairie* – accompanied as ever by identification and a utility bill – to complete a form, which will ensure that you're eligible to vote in the next election.

INSURANCE

You can often get a better deal by placing all your insurance (*assurance*) needs in the hands of one reputable agent. It's always best to choose a company with local offices or at least an agent you can conveniently meet in the event of any problems. If necessary, recruit a French-speaking neighbour to go with you or use the services of one of the many organisations currently being set up to help new residents through this difficult transition period. You will obviously have to pay for their services, but they could help you save money in the long-run by making sure that the insurance you're being sold is actually what you require. You can easily be sold products which either you don't need or which don't cover your specific requirements. Such services advertise in *French News*, *The Connexion* and the classified sections of *French Property News* and *Living France* (see **Appendix B**).

With property insurance, it's essential to check the small print concerning the type of security devices required. If you're burgled and make a claim, the assessor may insist on examining the whole house. Further information on property insurance can be found in ***Buying a Home in France*** (Survival Books – see page 287).

MEETING THE NEIGHBOURS

Wherever you live, good relations with neighbours are invaluable. In rural France, it's essential to get on with your neighbours, who can be a mine of useful information as well as a vital link between you and the local community. For example, your neighbours will probably know where your mains water supply valve is – very useful when you have an unexpected leak in the middle of the night! – and they will certainly be able to recommend trustworthy tradesmen. If your command of the language isn't up to telephone conversations, a neighbour may even make calls on your behalf. And if you aren't living in your property full time, neighbours may act as key-holders and empty your letterbox and even help organise workmen when you're away.

Introductions

The first contact with your neighbours will be often be 'in passing': you may be walking the dog as they're out in the garden or they may casually wander your way in the hope of seeing you and sating their curiosity. They will greet you with '*Bonjour, Madame*' or '*Bonjour, Monsieur*' and will expect you to do the same. If you haven't bumped into neighbours in a casual fashion after a short time, you might need to bite the bullet and knock on their door and introduce yourself.

Names aren't always given initially but, if they are, listen carefully to their pronunciation. Check whether a French person's name is French- or English-sounding, as in Patrice or Patrick, both of which are commonly used. And if, as is often the case, a name is 'double-barrelled' – e.g. Jean-Claude or Marie-Christine – **always** use the full name and **never** abbreviate to Jean or Marie.

Obviously, you must initially address your adult neighbours as *vous* and it may be some time before they ask you to use the familiar *tu*, whereas children are always addressed as *tu*.

Invitations

An offer from neighbours to join them for an *apéritif* or dinner is usually sincerely meant and will be backed up with a definite date and time. There can be confusion as to what to expect on these occasions and sometimes what at first sounds to be a casual snack can turn out to be a six- or seven-course meal. At other times you might only be offered strange things on bread or biscuits! Much depends on the hosts. Elderly neighbours in a farming community will have had their main meal at midday and will probably expect you to have done the same, and therefore dinner may be on the light side.

The time of invitation is usually early in the evening – again this may be peculiar to country living and a legacy of the 'early to bed, early to rise' mentality. If you're part of a large gathering, don't expect to be offered a drink until all the guests have arrived and don't be surprised to be offered a place around the dining table rather than on comfortable armchairs.

When you invite them, your neighbours will be pleased to have the opportunity to look around your home, especially if you've made substantial alterations since they last had cause to visit. (It isn't unknown for past inhabitants of your house to turn up un-invited just to see what you've done to the place!) You needn't worry about conforming to French etiquette: you call the shots and an evening of mulled wine and mince pies goes down very well at Christmas, for example. You could also try introducing them to the American idea of 'brunch' and provide scrambled eggs, smoked salmon and Buck's Fizz or even a typical English breakfast of imported bacon and sausage!

IMPROVEMENTS

It's a fortunate person who can move directly into a rural property which needs no improvement or alteration and, depending on the nature of your chosen project, you may wish to start planning improvements as soon as you arrive. With major schemes you would be wise to use the services of a professional adviser, which in some cases is a legal requirement. Using a consultant may also be a condition of planning permission being granted by the relevant authorities. When planning improvements, also bear in mind the following:

- **Be sure to use the services of professional builders and tradesmen, making sure that they're registered (i.e. have a SIREN or SIRET number).**

- Obtain two or three quotes and check that the work being quoting for is 'like for like' before opting for the cheapest.
- Reliable, registered tradesmen will give you a *devis*, pricing their proposal in detail, and it's in your interest to read it before signing, as once you've done so it becomes a legally binding contract. On the plus side, you know that you aren't going to be faced with escalating costs, as the price you've agreed to is the one you will pay and any unforeseen costs will have to be borne by the tradesman.
- It's quite usual for a 10 per cent up-front payment to be requested (and this can be as high as 30 per cent), but this should be mentioned on the *devis*. Any demands for stage payments should take the form of written invoices referring back to the quote and not just be a casual request for cash.
- The most unexpected of setbacks can occur. If, for example, during restoration work, you find that your rural retreat is already home to a family of bats, you could find your plans restricted by law and may have to wait until they've given birth and brought up their young before commencing any work. (For your legal obligations regarding bats, contact the Société Française pour l'Etude et la Protection des Mammifères, ☎ 02 48 70 40 03, 💻 www.museum-bourges.net, 💻 http://sfepm.ciril.fr or 💻 http://aptcs.ciril.fr, which will advise you who to get in touch with locally.)
- Choose the time of year carefully when considering when to commence work – winter isn't a good time to find half your windows being removed in readiness for an extension!
- If you're absent when work is being carried out, ask a neighbour to keep an eye on the job for you. It isn't unknown for even a respectable tradesman to slope off early and turn up late, which won't affect the price you pay (provided you've been given a *devis*) but will obviously affect how soon the work is completed.
- You should always personally check that work has been completed to your satisfaction and exact specifications before finally settling the account.
- If a builder asks for payment and promises to come back to finish off the odd job, which for one reason or another is still outstanding, make sure that you retain a portion of the money due to cover the unfinished work.

Doing it Yourself

Some improvements are within the scope of a competent handyman, and France has more than its fair share of DIY outlets. Most are competitive with builder's merchants and they have the advantage of carrying more stock. Some of their staff may be expected to speak English, so it's easier to ask questions about the suitability of a certain product if your French isn't up to it.

Make sure that you calculate the materials required for the whole of your project. The price of plaster-board, for example, is lower the more you buy – and you may even be able to negotiate free delivery with a large quantity. If not, remember to include the cost of delivery, the price of which varies considerably according to the distance from the depot to your home.

Swimming Pools

Finances permitting, rural properties in certain areas of France lend themselves to the addition of a swimming pool, especially if you plan to take in summer visitors to help offset the cost of living. With the ever-increasing numbers of holiday lets, a pool is often the only way to make your property stand out amongst the countless others on offer – especially during the summer holidays when it will entice parents of school-age children. When considering the possibility of a pool, it pays to bear the following points in mind.

- Is the soil structure or topography conducive to a ground-level pool or are you better considering an above-ground alternative?
- A pool may be relatively easy to construct, but planning permission is required for all constructions over 20m^2, i.e. anything other than a paddling pool! As always, it's essential that you visit the *mairie* to ensure that you adhere to local planning regulations.
- The type of pool liner chosen will affect not only the price of construction, but also its longevity. A flexible liner is normally guaranteed for ten years – again, it's important to check with the installer before giving the go-ahead.
- As with all building matters, make sure that you obtain several quotes before appointing a contractor.

- Make sure that a pool can be constructed within the time envisaged and at a convenient time – you don't want diggers in operation when you have guests booked for a relaxing holiday!
- It's a legal requirement to have your pool fenced or otherwise protected, even if you don't ever intend it being accessible to paying guests (see page 188), and the additional cost is substantial.

4.

Land & Its Uses

Most people considering buying a property in rural France think that the more land they have, the better. For those planning to make a living from their property, e.g. through tree cultivation, growing fruit and vegetables, or possibly the development of a caravan site (see **Chapter 10**), a certain amount of land is necessary. However, too much land can become a management nightmare. Although you may want sufficient land to grow vegetables, keep a few chickens or graze a goat, you're unlikely to need more than a couple of hectares. Much more than this and you will begin to need specialised maintenance equipment (see **Chapter 9**). A smallholding can be created slowly as and when you gain experience, but full-scale farming isn't for the beginner to rural life.

However, you shouldn't let the prospect of too much land attached to your ideal property put you off the purchase. If it's of reasonable quality, you can let land to a neighbouring farmer and put the rent towards paying some of your bills, but be aware that under French law if a landowner offers a farmer the use of land it can create a tenancy, which lasts for a minimum of nine years. Ground that isn't suitable for cultivation or grazing can have other uses, which are covered below.

VINEYARDS

Occasionally, properties become available on which a part of the land is given over to vines. It's tempting to think that, before long and with little effort, you will have your own limitless supply of wine and an instant source of income. Nothing could be further from the truth, as it takes years to become a *viticulteur*. To be successful you need not only to tend the grapes on a regular basis throughout the year, but also to buy and maintain all the equipment required for blending and production. Bad weather – in particular heavy frosts in April or thunderstorms in September – can ruin the whole season's crop. There's also a long time to wait before you can sell the wine you've made.

Meanwhile, you must become a chemist, blending the wine until it becomes drinkable, and then a marketer and salesperson, trying to persuade sceptical customers that what you've bottled is nectar, not nettle juice. You could try joining a co-operative, but it's unlikely that you will be able to supply enough grapes to interest them. You also need to be growing the type of grapes that are in the most demand.

There's a market for 'hand-made' wines cultivated from small plots (known as 'garage wines' in the UK market and fetching £150 per bottle or more) but you're only likely to be successful if you're in a prestigious and well-known area, and the average property purchaser cannot expect to achieve the required quality from a few inferior vines. There are also restrictions on planting new vines in many areas because of over-production.

Conversely, in other areas, some *communes* offer grants to anyone owning the ideal *terroir* – a generic term for the soil, subsoil, climate and proven wine-producing credentials. To find out whether you might qualify, it's necessary to get in touch with the relevant regional office of the Centre National pour l'Aménagement des Structures des Exploitations Agricoles (CNASEA) by contacting its head office, 7 rue Ernest Renan, BP1, 92136 Issy-les-Moulineaux Cedex (☎ 01 46 48 40 00, 💻 www.cnasea.fr). With only a few vines on your land, you would be better talking to your nearest *viticulteur* and suggesting that he manages and harvests your grapes in return for an annual rent of a few dozen bottles of the finished product.

It is, of course, possible to plant a few vines simply to produce wine for your own consumption. With little expertise, but time to experiment, you could end up with a year's supply of 'drinkable' plonk from a few rows of vines. Just don't expect to win any wine medals!

If, after reading the above, you're still convinced that you could make a go of running a vineyard, you're advised to read *The Ripening Sun* by Patricia Atkinson, which graphically illustrates the realities of producing wine.

WOODLAND

Where properties contain woodland, you may wish to plant more trees, which are not only a valuable commodity but also an important habitat for many of France's flora and fauna.

Possible Uses

In exposed areas, trees provide a good windbreak for the house and a source of firewood. Even if you've put in the very latest central heating system, a log fire provides a focal point and is a great centrepiece for entertaining and winter celebrations.

If you're planting for the future and looking to eventually keep yourself in logs, slow-growing native species produce a small amount of high-density wood, whereas quick-growing species produce a larger quantity of low-density logs. Just over 1ha (2.5 acres) of ground can supply enough firewood to last an average household for two years. The coppicing and pollarding of existing trees (see **Coppicing** on page 68 and **Pollarding** on page 67) may provide enough logs until new trees require thinning or lopping so that, with a little planning and organisation, it could be possible to be self-sufficient in firewood almost immediately.

It's unlikely that commercial forestry will be viable because of the length of time it takes a hardwood tree to mature. Softwoods are quicker, but you will still have to wait several years for them to mature (e.g. six years for hybrid poplars). Similarly, although it can add to the character of your home to include a beam cut from your own woodland or to use planking to build or repair buildings and outhouses, you must wait at least two years for the cut wood to season and dry.

If you want to shoot wildlife on your property, you will need at least 5ha of woodland; with just half a dozen or a dozen trees it won't be possible to do much more than use the branches for firewood, fit a couple of bird-boxes and string a hammock between the limbs you haven't used for burning. But however much you have, well-managed woodland is a haven to birds and other animals.

Improving Woodland

It isn't always necessary to plant a whole new wood – some scrub species such as birch (*Betula pendula*) and alder (*Alnus glutinosa*) do a very good job of planting themselves, producing a huge number of very small seeds that travel considerable distances and germinate where there's less competition from other, more mature, trees. They grow rapidly and will begin to produce new seeds themselves when as little as five years old. In contrast, species such as oak (*Quercus robur*) produce fewer seeds but the acorns contain lots of food for the developing seedling, giving it a good start in life, particularly if it finds itself under the canopy of other trees. In areas where there's too much canopy, transplant them to a more open part of the wood. Similarly, rather than letting all the self-sown trees survive, transplant or cut down the majority, leaving only the strongest to mature and replenish your woodland. If a few other, soil-compatible species are introduced, your spinney can be just as successful as if it were planted deliberately.

Individual trees or bundles of young plants (whips) can be bought from specialist tree nurseries (*pépinières*). Their addresses and telephone numbers are listed in yellow pages under *Pépiniéristes.*

Creating Woodland

If you're considering creating woodland, your choice of tree types will obviously be influenced by local conditions as well as the area of France in which the planting is to be done. Spend time looking around your area and identify the most common species before rushing out and buying vast quantities of whips or saplings. If you're planning to plant a large area, it might be possible to obtain a government grant, although this is unlikely unless you're contemplating commercial forestry. To find out if you're eligible, contact the local office of the Service des Eaux et Forêts.

Planting

Whips around 1m high should be planted in the autumn or spring into cleared ground and well spaced to allow for the roots. When planting trees, you should remove any competing vegetation. Special mats to suppress weed growth around the base of a tree can be bought, but a cheaper method is to save large plastic bags (e.g. for compost) or ask your local farmer if he has any plastic feed or fertilizer sacks he can give you, cut them in half and lay them around the base of newly planted saplings. Peg them the bags down well, or they will be blown away by the first gust of wind. This simple precaution gives a tree a great start in life, as not only are weeds suppressed but also condensation builds up underneath the plastic during dry spells to keep the roots moist.

Protecting Trees

It's essential that newly-planted trees be protected from rabbits, hares and deer until well established. If you're planting only a few trees, individual guards made of wire netting can be used. These need regular maintenance, however. Weeds should be pulled out, supporting stakes checked and any dead or diseased branches removed. This is ideally done in the spring, when trees have started growing. Don't set the guards so close to the trees that new foliage becomes entangled in the mesh or, worse, the wire becomes embedded in the bark. Several French manufacturers have developed rolls of plastic tree-protection netting that they claim to be bio-degradable; it is, but not for at least seven or eight years – by which time it will have bedded itself into the tree if positioned too closely in the first place. Spiral guards are another alternative, but they will protect only from damage caused by rabbits and hares.

The stakes used to support young trees should be sturdy. Don't be tempted to tie a tree to a stake with string, as this will eventually cut into the tree. Specially designed ties are available from garden centres, *quincailleries* and agricultural suppliers, although even these will need adjusting from time to time. Strips of hessian or webbing are good alternatives and can be attached to a stake with a felt 'nail' to prevent them from slipping up and down both post and sapling in windy weather.

If you have goats, sheep or horses and intend to let them graze close to trees, the trees will need to be protected by electric fencing – even with several hectares of good grass, animals seem to prefer browsing on branches! Sheep and horses will also treat your stakes as scratching posts.

Weeding between trees can be done in the autumn. Strimming is preferable to herbicide treatment as, if used carelessly, weed killer can kill the trees you've just planted, as well as damaging the environment.

HEDGES

Whether you're planning to plant a stock-proof hedge around part of your boundary, or merely a wind-break or decorative hedge in part of the garden, the same principles apply.

Legally, you must plant a hedge at least one metre from your boundary line, but the required distance can vary according to the likely height of the hedge; it's best to check with your *mairie*. There must also be enough room between the hedge and the boundary line for you to maintain the back of the hedge – should it encroach onto your neighbour's property, he will be entitled to cut it back without asking your permission.

There are many time-consuming aspects of planting and maintaining a hedge, such as preparing the chosen planting line and choosing plant species, bearing in mind the hedge's purpose. You should also consider how you will protect newly-planted shrubs from animals. In the wettest parts of the country, it may be necessary to build a bank on which to plant a hedge and possibly even dig a drainage ditch alongside it.

For general use, the thorn varieties (hawthorn/*Crataegus monogyna* or blackthorn/*Prunus spinosa*) are the most widely planted, as they will grow in almost every soil and climate. They can be grown from seed but are usually planted as nursery-grown 'quicks'. Wild rose (*Rosa canina*) is also worth considering, as is hornbeam (*Carpinus betulus*), which copes well with heavy soil. Beech (*Fagus sylvatica*) will also grow almost anywhere provided the soil isn't polluted. Holly (*Ilex aquifolium*) is slow-growing but is probably the most shade-tolerant of hedging plants. Planting in a double row rather than a single row will establish a solid hedge more quickly. A gap of 20cm (8in) between plants and around 45cm (18in) between rows is ideal for most varieties.

Just as widely available in France as it is in the UK, Leyland cypress (*Cupressocyparis leylandii*) provides dense hedging and is an excellent windbreak, its most tempting attribute being that it's fast-growing (in ten years, *leylandii* can grow 5m, whereas most other hedging species grow around 3m). If the tops are cut out once it has reached a suitable height, its growth will be controlled. If neglected, however, *leylandii* can become so 'leggy' as to be of no use as a hedge or can start to die, leaving unsightly brown patches and gaps. Because *leylandii* creates an evergreen canopy and adds acidity to the soil, no other species will grow near it. If you nevertheless feel the urge to plant it, you can buy container-grown shrubs around 30 to 45cm high for just a few euros from any garden centre. In spring, plants are often on offer in the gardening section of supermarkets.

There are other conifers which, although not as fast-growing as *leylandii*, will make an adequate hedge, provided the leaders are cut out once they've reached the required height. A useful hedging shrub is lonicera (*Lonicera nitida*), which is evergreen, cheap and quick to establish, and won't be eaten by rabbits, deer or hares. Note, however, that a mixed hedge is more interesting than one consisting of only one type of plant.

CUTTING

An essential annual task is cutting trees, hedges and bushes to contain growth and retain their shape. Growth rates in rural France are considerably greater than in the UK, for example, and trees and shrubs left to their own devices will soon become ugly and unmanageable. Don't be afraid to cut back hard, as you will rarely do permanent damage.

To cut wood thicker than your little finger, invest in some good loppers (known and sold in France as *coupe-branches*, *ébrancheur* or *sécateur deux mains*), preferably of the 'bypass' type, i.e. with blades that pass each other as they cut. Depending on the quality, these will cost between €17 and €25. If you intend to cut wood thicker than 2cm, you will need to buy a good pruning saw (*scie élagage*, *scie arbo* or *scie couteau devaux*); don't try to force secateurs or loppers through thicker material, as it's likely to rip the bark **and** damage the tool. See also **Pruning** on page 88.

Pollarding

Pollarding (*écimage*) was developed as a means of continually producing firewood without cutting down trees, which instead are lopped annually. This was especially important in areas where trees were in short supply, and the practice ensured good, straight branches above the reach of livestock. Since then, pollarding has evolved into a means of removing old growth and creating new for ornamental purposes or in order to keep large trees under control, e.g. along the streets of towns and cities.

Most deciduous trees are suitable for pollarding: dormant shoots lie in the cambium bark layer and are stimulated into growth after the branches have been removed. If you have a pollarded tree on your property, don't neglect to cut it back each spring – the best time is when the same operation is carried out in nearby villages and towns. If you leave a pollarded tree to grow unchecked, there's a danger that storms will break many of the branches with resulting damage to the tree and possibly your property or, worse, you or your family. (This is because new shoots are weaker at the joint than the original branches.)

Once a branch has been cut, smooth off any rough edges. The practice of painting wounds with tar or creosote went out of fashion many years ago (although you may find it advocated in older books), as research has proven that this seals in disease. Instead, leave the cut clean and the cambium or bark layer will gradually close over the wound.

Coppicing

The art of coppicing (*taillis*) was introduced for a similar purpose but, as it involved cutting back the main trunk to almost ground level so that side shoots would develop and eventually produce several trunks rather than a single one, it was generally used in areas where livestock couldn't graze and there were no deer (or they could be controlled).

The trees most suitable for coppicing are hazel, chestnut and alder. If you've inherited a wooded area containing such species and you wish to maintain it, you would do well to continue the practice (see **Creating Woodland** on page 64). There are many incidental benefits to doing so: improving the habitat and its suitability for wildlife, especially woodland butterflies; prolonging the life of the trees; lessening the risk of disease by removing affected stock; and obtaining timber for firewood, beanpoles, pea sticks and fencing stakes (chestnut makes the best fence posts, as it's the longest lasting and has a straight grain, making it easy to split into half-round stakes or even rails).

Traditionally, trees are cut back every three to five years – a five-year cycle is ideal. If your woodland has been left unmanaged for longer than this, you should coppice it as soon as possible. To find out the last time coppicing has been carried out, ask a neighbour or look at the diameter of the previous scar tissue and compare this with the diameter of a new shoot. If in doubt, cut back and begin a new cycle.

The best time for cutting is between early November and the end of February. A hand saw (*scie*) or, more usually, a chainsaw (*tronçonneuse*) is used, and each cut should slope downwards so that rainwater will run off, thus preventing a build-up of moisture and consequent rotting of the stump. Be careful also not to damage the bark on the stump below the cut, which will not only affect future growth but also encourage infestations of harmful insects, bacteria or fungi.

Coppicing should result in fast and prolific re-growth from the stumps (properly called stools), especially when the cuts are made as close to the ground as possible, encouraging new shoots to develop their own root structure. Coppiced hazel and chestnut stools remain productive for up to 200 years and it's only when the practice stops that the trees begin to fail as a result of rot from broken branches. In a garden, coppicing is unlikely to produce enough timber to be of much value, but hazel makes a better shaped bush if coppiced from time to time.

Layering

Cutting the top shoots (leaders) of any hedgerow species (even if it's growing as a single shrub or bush) can only be beneficial, as the operation will encourage vigorous growth from the side shoots. A stout pair of gloves and a billhook (*serpe*) are all that's required to layer a hedge in the traditional way. Try to find someone to show you how to do the job properly (which is likely in many parts of France, where many farmers still use old-fashioned methods); if you cannot, an adequate result can be achieved by merely chopping most of the way through young, strong branches and gently bending them in the direction of the line of the hedge. It's important not to cut too far or the branches will break as you bend them and then die. In a badly neglected hedge it may be necessary to use a chainsaw as opposed to a billhook, but there's more chance of cutting right through the growth.

Like most cutting operations, this work should be done during the winter months, when the sap is at its lowest and cutting isn't likely to cause damage to new shoots. In a very short time (certainly by the end of the second year), the areas that have been layered will be producing substantial new stock, which may itself need layering.

SURVIVAL TIP

A chainsaw is an extremely dangerous tool and should be used only by competent operators (see page 182).

MEADOWS

You cannot just leave a patch of land in the hope that it will miraculously turn into a glorious wild flower meadow. If you do, you're likely to be rewarded only with weeds, stinging nettles and brambles. To create a natural meadow requires long-term care and attention, and even then the flowers will take some years to become established.

The grass should be cut once a year after all the plants have set seeds (as for hay). Leave the grass until it has dried and all the seeds have fallen onto the ground and then rake it all up. This will ensure that the last of the seeds are knocked off the stems. It's important to remove the grass; otherwise, as it rots, it will release nutrients back into the soil and encourage the grass to grow again, thereby creating competition for the flowers when they appear. If you have goats (see **Goats** on page 144), dried grass is perfect for them (turn it several times while it's drying); otherwise, just leave the rakings in a pile ready for autumn burning. **Never feed goats fermenting grass cuttings, which can be fatal!**

Although planting wild flowers (*fleur sauvage*) isn't as popular in France as in the UK, for example, it's possible to buy packets of wild flower seeds in some large garden centres. The inclusion of a few packets will help to establish a meadow, but make sure that they contain plant varieties that grow naturally in your area. Plant them by 'sod-seeding': cut and lift a flap of turf with a spade, sprinkle some seed and let the turf fall back into place. Note, however, that if field voles find them you may have to do it all again, as they're extremely partial to wild flower seeds!

If a meadow has uneven areas it's advisable to level it with subsoil before planting seeds, but don't use good topsoil which is of more value in the garden and too high in nutrients. A few clumps of nettles should be left – they're an important source of food for some of the most spectacular butterflies (see **Moths & Butterflies** on page 223) and insects that will not only give pleasure but also help pollinate the flowers you're trying to encourage.

Ideally, animals shouldn't be grazed in a wild flower meadow, as their droppings re-introduce fertiliser and nutrients, neither of which is required.

PONDS

It's likely that your newly-acquired land will contain a pond (*étang* or *mare*). These are popular in rural France, where they're used for coarse fishing (see **Fishing** on page 209) and as a supply for irrigating fields. If it doesn't, you may want to consider creating one as an amenity and/or a home for wildlife.

Creating a Pond

It's possible to create a pond by digging a hole, lining it and filling it with water, although this is hard work, expensive and not guaranteed to succeed. If, on the other hand, there's a stream or river running through your property, it can be relatively simple to turn part of it into a pond.

Even if not obvious, there may be an underground watercourse near the surface. To find out, consult the map of subterranean watercourses at the Bureau Régional Geologique Minier. An alternative is to engage the services of a water diviner (*sourcier*). Good diviners can be surprisingly specific and accurate in their findings.

If your intended pond is to cover less than 2,000m², you don't need permission to create it, but as in all such situations in rural France it's best to inform the *mairie* before you start work. If it's going to be larger than this, you must obtain permission from SAFER (see page 32) as well as employing an engineer to provide plans and supervise the project.

A pond should have a few deep points – especially if you intend to stock fish in it. Coarse fish can generally survive in shallower ponds than trout, which require a depth of around 2.5m (8ft) in order to have enough oxygen in the hottest weather. If there's a raised piece of ground around which water can be diverted, this will make an attractive island.

It isn't enough to dam a watercourse and hope for the best. A log laid across a stream supporting a few sheets of corrugated tin driven into the ground won't work – not because the dam will burst but because water will seep underneath or around it. A dam must be solidly constructed and of a height no less than the maximum depth of the pond. It should also include a sluice gate. This might seem an unnecessary refinement, but it will help you cope with the inevitable floods and flush away silt deposits.

The sides of a pond should be grassed to resist erosion. If your pond attracts unwelcome coypu (*ragondin* – see page 226), which will undermine its banks, you can ask the *mairie* to have the local Féderation des Chasseurs set traps for them. Coypu runs are easy to spot, being muddy and greasy like those of rats.

MANAGEMENT & MAINTENANCE

To make sure that your land doesn't degenerate into a wilderness, you will need to manage and maintain it. After the *Maire*, your local farmer is probably the most important person to keep on the right side of when living in rural France. He might be willing to spray weeds, apply fertiliser and bale your hay at the same time as carrying out similar operations on his own land. Most are only too happy to help once they've seen that you're making an effort to integrate and do things correctly.

Fencing

Provided you've taken care to include it in the purchase contract, you will inherit some kind of fencing with your property. Whether it's adequate for your purpose is another matter and, even if it is, it will need regular maintenance and eventual replacement, which can be costly. In the long term, hedges or posts and rails are a more satisfactory solution for cattle and horses than wire fencing, although other animals may need specialised fencing (see below).

Boundary Fencing

Your boundary fence is the most important and must be properly maintained. If internal fencing fails and your sheep or goats eat all your precious vegetables, it's only you who suffers. If your boundary fence gives way, you may have to pacify and possibly compensate an irate neighbour whose trees have been stripped of their bark!

By far the most effective boundary fencing is stock fence. This is 1m high, galvanised wire mesh that can be bought in 25m or 50m rolls. The square holes at the bottom are smaller than those at the top to prevent lambs or piglets from getting through. The mesh should be clipped with wire ties to strained plain wire that has been fixed at the top, middle and bottom to pressure-treated timber posts, firmly driven into the ground every 5m. The posts should be long enough to protrude above the fencing by at least 25cm, as this will be required to carry two strands of barbed wire. If the straining wire isn't tight, stock fencing soon becomes slack, so you should tighten the wire with tensioners, obtainable from your local *quincaillier* in the '*outillage agricole*' section, rather than rely on fencing pliers.

As the corners of your fencing will take a considerable strain, you should dig in a substantial corner post with diagonal braces nailed to it along the line of the proposed fence. Dig a good-size hole – at least 60cm (2ft) deep – and fill it with pieces of stone or even cement once the post is inserted. If the intended run is more than around 50m, another 'strainer' should be fitted halfway along. The braces should also be pressure treated.

A fence of this type should contain all but the most determined of stock (but see **Livestock Fencing** below) and, if constructed properly, should last for at least 20 years. If you have a rabbit problem, clip half a metre of wire mesh netting to the base of the stock fence.

Livestock Fencing

If one of the intended uses of your land is to keep livestock, your property may require specialised fencing. For details of fencing for poultry, see **Constructing a Pen** on page 117.

Goats are inquisitive and know that the grass (or bush or tree) is always greener on the other side of the fence. To prevent them climbing out of their enclosure, use stock fencing (see **Boundary Fencing** above) raised around 15cm (6in) off the ground with an extra wire 15cm above the top of the fence. The corner posts must obviously have wire rather than wooden braces, which would allow an active goat to climb to freedom. A similar fence, but with wooden corner posts, will suffice for pigs – with the addition of an electrified wire (see below). Note, however, that goats and sheep with horns can get their heads stuck fast in stock fencing.

It's wise to cut back bushes and other potentially edible matter a metre or so from the outside of a fence so that there's less temptation for animals to push against or climb it.

Electric Fencing

There are two types of electric fencing: a single strand of electrified wire (*fil électrique*) and electrified mesh (*clôture électrique mobile*). The latter is made of nylon, through which are woven strands of electricity-conducting wire. The bottom strand isn't electrified, to prevent a short to the ground. It's important to keep vegetation away from either type in order to prevent accidental shorting. Power is supplied by a battery-operated unit, which costs around €120 and must be kept charged or regularly replaced. Coils of single strand wire cost around €75 for a 400m roll, and you should expect to pay €75 for a 50m length of electrified mesh.

SURVIVAL TIP

Electrified mesh shouldn't be used for animals with horns, because if they get them stuck in the mesh, they will suffer constant electrification until they manage to free themselves, shredding your fence in the process.

If you already have a fence but don't think it's strong enough to withstand a daily battering by goats and constant rubbing by sheep, a single strand of electrified wire at a strategic height will keep them away from it. An electric fence will also help protect your property against deer, but the strands need to be set higher. On the other hand, don't set the bottom wire too high, as deer will learn to crawl underneath.

A stock fence (see above) intended for pigs should also have a single electric strand running around the interior to prevent them from rubbing against the posts or trying to dig under the netting. As an alternative, pigs can be 'folded' in any part of your property that needs turning over periodically by a single- or double-strand electric fence.

Drainage

Most French properties are well drained. (The average French landowner seems to care more about drainage from his land than about drainage from his house!) The main factors in drainage planning and design are the relationship between rainfall and evaporation and their seasonal pattern. Obviously, low-lying land is more susceptible to drainage problems, but any area of relatively flat land will tend to accumulate water.

The cheapest method of drainage is an open ditch system, and most properties have one or two ditches running though them. An alternative is to use plastic field drainage pipes, which have small holes in them for water to seep through.

If you're intending to dig a ditch, its dimensions will depend on the soil type and land gradient, but as a rule of thumb it should be at least 25cm (10in) below any existing drain or pipe outlets. The gradient should be 1/100, i.e. a fall of 1m for every 100m length. The width of the ditch at the top should equal the sum of the width at the bottom and its depth (for example, a ditch 0.5m wide at the bottom and 1m deep should be 1.5m wide at the top) in order to prevent the sides falling in. Obviously, the top of the ditch will need to be progressively wider as the ditch becomes deeper. A ditch should be cut in as straight a line as possible and the soil moved well away so that it cannot be washed back in.

Plastic land drainage pipe can be bought from Espace Emeraude, Point P and larger branches of Mr Bricolage (look under *Matériaux* in yellow pages). It's available in 6m (20ft) lengths – the ends of which are either tapered or enlarged so that they slot inside each other – or in 200m rolls. The latter option requires hiring a pipe-laying machine and operators but saves hours of digging and may be worth considering if there's major drainage to be done.

Clearing and maintenance should be carried out regularly. It's important to keep open ditches clear of debris and to ensure that any bank slippage is repaired immediately. A reasonable period between ditch bottom cleaning is five years, but annual attention should be given to the vegetation on the banks.

Grassland

If you inherit an area of grassland, you cannot sit back and do nothing. Before long it will become overgrown and eventually revert to scrubland, which is good for wildlife but won't endear you to neighbours if, for example, they're growing cereal crops and weed seeds drift from your garden to their fields. The presence of scrubland will also reduce the value of your property should you decide to sell – a house with well-maintained grassland is a much more attractive proposition to most would-be house buyers. Regular cutting will rejuvenate grassland – when grasses are able to 'tiller' freely, they spread over the ground to form a dense sward.

A field, even if grazed by your own or a neighbour's sheep or cattle, will need 'topping' (*fauchage*) at least once every summer. Unfortunately, animals eat some vegetation in preference to others and anything not grazed is left rough and unkempt. Horses and donkeys are the worst offenders and won't eat areas contaminated by their own droppings. If you decide to make your field available to horses, it's therefore important that you insist on their owners removing the manure on a daily basis. If you ask them to stack it near to your vegetable garden, it will prove a useful addition to your autumn digging. You could make it part of the conditions of rent that a farmer cuts the field once his livestock have been removed. Land used for grazing should be harrowed after use to spread the droppings and avoid clumps of coarse grass.

Fertilising

Soil is able to supply some or all of the nutrients for grass growth, but fertilisers help make up the difference between what's present naturally and what a particular crop needs to grow. Unlike a wild flower meadow, where extra nutrients aren't required (see **Meadows** on page 70), grassland needs the addition of nitrogen. Grazing animals re-circulate a high proportion of nitrogen, but it may pay to give your paddocks a good dressing of artificial fertiliser during the early growing months (i.e. in late spring). If they're small, you could spread nitrogen by hand – it comes in granular form and it's a simple operation to scatter it across a field from a bucket. Make sure you wear rubber gloves, however. Although nitrogen isn't normally harmful, it can cause cut or damaged skin to sting. Use no more than 50kg per hectare.

Weed Control

Just as they will invade your garden unless checked, weeds are likely to infest open patches of uncultivated land. The nature of weed problems varies greatly throughout France. In some cases, a weed infestation may consist of a single species, which can be dealt with by a specific herbicide. If there's a wide variety of weeds, however, you will have to use a broad-spectrum weed killer (these normally contain a mixture of up to four herbicides). Wherever possible, you should select the weed killer least likely to be harmful to animal life (although the French attitude to pesticides and herbicides is generally 'the stronger the better'!). Herbicides differ in their reaction to low temperatures, so it's important to check the suitability of a product if using it in cold weather.

SURVIVAL TIP

Ragwort, easily recognisable by its yellow flowers and serrated leaves, is extremely poisonous to livestock and should be pulled up by hand (wearing gloves) to prevent it spreading.

Animals won't attempt to eat ragwort when it's growing (unless they're very hungry) but will become interested in it when it's cut and dried. It's therefore important that none is included in a hay crop and that pulled plants are stacked out of reach of livestock until they can be burnt.

If you have an orchard, the grass surrounding the trees needs cutting at least twice yearly to prevent the growth of brambles and other weeds – more often if you want it to be an attractive area.

Anne's
HOME MADE
Jams

5.

Flowers & Fruits

Having acquired your dream home in rural France, you will sooner or later need to tackle the garden. If you're an experienced gardener the prospect shouldn't be daunting. If you're new to gardening or have had little interest or previous experience, it's advisable to bring one or two general gardening books with you and ask your French neighbours for advice. Unless your grasp of French is good, trying to translate gardening advice from French books from your local library or book shop will be a frustrating task. However, don't despair, as with a bit of effort (or a lot if it's a jungle) your plot will soon be home not only to attractive plants and flowers, but also to fruit-bearing shrubs, vegetables and trees.

PLANNING

It's possible to create a low-maintenance garden quite easily, but short of covering the area with a six-inch layer of concrete, **there's no such thing as a no-maintenance garden**. With this thought in mind, your next consideration should be whether you will be living permanently in France or just visiting for holidays.

Many a holiday homeowner has regretted failing to plan his garden and subsequently spent the first ten days of a hard-earned two-week holiday doing back-breaking work in the sunshine trying to bring the garden into some semblance of respectability.

With some careful thought the task can be made much easier. It's unlikely that you will have a blank canvas on which to design your perfect garden – if you do, you're extremely lucky. Most buyers inherit established gardens in various states of neglect – particularly if the property has been on the market for some time. If you've purchased a house in need of complete renovation, the garden will almost certainly need similar treatment and by the time you've restored your new home to its former glory, the garden will have become a jungle.

Design

Decide early on what you want from your garden: a sunny sitting area, an area of lawn for children to play on, decorative borders, a vegetable plot or *potager* (see page 98) ... Having decided, keep the design simple. A lawn dotted with flower or shrub beds may look beautiful, but beds are notoriously high-maintenance and also make mowing difficult. There are ways of reducing maintenance work (see **Preparation** on page 83), but beds will still need attention. Consider making the grassed area suitable for a ride-on mower. Create gentle sweeping curves and open areas rather than narrow paths and spaces between shrubs, as this will make mowing much easier. Areas covered with chippings or gravel can look attractively rustic, but they require constant raking, spraying or weeding to keep them from becoming overgrown. (Although the grass may stop growing in the hot months of July and August, weeds never seem to!)

Before making any final decisions, it will pay to observe where the sun strikes the garden at different times of the year. Whilst sunshine is important, particularly in the morning and evening, its heat in the middle of the day is to be avoided. Dappled shade beneath mature trees will become a valuable asset, so don't be in too much of a hurry to remove trees before working out how this would affect the garden (see **Overhanging Trees** on page 84).

Soft Fruits

It would be a pity not to take advantage of the generally sunny weather in many parts of France and grow soft fruits, such as red- and blackcurrants, strawberries, raspberries, blackberries and gooseberries. A fruit cage in which you can grow all these without the risk of their being stolen by birds could be made to fit an odd corner but a bit of thought should be given to its position. Most soft fruits enjoy a fair amount of sunshine, so it's important that the taller bushes don't shade the smaller ones. Start with strawberries at the front of the plot (which should face south, if possible) and work up to the highest (probably raspberry canes) at the back. Ideally, a fruit cage should measure at least 5m by 5m. There are many ready-made sectional cages available, the longest lasting (but least unobtrusive) being made from tubular steel. Some come with netting fixed to the side panels; others require a net draped over the framework.

Fruit Trees

When planning for fruit trees, look for a fairly open site well away from the roots of other trees and shrubs that could compete for the soil's nutrients. Alternatively, most fruit trees – but especially peach, apricot and fig trees – will grow well against a wall, provided that their roots are firmly fixed in a good bed of soil. The heat reflected from the wall will help to ripen the fruit. Apples and pears grown either as individual trees (cordons) forming a hedge or as a 'fan' (espalier) against a wall will take up little space.

Irrigation & Weed Control

Finally, don't forget the question of watering; although perhaps not as crucial as in a vegetable garden (see **Watering** on page 103), watering will be necessary at certain times – particularly in hot, dry areas – and carrying a watering can long distances or unravelling lengths of unsightly, tangled hosepipe will soon lose its novelty value. If your plants are some distance from an existing tap, consider installing an underground pipe and a concealed tap when you lay out your garden.

If you're likely to be absent for long periods during the summer and don't have a friendly neighbour to water your plants, you will need to make alternative arrangements, e.g. install an automatic watering system. A particularly good system is made by Hozelock and consists of a battery-powered timer, a pressure-reducing valve and hoses. The small-bore hoses, which are fairly easily hidden, can be laid among and around precious or delicate plants (including those in tubs, pots and hanging baskets). Each hose terminates with a drip nozzle, which can be adjusted to the needs of the plant it waters. Set the timer to the required frequency and duration of watering, switch on the water supply and away you go.

The only disadvantage of such a system is that it won't remove weeds – but there are ways of reducing weed growth. Consider using a landscape fabric (*toile de paillage*) or mulching film (*film de paillage*). This is usually made of fibreglass (or a similar artificial material) and designed to allow water and air to pass through it whilst suppressing the growth of plants underneath. It can be laid on a new bed and plants inserted through it or it can be cut tightly around existing plants. Covered with mulch such as chipped bark, it cannot be seen, and any weeds that manage to germinate in the mulch are easily pulled out. The saving in labour and water is remarkable and it's well worth the initial financial outlay, as sheeting will last for many years. Shop around before purchasing, however, as it comes in different roll widths and lengths; 1.40m x 10m rolls are suitable for small areas and cost between €5 (for film) and €25 (for heavy-duty fabric).

As a further aid to reducing maintenance it might be possible to install perforated hosepipe (*tuyau poreux*) under the sheeting or fabric. This lets water to seep out along its length (the connections can be tucked out of sight) and costs around €11 for a 20m roll. Watering then becomes a simple matter of connecting the hose to the supply and leaving it on for a couple of hours as little as once a week.

PREPARATION

It's vital to prepare ground thoroughly before planting. Unless you have a private well, your water supply will be metered and you will have to pay for it. It therefore makes sense not only to reduce waste by careful planning (see **Irrigation & Weed Control** above) but also to prepare your garden so that it can survive under all weather conditions (planting varieties suitable for the local climate will obviously also help). This is best done by soil improvement.

Soil Improvement

As in other countries, most soil benefits from the addition of peat and peat substitutes, compost and farmyard manure (FYM). In rural France, there appears to be an almost limitless supply of manure (*fumier*) and most farmers are willing to sell it cheaply. Manure is best obtained in late autumn, after the harvest, or during winter when the farmer is hauling it to the fields. Expect to pay around €20 to €30 for a trailer load (around 5m^3), including delivery.

If manure is too fresh it will burn plants, so it should be stacked for a while, but older (and less smelly) manure is usually obtainable – if you insist a little. It should be spread on the soil in the early winter – so that it has a chance to rot and be pulled down by earthworms – in a layer between 5 and 15cm (2 to 6in) deep. At this rate, one trailer load will cover between 7 and 20m^2. However, if you're turning over soil by deep digging (i.e. starting with a trench and back-filling from the soil in front of you, adding manure to the base of each trench), the area covered will be less than 4m^2 per load.

Dig manure in well; beds will immediately benefit, as it feeds and improves the soil and also helps it retain water. Well matured manure can be used as an inexpensive mulch, which will help further to save water and also to suppress weeds.

Should your garden be too small to justify a whole trailer load of manure (or if you're averse to the smell), an alternative is *terreau universel*, which is stocked by most garden centres and supermarkets. This is a type of compost and works almost as well as manure. It also has the benefit of being easy to use, as it comes in 25 or 50kg plastic sacks and is clean enough to be stored in an outhouse or shed. It's of variable quality and price, however, and generally you get what you pay for; the nutrient level of the best is about the same as well-rotted manure. A 40-litre bag should cover 2m^2 if laid around 5cm (2in) thick.

Fruit Beds

Beds for soft fruit plants such as strawberries should be well dug and have lots of well-rotted manure or compost added to them. Alternatively, incorporate a conditioning soil (*terre à planter*) or compost with a fertiliser already added (*terreau à lor brun*), which are suitable as a top dressing and soil improver for all plants. Prices range from €2 to €9 for a 40-litre sack and the rates of application for each type of job are listed on the back of the bag.

This process should raise the beds a little higher than adjacent paths. The soil can be kept in place by edging boards or by regular raking into sloping sides. Black polythene, through which slits can be cut and strawberries planted, will ensure that no weeding, no mulching and very little watering are required, especially if you bury the edges and install underground irrigation (see **Irrigation & Weed Control** on page 82).

Raspberries need some sort of climbing frame. The easiest way to create one is to hammer posts around 2m long into the ground 2 or 3m apart before stretching thick gardening wire horizontally between them at regular intervals. The plants can then be trained along these wires as they grow.

Overhanging Trees

If there's a mature tree that needs to be removed, check with the *mairie* before doing so. Officials like to be informed of any changes to the local landscape and can tell you of any restrictions or legal requirements that might apply.

If offending branches belong to a tree on a neighbour's property, you should approach him and ask whether he minds their being removed. Often, he will gladly help you and the task will result in an exchange of drinks and a new friendship. If the neighbour is reluctant or unable to help, say that you're prepared to cut the offending branch yourself, on the line of your boundary, and offer to return the cut wood, which technically is the neighbour's property.

Similarly, fruit growing on a neighbour's tree and overhanging your property belongs to the neighbour. On the other hand, if the fruit ripens and falls on your land, you're entitled to keep it. Once again, friendly discussion is much better than confrontation. (See also **Hedges** on page 66.)

PROPAGATION

In general, greenhouses (*serre*) are far less common in rural France than in the UK, for example, but many excellent models (including those familiar to British gardeners) are available at larger garden centres. However, their use is probably best confined to extending the season, as in summer they require heavy shading and forced ventilation to fulfil their potential. With a little heating, a greenhouse can allow you to over-winter tender plants such as orchids, which can be left outside from May to September.

A garden frame (*châssis vitré*) is an even more valuable asset. Garden centres and larger hardware stores stock a model called Nantes Lights. Similar to the Dutch Lights (*châssis hollandaise*) much beloved by professional gardeners, this consists of a ready-made frame about a metre square glazed with glass or rigid plastic. With a little scrap timber and some basic carpentry skill, a box frame can be constructed and the Nantes Lights fitted as a removable clear lid or roof. Alternatively, you can buy a complete garden frame, but it will obviously cost more than if you'd constructed the base yourself.

If a greenhouse or frame can be positioned near to an electricity supply, install a heater (fill the base with gravel and run a cable through it) to provide heat during the colder months for rooting up cuttings and protecting tender plants. During the spring it can be used to germinate seeds and later to harden off tender plants such as tomatoes and melons before exposing them to the rigours of the garden. In the early autumn, frames are useful for drying onion and garlic bulbs.

Use specialised soils for propagating and planting out seedlings. Sterilised soil (*terre dite de bruyère*) is ideal for use in a garden frame, while *terreau rempotage* should be used for potting and planting compost (*terreau plantation*) for transplanting to the garden. Prices range from €2 to €9 per 40-litre bag.

PLANTS & FRUIT TREES

It's commonly believed that there's no restriction on bringing garden plants from the UK to France, as most pests and diseases are common to the two countries. In fact, there are prohibitions on certain plants and, as a general rule, all plants and plant products should be offered for inspection by officers of the Plant Health Inspection Service (*contrôle phytosanitaire*) at the port of entry. Endangered or threatened species are also covered by the provisions of the CITES Convention and require an export permit from the country of origin and a French import permit issued by the Ministère de l'Agriculture et de la Pêche (175 rue du Chevaleret, 75646 Paris Cedex 13, ☎ 01 49 55 81 53). Anyone harbouring thoughts of bringing in hemp-related products is advised to check the legality of doing so, although it's currently possible for UK-based businesses to send hemp seeds to France.

Choosing Plants

Don't rush into your garden centre and buy all the garden shrubs you require on one visit just because they're in flower. If you do, it's likely that every year thereafter you will celebrate the anniversary of your visit with a riot of colour in the garden, but you will have little to enjoy the rest of the time. It's important to choose plants and shrubs that will give you a succession of flowers and colour throughout the season. Consider also the winter months and include plants that will give winter interest, such as dogwoods (Latin: *cornus*, French: *cornouiller* – see below), which are available in red- and yellow-bark varieties. If it's cut back in early spring before the new growth appears, dogwood produces new shoots which, once the leaves have fallen in the autumn, provide glowing colour right through winter.

It's impossible to list all the common garden plants available in France. The best thing to do is look what your neighbours are growing. Walk around and see what appears to thrive and what doesn't before planning any purchases. Roses are popular in many parts of the country, where the differing varieties can be inspected at nurseries and garden centres. Note, however, that your favourites in your home country may have been bred specifically for that climate and may not thrive in France. Locally-produced varieties have been developed with topographical conditions in mind and will generally give greater satisfaction.

Garden centres carry a wide range of plants (although generally not as wide as in the UK), and staff are generally knowledgeable and happy to advise on the suitability of particular varieties. Plants are also available in season from larger supermarkets, but you may find that the best plants are on sale at your local market – and are excellent value.

Plant names can be confusing and it's wise to get into the habit of using the Linnaeus system. This was invented by the Swedish biologist Carl von Linné in 1735, who devised standardised Latin names for all plants and living organisms (see **Author's Notes** on page 13). It's a valuable tool, as the French name for your favourite plants may be very different from the English name, whereas the Latin name will be known by professionals. Look it up in a gardening book and make a note of it before visiting a plant supplier or garden centre and you will be sure of making the right purchase.

In addition to brightening up the garden, plants can be a practical asset. Herbs are an obvious example (see page 98): not only can they add flavour to your cooking but some are claimed to provide a natural solution to plant pests and diseases. For example, according to popular belief in France, mosquitoes can be kept at bay by planting lavender, rosemary, santolina and pennyroyal near your terrace, while marigolds supposedly keep whitefly at bay if grown between susceptible plants. And all the above attract hover-flies, the larvae of which are voracious feeders on aphids.

If you're ever in Paris, it's worth visiting the Jardin des Plantes to gain some useful ideas. Situated near the Gare d'Austerlitz underground station, the garden was created by the premier botanists of the 16th century. Today, it contains greenhouses and alpine and rose gardens housing some 4,500 different plants, all of which are clearly labelled.

Choosing Fruit Trees

Whether you can cultivate certain plants – particularly fruit trees – depends largely on the local climate. When it comes to hardiness, there's a rough scale that runs from the north to the south of the country: from grapes (which will grow almost anywhere in France – Normandy, for example, used to have extensive vineyards) to olives and figs (from central France southwards) and finally to oranges and lemons (in the south only). Obviously, hardy fruit trees that grow well in almost any country, such as apple, pear, cherry and nut trees, will flourish in France.

The problem is not with the tree itself surviving a severe winter, but with frost damaging fruit as it forms in the spring. Peach trees generally produce good fruit south of the Loire. Oranges and lemons will grow in Provence, although traditional gardeners in the south believe that neither will do well if planted a long way from the coast. Lemon trees have also been grown successfully in the western Loire region, but fruit is often lost as a result of cold winds rather than frost. If you're desperate to grow oranges but don't live on the Côte d'Azur, you might reach a compromise by planting the ornamental *Calmondin x Citrofortunella mitis*, which produces a decorative clementine-like fruit with the minimum of winter protection. Alternatively, it may be possible to grow a single orange tree in a large container, which can be kept in a protected area in winter. To ensure that a potted tree receives sufficient nutrients from the soil, use a pot compost developed for Mediterranean plants (*terre parfait* or *terre agrumes*).

Some fruit trees are self-fertilising, others require the purchase of male and female plants – although you might get away with a single tree if your neighbours have similar ones in their garden, as bees will transfer the pollen from one to the other.

Most apple trees are sold trained, as it's the first two to three years' growth that requires the most skill in cultivation. All you need to do is decide on the shape you want them to be and prune accordingly. The size to which an apple tree will grow depends on the type of rootstock to which it has been grafted. There's less choice with pears, as most are grafted onto a semi-dwarf quince stock.

Planting

Dig a hole at least three times the size that a tree's roots currently require and remove all stones from the excavated soil (a coarse riddle helps). Mix the soil with an equal amount of *terreau universel*, compost or well-rotted FYM and a handful of bone meal. Break up the bottom of the hole before adding a little compost or FYM and mix it in well. If the roots of the plant have encircled the pot, tease them out gently, making sure that the root ball is moist before planting. As you fill the hole with the new soil mix, firm it in around the roots and the base of the plant. Fruit trees will need staking so that the wind doesn't cause the roots to move. Finally, give the tree a thorough watering – attention to detail now will avoid disappointment later. All that should then be required is regular watering to ensure that the roots become well established.

PRUNING

One of the most important things for the novice gardener to learn is how to prune. Growth rates in rural France are considerably greater than in the UK, for example, and plants and trees left to their own devices will soon become ugly and unmanageable. Some plants, such as lavatera, flower on the current year's shoots and, as soon as the leaves start to drop, should be cut down hard. Next spring, new shoots will rise from the rootstock and produce masses of blossom from a tidy shrub. Do this with forsythia, however, and you will never get flowers, as it blossoms on the previous year's shoots. It needs cutting down hard after it has finished flowering in the spring in order to give it a chance to produce new shoots during the summer. Once you've identified the right time of year to prune a particular type of plant or shrub, don't be afraid to cut back hard, as you will rarely do permanent damage.

Perhaps the worst thing you can do is to cut parts of branches off just because they're growing over a path or otherwise obstructing. If you must cut a branch, do so in the autumn or winter, when the sap has dropped back into the base of the trunk. Take the offending branch back to a joint, not just to where appears convenient, and cut it neatly. Leaving 'snag' wounds from the teeth of a saw invites disease and makes a well-shaped shrub look like an untidy hedge. Buy a quality pair of secateurs; there are many good makes available in France. See also **Cutting** on page 67.

Fruit Trees & Bushes

Fruit trees need careful attention if you wish to maintain them and obtain good crops. In addition to winter pruning, to remove diseased and crossing branches, summer pruning is vital. This is done when the sap has risen so that cuts heal quickly, thereby reducing the risk of fungal spores entering the wound. The object is to make a tree produce short fruiting spurs, and failing to carry out this task will eventually lead to long, thin branches laden with fruit and bending to the ground. Shortly after congratulating yourself on your magnificent crop, you will find half the branches torn off by the weight and the tree spoiled for years until you can re-shape it.

Plums or cherries 'fan' trained against a wall simply require their side shoots tying back against canes or to horizontal wires fixed to the wall. In the winter, all you need to do is shorten the main stems and branches by roughly one-third of the current year's growth to encourage new side shoots.

Gooseberry bushes over three years old should be pruned in the winter. The best way of doing this is to cut out one in three of the thickest stems at the base of the bush. Red- and blackcurrants will benefit from a little winter pruning but only around 8cm (3in) should be removed from the tips of the main stems.

As with most garden tasks, forethought and simple maintenance will produce good results; neglect only leads to tears. Most gardening books have a chapter on pruning but they may not give specific dates, as these vary with the region. In France, the ideal time could be a month or more ahead of the UK, for example.

FRUIT PESTS

In addition to the pests that affect plants generally (see **Controlling Pests & Diseases** on page 106), there are some that are specific to certain fruits and fruit trees. A general spraying programme is often advised but many common fruit pests are difficult to control by this method, as they arrive on the wing and disappear as soon as they've laid their eggs. Nevertheless, it won't hurt to apply a fenitrothion-based spray (the chemical name is universal), but don't use fenitrothion on cherry trees when they're flowering. The old gardener's tip of a winter tar oil spray may help and will certainly kill off any dormant eggs; it should be done in December or January.

Moths can be a major pest. Codling moths (*carpocapse des pommes*) are particularly troublesome on apple trees, where they lay their eggs on the immature fruit. These turn into small maggots that burrow into the apple as it ripens. Many garden centres and agricultural suppliers stock traps that use the pheromone smell of the females of species such as codling moths to attract the males, which are caught on a sticky material, as on a sheet of flypaper, and therefore unable to mate with the females, who in turn are unable to lay eggs. (Each supplier has its own trade name for these traps, but it's easy to see what they're for from the pictures on the box.) One trap for every four or five trees, left hanging throughout the summer, is usually enough. They're also effective against other similar pests and well worth the investment of a few euros. Grease bands (*bande de graisse*) placed around the trunks of apple trees will trap the grubs of winter moths as they attempt to hibernate in the ground at the base of the tree in the autumn.

Hazelnuts can be affected by the hazelnut weevil. Its eggs are laid in young nuts in May and June, and in late summer they bore circular holes through the shells in order to reach the ground and pupate. There seems to be no chemical means of control, but in most years only a small proportion of the crop is affected.

RURAL
LIFE

SEEDLINGS
SEEDLINGS
SEEDLINGS

6.

Vegetable Garden

Even the least enthusiastic of gardeners often find that with ample land, favourable weather and the simple fact that everyone else is growing vegetables, they're overcome by an urge to be self-sufficient. However, if you've been invited by neighbours for an *apéritif* and they're keen gardeners – as most French country dwellers are – you may well be envious of their rows of immaculate vegetables. Certainly, the BBC's 'Ground Force' team would be given short shrift if they suggested to the average rural French person that a garden could be produced in just two days, as there are no quick fixes or shortcuts when it comes to vegetable production. Not for them is it a question of merely sticking a plant or seed into the soil and hoping for the best. When they plant, it's in soil that has been carefully prepared and nurtured over several years. Good gardening practice is a serious science, as is evidenced by French seed packets, which provide spaces in which you can note the time of sowing, as well as the weather, the phase of the moon (see **Planting by the Moon** on page 101) and the date of the first harvest.

Nevertheless, creating a vegetable garden shouldn't be a daunting prospect, and in doing so you will show the neighbours that you, as well as your plants, intend to put down roots. Two of the greatest advantages you will have if you've moved from a more northerly country are that in most areas the growing season is longer (an average of six weeks longer than in the UK) and a greater variety of vegetables and fruits can be grown. The exact length of the growing season obviously depends on the local climate – there may be little noticeable difference between southern England and northern France, for example, but south of the Loire the difference is considerable. Like many other parts of France, the western Loire area is blessed with a microclimate conducive to market gardening, and it has good reason to be known as 'The Garden of France'.

Skilful planning and rotation might enable you to produce as many as three crops from each plot in a year. And a longer season means that even mundane crops such as outdoor tomatoes have time to reach maturity, so you won't have to resort to making vast quantities of green chutney from unripe fruit. Peppers, melons, cucumbers, aubergines, figs, peaches and even kiwi fruits can usually be grown outdoors, although some fruit trees will need to be covered with fleece in the winter.

NEIGHBOURS & ADVICE

Neighbours are the best people to ask for advice, especially if they've lived in the area for a long time. For example, in particularly dry areas of the country, they might suggest that you plant your haricot beans especially deep so that they reach the available moisture for longer and have a better chance of germinating.

On the other hand, try discussing parsnips (*panais*) with a neighbour and you're in for some blank looks, as the French don't recognise these as a separate vegetable type, but merely as part of the turnip group (*navet*) – if indeed they recognise them at all. Sweetcorn or 'corn on the cob' is known simply as maize (*maïs*) by the majority of French people, who consider it to be nothing more than cattle feed.

Chicory can cause linguistic confusion between French and English. The roots grown and roasted for coffee are called *chicorée* but the roots saved and forced in order to produce vegetable buds are called *endive* (but chicory in English). A close relative, which, on the market stall, looks like a lettuce and is usually blanched in the middle to reduce its bitterness, is known as *chicorée frisée* but endive in English.

Although knowing what your neighbours are growing will tell you what varieties are most likely to be successful locally, you should be imaginative with your vegetable growing and take advantage of the fact that the climate will probably allow you to cultivate varieties that you couldn't even attempt to grow in your home country. If you're unsure what plants are best suited to your soil and there's no one to ask, you could try scattering a mixture of various seeds and see what thrives – remembering that, planted properly, they would be sown at different depths and that each variety has a different germination period. What it lacks in scientific rigour, this method gains in empirical simplicity. Good luck!

CREATING A PLOT

Assuming that your rural property has the average amount of land, it should be possible to find an area suitable for vegetable growing. But whether you choose a traditional plot or raised beds (see **Raised Beds** below), some thought needs to be put into its position.

A south-facing area, level and sheltered from the wind, is ideal. It should have plenty of sunlight (i.e. for at least half the number of daylight hours), and rich, finely-textured soil will be an enormous advantage. If your potential plot has none of these attributes, you will have to put in a great deal of physical labour to achieve the desired results, although there are ways of compensating for a plot's deficiencies, including the following:

- **Poor Quality Soil** – Soil can be improved by the addition of compost, farmyard manure (FYM) or the contents of cheap grow-bags (see **Soil Improvement** on page 83).

- **Insufficient Sunshine** – Too much shade can sometimes be cured by the (admittedly drastic) step of cutting down a tree, but it's best to check your legal position at the *Mairie* before you do so (see also **Planning** on page 80).
- **Too Much Wind** – Exposure to wind can be avoided by planting a hedge, but make sure it isn't of a type that will create shade in later years or leach all the nutrients from the soil. Rolls of windbreak (*brise-vent*, *abat-vent* or *volis*) material can be bought from supermarkets, garden centres and DIY centres as an effective temporary measure.
- **Sloping Ground** – On sloping ground, it may be necessary to dig out terraces on which to grow your vegetables and, to prevent the edges being washed away, fit boards, breezeblocks or lengths of tree trunk.

Most vegetables need an ample and regular supply of water to mature successfully, so if possible site your plot or raised bed within easy access of a water supply.

Basic Cultivation

Such is the generosity of the average French farmer that it won't be too great an imposition to ask him to plough and cultivate your plot – and to supply some FYM into the bargain. Most farmers have at least one small tractor – especially in wine-growing areas – and, provided your patch is large enough for him to manoeuvre in, your request will add little to his daily routine and he may well do the work for free. Nevertheless, a bottle of something will undoubtedly be appreciated – but check whether he has his own vines; it would be a serious insult to offer him mass-marketed wine when he's the producer of a *premier cru* and much safer to go for a single malt whisky. Nevertheless, if you're planning to have a large vegetable plot, it will pay to buy or hire a rotary tiller (*motobineuse*) to turn over the soil for the first time (see **Plant Hire** on page 174).

Ground that requires heavy cultivating could first be sprayed with a 'systemic' weed killer (*désherbant polyvalent*), which is taken in through the leaves of the plant and doesn't infiltrate the soil. It will then have to be left for a few weeks before digging.

When it comes to preparing your plot, you have a choice of timing: autumn digging will give the soil a chance to break down over the winter (and you the opportunity to improve its condition further by the addition of more compost); spring digging is likely to be easier, as the soil will be more manageable from the winter rain, but if it's too wet your planting programme could be delayed.

Raised Beds

Raised beds are an excellent way of growing produce in a small area. The advantages over a traditional plot include the following:

- They're always well drained; because they're small enough for you to work from the side, the soil is never compacted by constantly being walked over. (Although treading the soil can be beneficial when growing brassicas, e.g. broccoli, Brussels sprouts and cabbage, repeated tramping up and down breaks down the structure of the soil.)
- Because you don't need to walk between the rows, plants can be placed closer together.
- The soil can be altered to suit the types of vegetable you plan to grow – carrots (*carotte*), for example, need a fine, sandy soil while cabbages (*chou*) require a heavy soil – and beds containing different types of compost (*terreau*) can be rotated each season.
- They can be sited near to the house (or another source of water) to make watering easier.

Raised beds are ideal for the elderly or infirm, as they're more easily accessible from a chair or wheelchair.

Building a Bed

A raised bed consists of a soil-retaining wall (railway sleepers are ideal but difficult to obtain), within which good-quality compost is laid. Beds can be built on poor, stony ground and even on concrete. In the latter case, they need to be at least 60cm (2ft) deep in order to accommodate roots. On poor soil, half that height is ample, as the beds will contain enough good-quality compost to start off the seeds or plants and the roots will then push through into the soil underneath. A raised bed can be any length but shouldn't be more than 120cm (4ft) wide so that you can reach the middle from either side.

Growing medium can be expensive, so check whether there's any good-quality topsoil on your land and mix it roughly 2:1 with bought compost. The only disadvantage with this method is that the crops will rapidly use up the soil's nutrients unless you regularly add organic fertilizers (e.g. blood and bone, calcified seaweed and potash) or mix in a bag of new compost annually.

POTAGERS

A book dealing with life in rural France wouldn't be complete without at least a mention of the *potager*. Literally translated, *potager* means kitchen garden, but the French word implies a garden in which the ornamental aspect is every bit as important as its function as a producer of vegetables, fruit and herbs. To add to the ornamental aspect, you should therefore include a variety of flowers, rose bushes and shrubs.

The most famous example of the French *potager* is at the Château de Villandry – one of the last Renaissance houses to be built on the Loire. Vegetables and fruit trees are arranged in a multicoloured chequerboard, each of its nine squares enclosed by clipped hedges of box and yew. It's unlikely that you will aspire to such heights, but if your house lends itself to the creation of a *potager*-style garden and you're a glutton for hard work, you might enjoy creating one.

Layout

To achieve the required formality, the beds should be grouped in geometric patterns and be surrounded by dwarf hedging. Paths between the beds can be surfaced with stones or shingle and perhaps be partly covered by archways or small pergolas, over which roses or vines can be grown. Non-edible plants should be in the centre if the bed can be walked around or at the back if not. Coloured and variegated lettuce, such as lollo rossa, the fronds of carrots and the bright flowers of courgettes and runner beans (*haricot à rames*) will add to the ornamental aspect. To ensure that there are never unsightly patches of bare earth, you must prepare young plants in pots and fill gaps as soon as a crop has finished. With careful planning, it should be possible to keep the *potager* filled with seasonal vegetables, but flower bulbs (e.g. daffodils, irises and tulips) will add colour in the spring.

HERBS

If you're planning to have a vegetable garden, you must also have a herb garden; French cooking depends on their inclusion, and salads are enhanced by the addition of a few fresh herbs. Home-grown tomatoes, sliced and laid between alternate layers of onions, mozzarella cheese and basil, are the perfect summer lunch – accompanied, of course, by a glass or two of wine from your local *viticulteur*!

Planting

It's best to have a dedicated herb garden rather than plants interspersed amongst vegetables, and it's important to create it as near to the kitchen door as possible. You will probably need a daily supply of herbs and it isn't much fun having to rush to the far end of your property to collect them in the middle of a complicated culinary concoction – or a thunderstorm.

Many herbs are Mediterranean in origin and will do well in southern parts of the country, but some are only half-hardy and will need winter protection in other areas. Most herbs need a sheltered but sunny spot. If the walls of nearby buildings don't give any protection, you could plant a 'hedge' of taller, hardier herbs around the patch to act as a windbreak. Soil needs to be well drained, and you can lighten heavy soil by adding sand, grit or compost. If you're in an area where mushrooms are grown, most producers will sell you spent compost for just a few euros, and this makes a good addition to the soil.

As some herb varieties are invasive – notably mint (*menthe*) – it pays to divide the bed into discrete compartments and bury some form of shuttering between them to prevent the roots from spreading. Large pots, sunk into the ground, will help contain roots. You could, of course, simply grow your herbs in containers around the kitchen door; provided they're well watered, they will do as well as they would in the ground.

Cuttings & Wintering

Most herbs can be raised from seed but, as young plants can be bought cheaply from a market, there's little point in spending valuable time doing so. It's possible to buy herb plants (such as parsley and coriander) in the spring, but beware of the puny varieties sold in supermarkets, which may last no more than a week.

Once they're established, you can take cuttings from some of the woody types, such as rosemary (*romarin*) and sage (*sauge*), to create more plants. This is best done in the autumn. Simply break off a piece that has new growth near its tip and either push it into a pot of good-quality compost or put it in a glass of water until you see roots appearing.

Some perennial herbs, such as chives (*ciboulette*), die back in the autumn but, provided they've been regularly fed and watered the previous summer, will reappear the following spring. You can try to keep them growing during the winter by covering them with a cloche (see page 105) or potting a clump and bringing it indoors. Shrubby herbs, such as tarragon (*estragon*), will benefit from a 'haircut' in the late summer, as this will stimulate new growth. When you cut them back, sprinkle some general fertiliser around the plants and water it in, as this will encourage faster re-growth.

Drying

During the growing season, you will normally pick herbs as and when they're needed. For winter use, however, you will need to dry them – and most herbs can be dried. Do this by hanging them in bunches or laying them out on a tray in the sunshine. In cool weather, you can cover them with a cloche (see page 105) to increase the temperature. After a couple of days, leave them at room temperature for two weeks, but turn them regularly until they're crisp and flaky. The leaves can then be crushed and stored in airtight containers until required.

STAKING

It's necessary to stake or train (*tuteurer*) some plants in the vegetable garden. Note that a cane is a slender stick used to support a plant, a stick is a thin branch cut from a tree, trimmed and used as a support, and a stake is a stout pointed stick for driving into the ground.

Thin canes (*canne*), which can be bought from a supermarket or garden centre, will do for tomatoes. Bamboo is the best material, as it's light, strong and neat. You can buy bamboo canes in any length and they can be used for several years. Sticks (*rame*) are needed for peas and beans. Other vegetables require supporting with a stout stake driven into the ground. For example, broad beans and larger greens can become untidy if left unstaked, especially in exposed gardens.

You can cut branches from a tree and trim them for use as sticks or stakes (according to their thickness). In some rural areas, there are woods of hazel trees, whose stems and branches are ideal. Find out who owns a wood and you're likely to be allowed to gather a few, especially if you offer to cut some for the owner. This needs to be done in the autumn or winter, before the sap rises. At the end of the growing season it's best to burn hazel sticks and stakes, as they will probably be covered in fungus spores.

For crops that need individual stakes, such as tomatoes and sweetcorn, you should always match the stake to the plant and allow for maximum growth. Make them firm, especially those at each end of a row. A length of garden wire attached to each end stake and wound along the others will stabilise them. Try to insert stakes before planting, to avoid damaging roots. Large-mesh nylon netting, stretched taut between posts, is a neater support for peas; alternatively, you can use wire netting, provided it's new enough to stretch flat.

PLANTING BY THE MOON

Gardeners have always sown seed and transplanted with a waxing moon, never a waning moon. Scientists have recently caught up with them, discovering that the effect of lunar rhythms on the earth's magnetic field influences growth. They've established that all water on the planet, including that contained inside even the tiniest living organisms, moves in tides like the sea. Even potatoes grown under laboratory conditions show a growth rhythm reflecting the lunar pattern. The moon also affects the earth's atmosphere, so that it's more likely to rain heavily immediately after a full moon than at any other time. Without statistics or scientific knowledge, the gardeners of yore learned all this from experience, and the principle is still widely applied in France. You have nothing to lose by following it yourself.

When to Plant

Lunar planting and harvesting times are very precise. Every February, the gardening magazine *Rustica l'Hebdo Jardin* publishes an edition that includes tables, dates and 'planners' indicating the optimum times for planting and harvesting all vegetable varieties as well as a calendar that indicates not only what should be done in the garden on each day of the year but also between which hours the work should be carried out – all in accordance with the various lunar stages and astrological coincidences (order your copy now!).

Essentially, Capricorn, Taurus and Virgo govern the root crops and the root systems; Pisces, Cancer and Scorpio the top growth, stems and leaves; Aquarius, Gemini and Libra the flower development; Sagittarius, Aries and Leo the fruit and seed production.

If you're tempted into giving this curious mixture of science and folklore a try, remember to take into account local climatic conditions and prevailing wind directions.

COMPOST

Compost is an essential regular addition to soil, which has much of its nutritional value depleted by plant growth. A compost heap can be started in any corner of a garden that's accessible to a wheelbarrow, but there's an art to it if you don't want to end up with compost that's either wet and slimy or as dry as fibre.

Start by making a three- or four-sided structure of wood (for the advantages and disadvantages of each type, see **Composition** below), corrugated tin or simply four posts banged into the ground and surrounded by wire netting. Don't be tempted into making the structure too large or the contents won't 'work'. Most gardeners recommend a heap of roughly a metre square. A base of wood or heavy plastic (builder's) sheeting will help retain the heat and moisture necessary to activate the breakdown of waste and turn it into good, friable compost. If properly constructed and managed, a heap started in the spring should have broken down well enough to be put back onto the garden the following autumn.

It's best to have two bins: seal the first when it's full and, by the time the second is full, the contents of the first should be ready to use and you can start re-filling it.

Composition

Just about any vegetable matter can be added to a compost heap, but avoid the roots of persistent weeds such ground elder and couch grass, as they will continue to grow rather than rotting. Cooked food shouldn't be put on a compost heap for the simple reason that it attracts vermin. Also, avoid anything that's coarse or woody, including leathery evergreen leaves, as they don't rot at the same rate as softer material. Grass cuttings are excellent components because they heat up quickly; on the other hand, they form a dense mass which air cannot penetrate and can end up as a slimy mess rather than quality compost; the addition of dry, bulky material such as straw from a chicken house will prevent this.

Once the first bin is full, cover it with straw, thick cardboard or a piece of old carpet and begin filling the second. After about a month, the compost needs turning (once should be sufficient). This job is easier with a three-sided bin, as all the contents must be removed, turned and put back again, but the more controlled environment created by a four-sided bin makes for more rapidly broken down compost.

WATERING

Whatever type of bed or layout you choose, your vegetable garden will require watering during the growing period, especially in hot regions. Raised beds will need even more water than traditional beds, owing to their self-draining design.

Wells & Bore Holes

Well water is preferable to tap water (as well as cheaper), as it usually contains beneficial minerals. If you're fortunate enough to have a well on your property, it's worth spending a few euros on a pump. Make sure that the pump is powerful enough not only to lift water to the top of the well but also to force it along the hosepipe leading to the bed. Prices vary from €50 to €120 depending on quality and power. Garden hose (*tuyau d'arrosage*) is generally sold in 10 to 20m lengths and is likely to cost between €1 and €4 per metre, depending on its diameter and quality.

If you don't have a well and want to avoid the cost of mains water, it might be possible to have a bore hole (*forage*) drilled. First you must find out whether there's water under the property. Ask locally if anyone has a bore hole and, if so, how deep it is. Even if a nearby property has a bore hole, however, there's no guarantee that the supply will also be available to you; it depends whether it's a spring or underground river, or a lake or 'table' (*nappe phréatique*). There are two ways of finding out:

- Go to the Bureau Régional Géologique Minier (BRGM) and ask to consult the relevant map of underground watercourses, which usually specifies locations to within around 5m but isn't always reliable; there should be no charge for this.
- Employ a water diviner (*sourcier*), although these are few and far between (ask a company specialising in wells and bore holes). He will charge between around €75 and €150 depending on the distance he has to travel and cannot always be relied upon to find water. (You could always try your hand at water divining yourself, with a forked hazel stick or a metal coat hanger!)

If there's water under your plot and it's less than around 20m below the surface, it may be worthwhile having a bore hole drilled; if the water is more than 20m down, the cost will probably be excessive, although it's possible to drill down to 100m.

Dry weather in many departments over the last two years has led to periodic hosepipe bans. These also apply to the use of water from wells and bore holes, as its extraction affects the water table.

Rainwater

The rain that falls on the roof of your house can be put to good use in watering your vegetables, and there are various ways of storing it. Plastic water butts are useful but unsightly and expensive (between €50 and €100 for a 2,000-litre/45-gallon container). In wine-growing areas, it might be possible to purchase old wooden barrels that have been discarded in favour of more modern containers. Farmers often buy chemicals in plastic tanks; provided the chemicals are washed out thoroughly (and away from any natural water source into which they might leak), these can be used for rainwater storage. Old baths work well as water butts but, if you use them as such, make sure that you wedge a log or plank of wood on the inside to allow lizards and frogs to escape if they fall in. In fact, it's best to cover any water container – not only to prevent accidents but also to minimise evaporation.

Technique

Watering isn't always as simple as it sounds. Too little watering will cause a plant's roots to grow upwards in search of moisture rather than down into the ground with the result that they will either become exposed and be scorched by the sun or produce plants that run to seed. Conversely, too much watering will cause the surface to form into a thin but hard crust or cap, underneath which the soil remains bone dry, although regular hoeing helps prevent this, as does mulching on either side of the rows of plants.

The rule is to water gently but frequently during the critical period, i.e. between flowering and harvesting for beans and peas, and from the seedling stage right through until maturity for green crops. Whereas in the UK, for example, watering generally needs to be carried out only weekly, even during the warmest weather, in France it may be required on a daily basis. When possible, water either early in the morning or late in the evening, when it's cooler and the soil therefore has a better chance to absorb the moisture.

CLOCHES & POLY-TUNNELS

Many French gardeners use small poly-tunnels (walk-in, plastic-covered, hooped greenhouses) to get an early start to the season. They're very useful for propagating early crops before transplanting them outdoors, but they're also good places to experiment with exotic winter salads and other crops. If you're a keen vegetable grower, a poly-tunnel will extend the season and make self-sufficiency easier to achieve.

A cloche is an individual plant cover, made of glass or polythene. Polythene cloches are cheaper than glass ones, as well as lighter and easier to use. The polythene will eventually split but you can buy polythene that has been treated so as not to go brittle in the sun from France Rurale, Gamm Vert, Jardiland, Mr Bricolage or any similar outlet, and replace it.

The soil under cloches and poly-tunnels must be in good condition, as it will be used intensively. It's wise to lay a moisture-retaining base, using material from your compost heap or leaf mould. You could also cut a shallow channel around the base of cloches to let the rain seep in, or place them over ridges so that the furrows in between channel rain underneath.

With such protection, all early crops can be sown outside three or four weeks earlier than they could otherwise, and summer vegetables, such as French beans, can be sown later and cloched for a late autumn/early winter crop – which would be impossible in the UK, for example. The seeds of half-hardy vegetables – dwarf tomatoes, sweetcorn, marrows, cucumbers and celery – can be either raised under a cloche or poly-tunnel and planted out in May (when there's no longer any danger of frost) or sown directly in their cropping positions in early April. The latter method might not give such an early crop but it saves planting out.

SURVIVAL TIP

Tradition has it that from the day of St Glace – which is 10th, 11th or 12th May, depending on the moon – there will be no more frost and it's safe to plant out.

CROP ROTATION

Talk to any French gardener and you will find that he thinks crop rotation one of the most important aspects of vegetable gardening. If you grow the same type of vegetable in the same place year after year, two major problems are likely to occur: first, soil-living pests and diseases that depend on a particular crop for their existence may develop to epidemic levels; second, a soil nutrient deficiency will be created that no amount of added compost can rectify. Rotating crops means that each uses nutrients left by others and replaces them with its own. Peas, for example, are known to leave deposits of nitrogen in the soil, which proves advantageous to varieties that need it for leaf growth.

Most gardeners use a three-year plan, splitting the plot into three sections: one containing roots (beetroot, carrots, parsnips, potatoes, etc.), another brassicas (broccoli, Brussels sprouts, cabbage, etc.) and a third salad crops plus marrows, onions and sweet corn. Each year the crops are rotated until, in the fourth year, they return to their original sections. A perfect overall nutritional and acid/alkaline (ph) balance will be achieved by the end of the third season. In the first two seasons, however, you may need to add nutrients as required by each type of crop.

CONTROLLING PESTS & DISEASES

Gardening is supposed to be a relaxing pleasure and so it may pay to adopt a Zen-like attitude towards pests and diseases. Growing more plants than you need so that it doesn't matter if birds, disease, rabbits or slugs take a few is one option, but there are other ways of ensuring that all your hard work isn't wasted.

The pests that cause most trouble in the vegetable garden are aphids (*aphides*) – of which there are types peculiar to various crops, e.g. bean aphids, cabbage aphids, peach aphids, plum aphids and potato aphids – and cherry black-fly and green-fly (*puceron*). All these creatures reproduce rapidly in warm conditions, and many of them are winged and migrate from plant to plant. Others to watch out for are caterpillars (*chenille*), slugs (*limace*), snails (*escargot*), wireworm (*larve de taupin*), millipedes (*mille-pattes*) and the grubs of egg-laying flies.

All can be destroyed with insecticides but when dealing with vegetables, it's essential that you don't use poisonous substances, as they can be absorbed into a plant's system. Certain insecticides can also cause great suffering to birds and are a danger to pets. To be on the safe side, use a biological preparation based on nematodes. A nematode is a microscopic worm that attacks and lives on larvae. In the UK, this form of treatment has a short season, as nematodes are effective only in higher temperatures, but in France, with its generally warmer climate, this biological approach works well for most of the growing season. Being organic, it's kinder to the environment than chemicals and is obviously safer to use around livestock and on plants grown for the kitchen. However, once they've fed on a particular infestation, nematodes die and you must re-apply them should another outbreak occur. Otherwise, a winter wash or spray with insecticide on some fruit trees will kill dormant eggs.

Identification & Treatment

Some pests and diseases commonly found in French vegetable gardens are described below.

- **Anthracnose** (*Marssonina salicicola*) – A fairly common fungal disease that affects dwarf and runner beans. Brown spots on the leaves and darker, sunken-looking spots on the pods can indicate its presence. Diseased plants should be removed immediately and the remainder sprayed with carbendazim.
- **Asparagus Beetle** (*Crioceris asparagi*) – Both adults and larvae feed on the new foliage and, in severe cases, completely strip the plant. Spray with derris or permethrin.
- **Bean Seed Fly** (*Delia platura*) – Small white maggots that eat into the seeds of beans, peas and sweetcorn. Only purchase seed that has been treated with a preventative.
- **Black-fly** (*Aphis fabae*) – Particularly affects broad beans in spring and French beans in mid-summer. They should be sprayed with permethrin as soon as possible. Many traditional gardeners suggest nipping out the tops of broad beans once four flower trusses have formed, as this is supposed to help prevent an attack.
- **Boron Deficiency** – A lack of boron (*bore*) in soil may cause the hearts of beetroot and swedes to turn brown. Brown cracks appear across celery stalks, and the leaves turn yellow. General watering with a trace element-based product early in the season should help but a severe boron deficiency will need to be corrected by a direct application of borax.
- **Cabbage Root Fly** – Small white maggots (of the *Delia radicum* fly) eat the roots of all brassicas, not just cabbages. Infected plants wilt, especially in dry weather, and leaves may take on a blue tinge. In some areas of France, root fly is resistant to certain insecticides. Try applying a nematode-based product immediately after planting (see above).

- **Cabbage White Fly** (*Aleyrodes proletella*) – Also affecting all brassica crops, cabbage white fly can sometimes be seen during the winter (feeding on the underside of leaves). Treat regularly with permethrin or malathion.

- **Carrot Fly** – Damage is caused by larvae (of the *Psila rosae*). There's no treatment for this problem, but burning affected plants can significantly reduce the number of over-wintering pupae. Organic gardeners dust soot or lime along the rows of plants to deter the fly.

- **Caterpillars** – The caterpillars of many moths and butterflies can trouble the gardener. Some live in the soil and are root eaters, while others burrow into the plant stem or fruit, but most feed on leaves. Effective sprays and dusting powders are readily available but in addition to waging chemical warfare you can do a lot by way of prevention. Regular soil cultivation will expose the larvae to birds. You can also simply remove caterpillars and crush any batches of eggs found on plants.

- **Celery Fly** (*Euleia heraclei*) – The small, white, leaf-mining maggots of this fly burrow into celery leaves and seriously damage young plants, causing the leaves to shrivel, as well as making the mature plant taste bitter. Plants can be protected by the use of malathion.

- **Celery Heart Rot** – A disease that causes the inside of celery plants to turn brown and slimy. Dusting with copper lime was once thought to be a useful precaution, but most experts agree that there's no treatment. However, as the bacteria that cause it enter a plant through wounds caused by slug damage or careless hoeing and cultivating, you should take care when weeding and control your slug population (see **Birds, Moles, Mice & Slugs** on page 111).

- **Cock Chafer Beetles** (*Melolontha melolontha*) – A very common problem in France, although they more often affect the flower garden than the vegetable patch. The grubs live in the soil and will damage the roots of almost any plant, causing it to die. Sprinkle bromophos onto the soil and lightly rake it in. Gamma-BHC dusts or sprays can also be used.

- **Club Root** (*Plasmodiophora brassicae*) – Most commonly found where soil is acidic, this fungal disease attacks most brassica varieties and also turnips and radishes. As the name suggests, the disease can be identified by swollen roots, but another sign is wilting leaves. Dipping the roots into a mixture of camomile dust and water when planting is a good preventative measure, as is liming the soil, which helps neutralise its acidity.

- **Cutworms** – Cutworms are types of caterpillar from either of two moths (the *Noctua* or *Argrotis*) and can be grey or brown. Living near the soil surface, they eat young plants at ground level. Numbers can be reduced by regular soil cultivation and good weed control. A dusting of powders recommended for caterpillars will provide additional protection.

- **Eelworms** (*Ditylenchus dipsaci*) – There are several types of eelworm, each affecting a particular vegetable or vegetables. They're generally thin, transparent and microscopic, and live in plant tissue. The eelworm that causes the greatest problem in the garden is the potato eelworm (*Globodera rostochiensis*). There's no effective treatment and it's recommended that all affected plants be destroyed and that the same type isn't grown in the same position for several years.

- **Flea Beetles** (*Phyllotreta*) – All brassica plants are susceptible to attacks from flea beetles, which cause tiny holes on the leaves as if they've been peppered by gunshot. On warm days, you can see the beetles on the ground and they can be sprayed, although the plants will probably survive without treatment.

- **Leatherjackets** – Leatherjackets are the grub of crane-flies (*Tipula*). Normally of concern only to farmers of new grassland, they're known to tunnel into root crops. Methiocarb-based products can control them.

- **Mildew** – Mildew is a species-specific fungus (*Peronospera* and *Bremia* are among the most common) often resulting from mild, humid conditions and identifiable by a white, powdery coating of spores on the stems, leaves and fruit of some plants. It can be sprayed with the relevant fungicide.

- **Mosaic Viruses** – As with mildew (see above), there are several mosaic viruses that affect many vegetable crops. They usually show as pale green mottling on leaves. Although there's no treatment, spraying with heptenophos will help control the aphids that carry the virus.

- **Onion Fly** (*Delia antiqua*) – Onion fly attacks shallots and leeks as well as onions and is a serious pest, especially in dry areas. It lays its eggs on leaves and in the soil. The maggots burrow into a plant and can kill young plants. Onion flies are thought to be attracted by the smell of crushed leaves, so it's important to cause as little damage as possible when weeding. If you or the people you've bought your house from have had infestations in previous years, you could try treating with pirimiphos-methyl before sowing or grow your onions from sets rather than seed, as this seems to alleviate the problem.

- **Parsnip Canker** (*Hersonilia pastinaceae*) – This disease shows itself as a blackened area at the top of the parsnip root. During late summer, leaves may also be affected. There's no effective way of controlling canker, but growing in a deep, loamy soil, manuring with a balanced fertiliser and adding lime to the soil will all help. Some varieties are more resistant than others, so read the packet carefully for any clues before you buy.
- **Pea Moth** (*Cydia nigricana*) – Any caterpillars (usually pale yellow) found in pea pods are likely to be the larvae of this small moth. Early sowings usually avoid the problem but as an extra precaution you could spray with fenitrothion around a week after the first flowers appear.
- **Strawberry Beetle** – Sometimes birds get the blame for damage to strawberries when in fact it's caused by the carpid beetle (*Pterostichus*), which thrives in lush vegetation. There's no effective means of controlling them, so it's important that your strawberry patch is kept clear of weeds.
- **Tomato Diseases** – Tomatoes have so many potential problems that it hardly seems worthwhile going to the effort of growing them; that any survive at all is something of a miracle. Troubles include Mosaic virus (see above), moulds (spray with carbendazim), whitefly (treat with permethrin) and a host of problems that affect the fruit itself, none of which have a remedy.
- **Wire Stem** – This disease affects brassica plants such as cabbage and Brussels sprouts. In more mature plants, it shows as a browning at the base of the stem, but in younger specimens it can cause the roots to rot (known as 'damping off'). It's best treated with Cheshunt Compound. This can be purchased only in the UK, so keep some in stock. Alternatively, lime the soil or water plants and seedlings with sodium molybdate.
- **Wireworms** (*Agriotes*) – Wireworms are the larvae of the click beetle and a serious pest in potatoes, as they burrow into the tuber. They also cause damage to the stems of lettuce and tomatoes. For some reason, they're more active on newly-cultivated soil and so you will need to look out for and destroy them particularly in your first year of vegetable growing. There's no effective treatment, but applying primiphos-methyl to the soil before planting may help prevent the spread of wireworms.

Rabbits, Hares, Deer & Wild Boar

A low fence of chicken wire surrounding your vegetable patch will protect it from rabbits and hares, but it's a nuisance getting in and out with machinery unless you install a gate. If you do, don't forget to make it wide enough for wheelbarrows and garden machinery.

A fence to protect your property from deer needs to be around 2m high and is expensive to erect, but they can be deterred by rags soaked in wood preserver mixed with oil or diesel and hung at strategic points. Human hair tied in the toe of old tights is supposed to frighten them, as are lion droppings – unfortunately in pretty short supply in most areas of France! Wild boar can also be a serious problem, but if you fix two strands of electrified wire to the fence around your garden (see **Electric Fencing** on page 73), they soon learn to stay away.

Birds, Moles, Mice & Slugs

Birds, and particularly pigeons, love a vegetable garden. Blackbirds, for example, will pull out your beans and peas given half a chance. If you're creative, you could build a scarecrow, but you will need to move it from time to time or birds will get used to it. You can buy bird-scaring tape at garden centres and *quincailleries* or you can make your own by stretching old audio- or videotape tightly between garden canes. As the breeze blows, it makes a humming noise that frightens most birds for a time. Alternatively, stretch a length of fishing line, twine or strong cotton in zigzags a few inches above the ground over your bean and pea crops until they've germinated.

The French seem particularly keen on eradicating moles (*taupes*) and if you go into any branch of Bricomarché or a similar shop and look along the shelves stocking pest solutions, you will find several products for dealing with them. Sonic mole scarers that are pushed into the ground and emit signals which moles don't like are quite effective. They cost around €23. Smoke bombs work for a time and send moles into your neighbour's garden, but eventually they will return. On the plus side, earth obtained from a molehill (*taupinière*) and mixed with sand makes a good base for potting plants.

Mice like to dig up large seeds before they've even germinated, but the only alternative to poison or a cat is 'humane' box traps that catch them alive. These can be bought for a few euros almost anywhere (box traps, not cats!). You will need to 're-locate' any captured mice at least a kilometre away or they will be back in your garden before you are.

The mild winters in most parts of France encourage slugs, and they can be devastating as they work their way along your rows of carefully-produced plants. Organically, you have perhaps just two options: to use nematodes (see page 106) or to wander round the garden by torchlight, picking up any slugs that you see. If you have ducks you can feed slugs to them, or you can kill them by covering them in salt. A circle of ashes, soot or lime placed around plants helps keep slugs away provided the substance remains dry. Containers full of beer (which is cheap in France!) will attract and drown them.

Organic Insecticides & Prevention

Nettles (*ortie*) can be used as an insecticide as well as a fertilizer. The roots of many vegetables will benefit from a diluted liquid manure (*purin*) made from their leaves, and whitefly hate the taste of nettle sap. To obtain a good *purin*, pick nettle shoots just before they flower. (Otherwise, you will be spreading nettle seeds and end up with many more nettles in your patch the following season.) Chop them up roughly and fill a plastic bucket. Cover them with water, preferably from a well or stream or rainwater, and leave the bucket to ferment. Once the process is finished – how long it takes depends on the temperature – dilute the resulting 'juice' at a rate of half a litre to ten litres of water. Water your plants in the normal way and use the residue left in the bottom of the bucket as a mulch for tomato or courgette plants or, alternatively, add it to your compost heap.

Marigolds (*souci*) planted around the vegetable garden, especially between potatoes and tomatoes, are considered helpful in repelling whitefly and other unwanted pests, while crumbled mothballs will deter carrot fly larvae. Laying a length of tarred or creosoted string on the surface of the soil between the rows of certain plants is said to prevent aphid attack.

STORAGE

You're likely to have more vegetables than you can eat at once and so will need to store them. Freezing is the obvious answer for most crops, but many people make the mistake of freezing produce at the end of the season when it's fully mature. It's much better to freeze continually throughout the growing season as soon as vegetables are tender. Pick each day and alternate between eating fresh and freezing.

Tomatoes can be made into chutney, soup and pickles or can be frozen whole until you're ready to use them in cooking. Place them on a tray and freeze them individually. Once they're fully frozen, you can put them into freezer bags to save space.

To store soft-leaved herbs, fill ice cube trays with chopped and blanched leaves and top up with water. Freeze and then empty the trays into bags before returning them to the freezer. Then all that's needed is to add one or two cubes as required to your cooking. (See also **Drying** on page 100).

Root vegetables keep their flavour better if they're left in the ground and used as required, but if you do this you may lose them altogether. The tops die, making it difficult to find the vegetables, and, when you do, they may be honeycombed by insects. On balance, it's probably better to lose some flavour than the whole crop. Main crop potatoes ('Kerpondy', 'Ratte', 'Rosa', 'Roseval', 'Stella Bell' and 'Urgenta') take longest to lift and store; it's easier to lift them on a dry day and leave them out for an hour or two before storing them.

Potatoes, carrots, beetroot, parsnips and turnips can all be stored in a weatherproof place. Spread them out on the floor so that you can easily detect any that are going bad and remove them. If you have to store root vegetables outdoors, stack them against a wall and cover them with earth, sand or peat. Keep some sacking (*tontine*) or straw matting (*paillasson*) to hand as extra covering should there be heavy frosts.

Onions, winter marrows and haricot beans must have plenty of air around them, and the most convenient way of ensuring this is to hang them from the roof of a shed or sling them in nets.

FOXES KEEP OUT! OR ELSE!

7.

POULTRY

It isn't unusual to inherit some poultry with your rural French property. In any case it's a safe bet that at some stage you will want to keep a few chickens so that you can enjoy fresh, free-range eggs. (Note that the word chicken is used here to refer to hens, cocks and bantams.) Most rural homes in France lend themselves perfectly to poultry keeping. An orchard can be successfully grazed by a small flock of geese, while ducks look well on a stretch of water and are excellent organic controllers of slugs and other garden pests. Poultry are relatively easy to house, feed and rear and, provided they're kept in a clean environment, there's little chance of disease.

With the current spread of avian influenza (see page 137), it may be forbidden to import poultry into France and you should check the latest regulations with the relevant authority (DEFRA in the UK – see below).

If there's no ban in force, you will need to obtain an export health certificate for stock you wish to take to France from another country. Contact your veterinary surgeon a few weeks before you intend to move and he will be able to advise you of the necessary procedure. If moving from the UK, you can obtain information from the Department for Environment, Food & Rural Affairs (DEFRA, 💻 www.defra.gov.uk – click on 'Export').

FREE-RANGE OR PENNED?

Free-range poultry is a wonderful idea but the practice isn't as simple as it might seem. While many people dream of having poultry running around their back door, picking at scraps and living a contented life, in reality this isn't ideal and all poultry enjoy being on grass. Geese are even cheaper to maintain than chickens and a sufficient number will keep an orchard cropped better than any lawnmower, requiring no feed in the summer and just a little grain in the winter. They don't scratch and will eat any bugs, but they may also debark young fruit trees if other food is scarce. Geese are ideal for livestock paddocks and are quite happy to mix with a few sheep or a pony. They are also (along with guinea fowl) perfect 'watchdogs' and make a tremendous racket at the sight or sound of a fox or human.

A light woodland setting is perfect for all poultry types and hens will come to no harm in an orchard provided the trees aren't sprayed with toxic chemicals. Turkeys enjoy a paddock but they shouldn't be mixed in with other poultry. They're susceptible to diseases such as blackhead, which are carried by other fowl, although the latter may not be seriously affected themselves.

In the garden, free-ranging poultry will eradicate insect pests and slugs, but some of their habits may be unwelcome to an earnest gardener. All chickens love nothing more than a good dust bath, which helps rid them of parasites – and a well-prepared seedbed is an ideal place for dusting!

Ducks also keep the slugs down but will turn a rain puddle into a mud bath; they might also nibble your prize vegetables. Like geese, they will manure the ground wonderfully, but with copious liquid droppings that make it impossible for children to play without risking getting covered in muck. Geese love ground elder but are quite destructive in the confines of a garden.

All things considered, it's much better to allocate a section of your property to poultry pens and to allow birds access to the garden only when you're around to supervise them.

Constructing a Pen

Although initially expensive, a properly-constructed poultry pen will last up to 20 years. It needs to be at least 2m (6ft 6in) in height. The perimeter is usually made up of two rolls of small-mesh wire netting: 3.2cm (1.25in) for the bottom half and 5cm (2in) for the upper half. The bottom 30cm (1ft) is turned out and pegged down or buried, while the top 46cm (18in) is allowed to flop outwards in order to prevent predators from gaining access.

- Start by hammering in all the posts, which must be no more than four paces apart and sunk around 60cm (2ft) into the ground.
- Struts angled at around 30 to 40 degrees to take the tension of the straining wire should be fixed to the corner posts and gateposts. Some people prefer to support their corner posts by means of wire windlasses pegged outside the fence line, like guy ropes on a tent. This is a particularly useful technique where the ground is rocky or hard.
- Next, attach the top straining wire as tightly as possible before doing the same with the middle wire, onto which the top and bottom rolls of wire netting will be fixed by either thin garden wire or fencing clips. Remember to allow a gap for a gate when fixing the middle wire.
- Staple the wire netting to the top of each post and tread it into a previously dug trench or bend it outwards if it's to be pegged.

- Backfill or peg before attaching the top roll of wire netting and then connect both to the middle strainer.
- Pull the top of the roll upwards and clip or wire it to the top straining wire. It should then be possible to staple both rolls down each post, taking extra care around the gate.

To prevent foxes jumping over the gate, fix a netting fringe to the top of it. When building the gate itself, make sure that it's secure. A central bolt often seems safe but you must never forget that a determined fox or neighbour's dog pushing and scratching at its base could force an entry.

Even though you might not like the idea of confining your poultry in a pen, it's worth it for peace of mind. They don't need to spend all day in there, but keeping chickens in for the first half of the day isn't a bad idea, as mornings are generally when the majority of eggs are laid and it will prevent them wandering off and laying in places other than the nest boxes.

Dust Baths

Where chickens are confined in a wire run, they will soon make their own dust bath, either in the roots of a tree or, if they have access to it, under the poultry house, where the soil is dry and friable. Otherwise, an artificial dust bath is easy to make. All that's required is a small shelter around a metre high. Four posts and a sloping roof will do. Turn over the ground underneath and the chickens will do the rest. You might like to add some fine soil, wood ash or sand to the mixture but the important thing is to keep the area dry.

HOUSING

The French can be quite inventive in their choice of poultry housing, including disused buses and transport containers. One of the most original designs is the 'ladder system', in which a hen house the size of a large packing case is fixed to the top of an old telegraph pole or tree trunk around 2m off the ground. Access for the chickens is via a flimsy ramp, up which a fox is supposedly unable to climb, while access for the egg collector is via a ladder, which is laid on the ground when not in use. The idea is that chickens can be completely 'free-range': i.e. they don't need to be shut up each evening and let out every morning.

If your rural property includes outbuildings, which is likely, the most suitable one can be converted into poultry accommodation. It needs to be light, airy, well ventilated and fox-proof. In most parts of France, summers are considerably hotter than those in the UK and other northern European countries, and it's important that you take this factor into account when choosing a place to house your birds. Old stone buildings will be insulated from the sun, whereas modern sheds will become stifling in the heat of the day.

A coat of paint on the interior walls will reflect any available daylight, and it's surprising how much extra light can be gained simply by brushing away generations of cobwebs and washing windows. Lice and mites detest a well-lit house and thrive only where there are dark corners to lurk in. The hen house door should open and close easily, as it will be necessary to use it several times a day and there's nothing worse than dragging a heavy lump of wood, half hanging from its hinges, backwards and forwards in order to get in and out.

Hens tend to lay more sporadically in winter, when there are fewer daylight hours, but if they're in draught-proof surroundings and a sunny location they should be less affected. A light bulb switched on at dawn and/or dusk will extend 'daylight' hours and help egg production.

Flooring

A solid floor is better than an earthen one, as it's easier to sweep. If the floor is uneven and not too large, it's worth levelling it with concrete. As most French outbuildings were built straight onto the ground without any foundations, the floor is often insecure and foxes may manage to dig under the walls.

No matter what the floor consists of, a covering of litter is essential. The most common covering is wood shavings, which can be bought in compressed bales from suppliers of horse feed and equipment. Straw is probably even easier to obtain in rural France, and most local farmers will be able to sell it to you after the harvest, when it's at its cheapest (if you buy it at a later date, the price might be higher owing to storage costs). If you have barn storage space, buy your annual supply in the autumn. Note, however, that straw and hay are more likely to be bound into in huge round 'rolls' than traditional bales, which isn't ideal for the small poultry keeper. If you cannot find small bales, ask your farmer if you can bag up some of the loose material left lying in his fields. Bracken and leaves cut or collected in the autumn also make a good floor covering, in which birds will happily scratch.

Whatever material is chosen, make sure it isn't mouldy or damp. Mould can lead to serious respiratory diseases and wet litter is a perfect breeding ground for the *E.coli* bug. The litter base should be around 15cm (6in) deep and regularly raked to remove matted portions.

Nest Boxes & Perches

Inside the shed, fit some nest boxes – ideally one for every three laying birds. These needn't be elaborate and should be positioned in the darkest part of the house (usually under the windows), as chickens prefer a dark – and quiet – place to lay their eggs. Straw or hay makes a good liner but will need cleaning and dusting with louse powder regularly. Remove any broken eggs immediately so as not to encourage egg eating; once formed, the habit is difficult to break.

One or two perches running the length of the building will give chickens somewhere to roost at night. Note that light breeds of poultry (see **Choosing Stock** on page 121) often prefer to perch on the rafters of old buildings, which isn't to be encouraged, as the hard pads of the feet can be damaged by daily hard landings.

SURVIVAL TIP

If more than one perch is required, keep them all at the same height, or all the birds will try to roost on the highest one.

Sometimes, chickens will attempt to sleep in the nest boxes. Wait until dusk and place the erring birds on a perch. After a few nights, they should get the idea but, if the problem persists, block the boxes at dusk.

Ducks and geese don't roost (with the exception of the Muscovy duck) and so don't require perches or such a high-roofed building. Geese, being hardy creatures, don't really need any housing at all but, unless your property is protected by a fox- and dog-proof fence, it's a wise precaution to pen them at night.

Ventilation, Temperature & Humidity

Good ventilation is vital in preventing poultry from contracting respiratory diseases, as the moisture exhaled and sweated off by the birds has a chance to evaporate and escape in moving air rather than increasing the humidity of the atmosphere. Too high humidity encourages various pathogens, whereas hot, dry air dehydrates birds. Inadequate ventilation causes a strong smell of ammonia, which should be an indication that it needs improving.

Fold Units

Fold units are ideal for keeping poultry. They consist of a kind of ark with a run attached that can be moved periodically onto fresh ground. The interior requirements of the housing section are as mentioned above, but fold units have several major advantages over static housing: the chickens can be kept confined but still have access to fresh grass; if the unit is moved on a regular basis, there's little chance of a build-up of disease; your chickens can still be free-range but are protected from foxes and the neighbour's dog when you're away.

Any competent handyman can built a fold unit cheaply with a few lengths of timber and weatherboarding and some wire netting. The housing part usually takes up around a third of the overall length, the remainder forming the run. Traditionally, fold units are 'A' shaped with a door to the house and another to the run. As a refinement, the back of the run can be fully or partially covered, which will shade the birds from sun and rain. The roof spar should be cut longer than the house and the extra length left protruding at either end to form handles that will facilitate movement.

A fold unit is a useful addition to any poultry keeper's equipment and can be used to integrate new stock, house a broody hen and her chicks or fatten surplus cockerels (see **Fattening Poultry** on page 195).

CHOOSING STOCK

Before choosing species, you need to be clear about your aims. Are you interested in profit or self-sufficiency, or do you want to keep poultry simply for the pleasure of doing so? You might have had a long-time ambition to keep a certain breed of chicken or bantam, in which case your only problem will be to find out where to obtain young birds (see **Pure Breeds & 'Mongrels'** below).

There are three distinct types of chicken: 'light' breeds, 'heavy' breeds and bantams (*poule naine*, which, literally translated, means dwarf chicken). The light breeds are descended from the jungle fowl of Java, while the heavy breeds originated (thousands of years ago) from the Chinese fowl known as Cochin, Brahma and Chabos. Whereas the light breeds were flighty and roosted high in trees, the heavy breeds had large frames, shorter wings and no interest in roosting. What we now know as the heavy breeds – Rhode Island Red, Light Sussex, Maran and Faverolles – are good dual-purpose birds, laying well and producing meat. They're also more inclined to go broody. The lighter (and flightier) breeds, such as the Leghorn, Ancona (both from the Mediterranean) and Houdan, lay many more eggs, but aren't suitable as meat producers and rarely turn broody.

Bantams are miniature chickens. True bantams have no large fowl counterpart, but there are also miniature versions of large fowl. In the latter case, depending on whether a heavy or light breed is chosen, they can lay a surprising number of eggs. Generally, true bantams don't lay so well but are ornamental and make good children's pets.

Cockerels

You don't need a cockerel running with your hens unless you plan to breed. Many people are under the misapprehension that the presence of a cock increases egg production and keeps hens in order; hens will in fact lay the same number of eggs without a cock, and will find their own hierarchy. (The term 'pecking order' derives from the poultry world, as female birds establish a hierarchy by pecking, and one takes on the cock bird's role in taking all the tastiest morsels.) If you have neighbours close by, a cockerel could be a nuisance, disturbing them with his crowing, although normally they will have poultry of their own and will be used to an early wake-up call. Consider, however, whether you wish to be woken at 5am every day!

Pure Breeds & 'Mongrels'

It's always more interesting to start with pure breeds and, by choosing one of the rarer types, you will also be doing your bit to ensure the survival of the breed. Some, such as the Bresse, Crève-coeur, Faverolles, Flèche, Houdan and Maran, although now found in many parts of Europe, have their origins in the French towns of the same names. As well as their own and other European breeds, the French are fond of breeds common to the UK.

During the summer, there are many poultry sales – usually held as part of a *fête* – from which good-quality birds can be bought. The dates and locations of nearby sales are advertised on posters or in local newspapers. If you want something a little different, but are at a loss as to what to choose, these sales are a good place to gain ideas. Information can also be found on the websites of the Poultry Club of Great Britain (💻 www.poultryclub.org/home.htm) and the Bantam Club Français (Patrick Quillet, 2 rue de la fontaine de Jallanges, 37210 Vernou sur Breene, 💻 http://perso.wanadoo.fr/bantam.club.jcm), which has specialised in bantam poultry for over a century.

If you just want hens to lay eggs, geese to keep the grass down or guinea fowl as 'watch dogs', you should be able to find all you want at your local market, where there's usually at least one poultry seller. Expect to pay around €7 for hens at point of lay (i.e. around 16 weeks old) and €10 to €12 for young ducks or geese.

Checks & 'Quarantine'

All too often, birds are transported to markets in cramped crates and it's impossible to get a good look at what you're buying. Ask the vendor to show you his birds and choose your own rather than let him put the first one he picks into a box. A healthy bird must have:

- A good covering of feathers.
- Feathers that aren't dull or sweaty.
- No discharge from the nostrils or beak.
- A clean vent (anal region) with no signs of diarrhoea.

On your return home, confine the birds to their new quarters with food and drink and leave them resting quietly. Even if you're intending to give them free range at a later stage, it's important that they're allowed to settle in and get the feel of home. After perhaps 24 hours, they will be sufficiently well orientated to be allowed out.

FOOD & DRINK

Poultry have different nutritional requirements according to their age. Young chickens that haven't yet reached point of lay – normally at around 16 weeks – need much more protein. This is best provided via the use of chick crumbs, starter pellets and grower's pellets. Mash (*pâtée*) is available as an alternative to pellets (*granules*) but is more wasteful. Although preferred by poultry keepers in the UK, mash is time-consuming to prepare, and only as much as the birds can eat in around half an hour should be made at a time. If left for much longer, it will become sour and unpalatable. This is of particular consideration in France, where the weather is generally warmer than in the UK.

In France, chicken feed is generally labelled as follows:

- ***Poussin*** – Crumbs or starter pellets for chicks.
- ***Poulet*** – Grower's pellets or mash, fed to birds up to and just beyond the point of lay.
- ***Poule/Pondeuse*** – For laying and adult birds.

Most kinds of pellets and mash can be bought in 5kg or 10kg bags from the pet section of any supermarket. Larger quantities (e.g. 25kg sacks) are to be found in agricultural and gardening suppliers.

Ducks will do well on a much lower protein food than chickens but, whatever you feed them, try to keep food away from water containers, as ducks have a habit of trying to soak their food in water.

If you're keen on recycling and self-sufficiency, you may wish to feed your poultry household scraps and vegetable off-cuts. One way of doing so is to boil them and add them to mash. If you decide on this method of feeding, it's important that you make the resultant mixture moist but crumbly – not sloppy. The mash should break up easily when a mixing spoon is put through it.

Cereal Feeds

Pellets are a complete feed, but all types of poultry benefit from the addition of mixed cereal (*mélange de graines*). The best mix is wheat (*blé*) and corn/maize (*maïs*), but the ratio shouldn't be more than around 3:1.

Too much maize in a bird's diet is bad for its health, as fatty deposits can build up around the ovaries. If possible, avoid feeding newly-harvested wheat; until it has been stored for a few weeks, it can precipitate digestive upsets and scouring.

Barley (*orge*) is unpalatable to chickens and will be rejected in favour of other cereals but it's a favoured food of ducks. It's possible to buy bags of mixed cereals, which contain all of the above, as well as sunflowers, linseed and other, smaller seeds that help keep poultry amused. Bags of grain can be obtained from the same suppliers as pellets and mash (see above).

It's pointless giving a combined feed of pellets and cereal at the same time, as most poultry will eat the grain first and leave the rest. Being harder to digest, cereal is best given in the afternoon or early evening, thus ensuring that birds go to roost with a full crop. A little more cereal can be fed during the winter, as it helps birds to maintain their body heat.

Geese

Given plenty of grazing, geese normally require no supplementary feeding during the summer, but a handful of grain per bird, morning and night, during the winter is essential to keep them in good condition. If the grass becomes brown in the heat of summer, however, it will have no nutritional value, and geese need to be artificially fed. They're seasonal layers, generally starting in early spring and continuing for two or three months. To gain the maximum amount of eggs, either for consumption or for hatching, give them pellets from around Christmas onwards. The Toulouse goose is widely considered to produce the best meat but is also a prolific egg layer, hence its popularity throughout France – a point to bear in mind if you're contemplating rearing commercially (see **Table Birds** on page 195),

Grit & Vitamins

Poultry have no teeth (hence the expression 'as rare as hens' teeth'), and all food passes from the crop to the gizzard, where it's ground down in much the same way as wheat on a mill wheel. Without the help of insoluble grit (*graines*) in the gizzard, it's almost impossible for a bird to break down and digest any whole grains of cereal. Although birds naturally pick up grit when foraging, it's necessary to give them added material.

There are essentially two types of grit:

- **Oyster-shell (*coquilles d'huîtres*)** – Although this is often included in manufactured feedstuffs, it can be given to the birds separately and is also a means of supplying calcium, which helps harden the eggshells.
- **Ground Limestone & Calcium** – Sold in the UK as 'mixed grit'.

Birds should have access to both types of grit, which can generally be purchased from any agricultural supplier but not normally from supermarkets. (Supermarkets sell small bags of fine grit for cage birds, which isn't suitable for poultry.) Five kilo bags cost around €4.50.

Birds should be given grit monthly from around one week old, the size of the grains altered as they grow. (Chick grit is available for very young birds.) If this is done, there's little fear of gizzard impaction.

French people, including vets, often insist that chickens be given regular doses of vitamins. However, vitamin supplements aren't normally required, as the manufacturers of pellets and mash always add a certain amount of vitamins, and all birds that have access to grass will find sufficient supplements themselves. Vitamin products can be useful whenever a bird is likely to experience stress, such as when being transported to a new home. Should you ever become enthusiastic enough to exhibit your birds at shows and there's a chance that they will be affected by stress as a result, a course of soluble vitamins, obtained from your local veterinary surgery and added to drinking water for five to seven days will help calm them. French vets usually recommend *Biotesse* or *Vitavia*. Alternatively, a vitamin product known as AD3 EC can be bought over the counter for €27 per litre bottle. Vitamins are also valuable when birds seem off colour – although there's always the risk that giving vitamins at this stage may mask the symptoms and delay the detection of a disease. If you decide to give your chickens vitamins on a regular basis, remember to change treated water at least once every 24 hours.

Greenstuffs

Free-ranging birds will obtain most of their greenstuffs naturally from grass and weeds. Long grass is useless, however. It should be cut if too long and raked up, as there's a danger that poultry, especially chicks, will choke when attempting to digest long strands. Young ducks and geese can be given lawn cuttings or chopped lettuce. In grassless runs and houses, a few turfs of short grass can be thrown in at intervals. Some weeds can be an advantage in the paddocks. Nettles, for example, are good fodder for poultry when cut and wilted. Chopped dandelion leaves and chickweed are ideal for chicks, and goose grass is liked not only by geese but also by turkeys and chickens.

Many crops can be grown especially for feeding to poultry. Well known to French poultry keepers is *chou fourrager*, a large cabbage-like plant that can be sown at intervals during April, May, June or July and can be harvested from September until February. Other useful greenstuffs that could be specifically grown include lucerne (*lucerne*), vetches (*gesse*), green cereals, kale (*chou*), millet (*millet*) and clover (*trèfle*).

The outer leaves of cabbage, cauliflower, beet, lettuce and sprouts can also be given to chickens before the rest of the vegetable is harvested for cooking. Some French poultry keepers also feed the greens of garlic and onions to their stock, believing them to have a cleansing effect on a bird's intestinal tract, but it's best to be sparing with these, as they may taint the flavour of the eggs if fed in large quantities.

Water

Water is the most important part of any diet for all poultry. It must be supplied on an 'ad lib' basis, clean and fresh every day. If limited, the first effect is a depletion in egg or meat production; the second is dehydration.

EGGS

The number of eggs you can expect from each hen depends on several factors: its age, available food, the size and type housing and the amount of light admitted (see **Housing** on page 118), and whether the hen is subjected to extreme heat or cold. A bird in its first season of production will lay the most, but it should continue to lay well for four or five years, although the older the bird, the fewer eggs it will lay. Fed a balanced diet (see **Food & Drink** above), the lighter breeds can be expected to lay daily for most of the year, stopping only when they moult (see page 132). Heavier breeds might not be quite as prolific and take the odd day off! As a general rule, half a dozen hens should lay four eggs each day, except when moulting. Obviously, on some days and at certain times of the year production will drop below this.

BREEDING

As your enthusiasm for poultry keeping increases, you may want to rear a few chicks from your own stock, either to replace aging birds or so that you can go into meat production – if not just for fun. It goes without saying that your first requirement is a cock bird. You must then decide whether to use the natural method of production (see below) or an artificial method (see page 129).

Note that eggs to be incubated don't need to be kept warm until placed under a broody hen or in an incubator. Even before a fertile egg has been laid, development has started. Development ceases when the egg is laid, provided the surrounding temperature is below 20°C. If, within seven to ten days, the egg is brought back up to that temperature, either under a broody hen or in an incubator, the arrested development continues.

Natural Method

Geese make perfect mothers, brooding their eggs and rearing their goslings without any help. All you need to do is to make sure that only one goose has been laying in the nest; otherwise, the eggs will incubate at different times. The mother goose will desert the nest once the first few eggs have hatched, leaving the other embryos to die in their shells. One way of avoiding this is to mark the eggs with a pencil as soon as you notice that a mother goose has gone broody. It's then a simple matter to remove the unmarked eggs each day, leaving only those on which you intend her to sit.

For most other species of poultry, it's best to take the eggs away on a daily basis until you notice that one of your hens is staying in the nest box longer than normal. If she's in there for a couple of days, you know she isn't laying and if, when you put your hand under her, she tries to peck at it, ruffles her feathers and squats tighter into the nest, you know she's broody and ready to hatch some eggs. Once you have a broody hen, begin collecting eggs for her to hatch.

SURVIVAL TIP

It can be useful to have an old bantam in your flock, as she may lay only five or six eggs before going broody and can be used to sit the eggs of other birds and act as a foster-mother.

Prepare a nest box away from any disturbance, perhaps in another outbuilding (make sure it's rat-proof). A coop and run is best of all if you or neighbours have one. Cut a grass turf the same size as your nest box or coop and place it upside-down in the bottom. This prevents eggs from rolling out when the rest of the nest is built up with hay and also helps to retain moisture and humidity – an important point when dealing with any type of egg. How many eggs to incubate will obviously depend on the size of the hen, but there's a school of thought that an odd number should always be set, as this makes it easier for the broody hen to turn them.

Broody hens shouldn't be removed from the poultry house to the sitting box in daylight. The move must always be done at dusk, and the bird handled with great care. If, after 24 hours, she's sitting happily and tightly, she should be encouraged out for food and drink. You may have to lift her off, in which case, check that no eggs are tucked in her feathers. She should leave the nest once a day from then on in order to feed and empty herself. Keep an eye on her and don't let her stay off the nest for more than 20 minutes or so.

The following table gives the incubation periods of eggs of various poultry types:

Poultry Type	Incubation Period (days)
Bantams	19–21
Ducks	28
Geese	28–35
Guinea fowl	28
Large fowl	21
Muscovy duck	35
Turkey	28

Once the eggs begin to hatch, the broody should be confined to the nest box and left alone. As soon as the hatch has finished and the chicks are dry, clean the nest and replace the hay with a handful of wood shavings. (Small amounts, sufficient for this job, can be bought in supermarkets, where they're sold as litter for rabbits and guinea pigs.) If the box is in a shed, make sure that the hen is prevented from taking her chicks too far from the nest by building a temporary pen. Ensure that the sides are tall enough to prevent her flying over them, or the chicks will be left behind and become chilled. If they've been hatched in an outdoor coop, it should now have a run attached and be moved onto fresh, short grass. Feed them on proprietary chick crumbs for the first three weeks and give water in a shallow container so that the chicks cannot drown.

If hatching duck eggs under a broody hen – because you've bought or acquired a clutch of duck eggs or because you know that ducks make unreliable broodies and worse mothers – don't be tempted into giving the ducklings water to swim in. They shouldn't be allowed near any water in which they can cover themselves before they're almost fully feathered, as it's possible for even ducklings to drown. A mother duck has oil on her feathers, which is transferred to the ducklings' 'down' as they creep under her for warmth.

Artificial Method

Hatching with an incubator can be quite complicated and the results are nowhere near as successful as those you will achieve by using a broody hen. If you're intending to rear poultry on a commercial basis, however, an incubator is essential, as broody hens cannot be guaranteed to be around when you want them.

Choosing an Incubator

Small electric incubators can be bought in France. **Each model is different and it's essential that you read and understand the manufacturer's instructions.** There are essentially two types of incubator, as described below.

'Still-air' Machines (*incubateurs statiques*): These are used widely and successfully by small breeders. They have few working parts to go wrong, and the mechanism is easy to understand and cheap and simple to maintain. It's this kind of machine that's more commonly sold at shows and poultry sales. Older models are usually heated by paraffin, but most modern machines are electric. You may be lucky enough to find a paraffin machine, normally made of wood, at a car boot sale or Sunday market (*foire à tout*, *brocante* or *vide-grenier*). The most famous make is Felmon, whose nameplate includes the words 'Gentilly, Seine'.

Still-air machines incorporate a hatching or nursery tray below the setting tray. The setting tray is shorter at the front and, as the newly-hatched chicks dry out, they're attracted to the light coming from a narrow window in the door. In walking towards it, they fall off the setting tray onto the tray below, where they cool off and are unable to interfere with or soil the remaining eggs. Humidity is supplied by two sliding water trays, which must be kept full at all times. At the base of the machine are two or three felts. These are removed one by one at intervals of a week and let out stale air.

Eggs must be turned at least twice daily by hand, in order to prevent the developing embryo from sticking to the side of the shell.

SURVIVAL TIP

One way of ensuring that each egg has been turned is to mark them with 'X' on one side and 'O' on the other; then simply make sure that all 'X's are showing in the morning and 'O's at night.

Most modern incubators have an automated turning system and you need only check daily (by noting the position of the trays or eggs) that the turner is working.

Cabinet Machines (*incubateurs ventilés*): These usually have more than one level of setting trays and differ from still-air machines in that they incorporate a fan, which ensures that there's an even temperature throughout. Because of their size and capacity, however, they're normally used only by commercial breeders.

Using a Brooder

Once the chicks have hatched in the incubator, they should be kept under the heat of an artificial brooder (*parquet d'élevage*). It's assumed that you have a shed, the corner of which can be sectioned off in order to house a brooder. These come in many shapes and sizes and the heat source (*appareil de chauffage*) can be powered by electricity, gas or even heating oil. Small-scale poultry rearers normally use calor gas heaters (*réchauffeurs de gas de calor*) or infra-red electric lights (*lampes infra rouge*). For only half a dozen or so chicks, a light bulb, fixed in an upturned terracotta plant pot, will give off sufficient heat and chicks will cluster happily around it.

SURVIVAL TIP

If rearing ducklings under infra-red light, make sure you use a dull emitter (*émetteur mat*) rather than a bulb, as they're fond of splashing even the smallest amount of water about, and water will cause a hot bulb to shatter.

Chicks need to learn immediately where the heat source is. When rearing is carried out in a large building or shed, this is best achieved by confining them within a surround of cardboard or hardboard. Once they've learned where the heat comes from (usually after a few days), the surround can be moved outwards to give the birds more space before eventually being removed.

The heat source is usually suspended from the ceiling and its height should be adjusted so that it creates a temperature of around 32°C (90°F) on the floor directly beneath. Each week, it's progressively raised until, by the third week, the temperature is down to 21°C (70°F). In hot weather, check the temperature, especially around midday, and if necessary turn off the heater and create a through-draught. You can tell whether the temperature is right simply by watching the chicks: if they're huddled under the heater, they're too cold; if they're right up against the surround, they're too hot and either the ring should be enlarged or the heat source raised. If only small numbers of chicks are being reared and the weather is hot, you could take them to a small pen on the grass outside for a few hours. It should be cat-proof and situated in the shade – and beware of sudden thunderstorms!

Feeding

Feeding and drinking vessels should initially be placed around the heating area so that the chicks don't have to go far to find them. Proprietary plastic 'chick drinkers' are available in the animal section of most garden, agricultural and hardware suppliers', but almost any small container (e.g. a jam jar) will do. Similarly, you can buy bespoke feeders but almost any shallow pan is adequate, provided that the chicks aren't able to scratch the food onto the floor.

Without a mother to show them what to do, chicks might need to be encouraged to eat, which you can do by 'pecking' at the food with your finger. The inclusion of some finely-chopped hard-boiled egg, sprinkled over the chick crumbs, will arouse their curiosity and has the added advantage of providing extra protein for the first day or so. You shouldn't mix too much egg at any one time, however; like mash (see **Food & Drink** on page 123), it will rapidly go sour.

MOULTING

Most poultry shed their feathers in the late summer or early autumn. This can be quite alarming at first – particularly with geese – as there are suddenly feathers all over the place and you might think that a fox or the neighbour's dog has taken one of your precious birds. Sometimes a partial moult occurs in the early part of the year, and young chickens moult twice during the first six months of their lives.

If properly cared for and housed, and fed on a balanced diet, a healthy young bird takes around six weeks to change its feathers; older birds can take as long as 12 weeks to complete the moult. Lighter breeds generally take less time than the heavier, dual-purpose types (see **Choosing Stock** on page 121). The large wing and tail feathers of all poultry are replaced slowly in a specific sequence over an extended time.

Normally, hens stop laying during the moult; if they don't, the numbers of eggs you collect each day will be considerably reduced.

DISEASES & PARASITES

Good hygiene is essential to birds' health and productivity. At least twice a year, their housing should be scrubbed out and disinfected, starting at the top of the roof and including every nook and cranny. This will help destroy mites and fleas, although corners of perches and the insides of nesting boxes should also be treated with powders – available from a vet or a pharmacy (*pharmacie*) – on a more regular basis. If the housing has no floor, the ground on which it rests will be difficult to disinfect. You can mix a powerful disinfectant with oil so that it soaks into the soil, then cover it with polythene before laying fresh litter.

Grass runs benefit from resting and periodic liming. If they're well covered with grass they shouldn't need disinfecting: it's better to rely on breaking the disease and parasite cycles by resting and maybe even Rotovating and cropping them before re-seeding. For this reason, it's preferable to have two grass runs that you can alternate.

A tendency to be alone, a droopy, hunched, ruffled appearance, nervousness, excessive thirst, lack of appetite, changes in droppings or a loss of weight and condition are all pointers to general ill health, as well as possible indicators of more serious sickness.

Parasites

Poultry are frequently the victims of parasites – external and internal. These can cause a lower resistance to disease, irritability and a disinclination to lay.

Fleas & Lice

Poultry fleas tend to live in the dust, especially of nest boxes. The females lay their eggs in any dirty area and they can hatch in a week, maturing in a month. You can control fleas in the hen house by cleaning, disinfection and the regular use of an insecticide powder (*insecticide en poudre*), costing around €4.50 per container. Dust your birds monthly with an anti-flea product (*antiparasitaire*), which can be bought from pet shops, over the counter at most pharmacies, or from your vet, for around €9 per container.

The most obvious sign of lice is a white crust (composed of lice eggs) around the vent as well as in the feathers under the wings. By parting the feathers, you may see small light-coloured lice running over the skin. Treatment is either by liberally dousing affected birds with louse powder or by using a chemical spray.

Mites

There are several species of mite. The most common is the red mite, which is in fact normally greyish-white, only becoming red when full of blood. Red mites live and breed in crevices as near to their food source as possible – hence their fondness for the ends of perches and the interior of nest boxes.

Similar in size to the red mite is another species that's grey to black and usually takes up residence on birds rather than in the hen house. It's most commonly found around the vent. Birds suffering from a heavy infestation tend to become scabby around the facial parts.

The scaly-leg mite differs from other mites in that it affects the legs and feet, burrowing under the scales and creating tunnels in which to breed. As it does so, the scales lift and distort. Left untreated, the legs may become swollen and crusty, eventually making a bird lame. Old-fashioned remedies include sulphur ointment, paraffin and linseed oil. Vaseline works well, as it seals the gaps in the scales and prevents the mite from breathing. Vets suggest an application of Gamma Benzene Hexachloride.

All mites can be treated by means of a pyrethrum-based spray. Effective mite-killing sprays are sold for use on pigeons and cage birds; although the manufacturers aren't allowed to claim that these sprays are suitable for poultry, they do a good job.

Worms

Worms are a common problem, especially on land that has been used for poultry for several years. The two main types are tapeworm and roundworm. The latter is round and smooth, the former segmented. Left untreated, they can prove fatal, as certain types block the windpipe and inhibit breathing. Others live off the host, taking all the protein which the bird has ingested via its food, causing it to become thin and listless. Birds that are suffering may increase their appetite while egg production decreases. Combs will turn from red to pink.

Like many parasites, worms normally pass from one bird to another by means of their droppings: fertilized worms are excreted and either eaten by snails and beetles, which in turn are eaten by poultry, or picked up directly by other birds. Poultry suffering from a heavy infestation of roundworms will excrete bundles of dead worms. Tapeworm eggs may also pass via the droppings or be retained within the rear segments of the worm, which periodically break off and are excreted.

Gapeworms are rarely seen in poultry unless they're kept on ground that has been infected by pheasants. The female worm lays her eggs in the bird's windpipe, causing difficulty in breathing. They're eventually coughed up and then swallowed, eventually being excreted; the larvae then develop before being picked up by other birds or ingested by earthworms.

Worming is normally carried out by the inclusion of a drug in the feed. Flubendazole is the most commonly used, both as a preventative and, at a higher strength, as a curative.

Diseases

As with all other animals, the diseases that affect poultry are caused by bacteria, viruses or fungi. They aren't always easy to identify, so you should always be on the look-out for unusual behaviour, which may indicate that a bird is diseased.

A complete list of poultry diseases would make a book in itself and, like a book of human diseases, do little more than convince readers that their poultry is suffering from every problem known to Man. Some of the common diseases and recommended treatments are, however, detailed below. The titles of some recommended books dealing specifically with poultry and containing information on identifying and treating diseases can be found in **Appendix B**.

- **Aspergillosis** (*Candidose*) – A respiratory infection usually resulting from inhaling fungal spores generated in damp or mouldy conditions, which are often found in badly-stored hay or straw. Damp shavings, especially those purchased in bale form rather than loose in bags, are another possible source. Chicks are particularly susceptible, and the spores can penetrate the shell of an incubating egg. Symptoms include laboured breathing, lethargy and increased thirst. Birds are sometimes unsteady on their legs, maybe even walking backwards with their head to one side. As there's no effective treatment, it's important to ensure that bedding and litter are kept dry and the poultry house regularly cleaned.

- **Coccidiosis** (*Coccidiose*) – All land contains the occysts of coccidiosis and, unless properly rested, develops a high count, which can cause infection in young birds reared there, although chicks reared under a broody hen are immune and the disease normally affects birds between three and ten weeks old. An affected bird may lose its appetite and become dejected, with ruffled feathers and white, sticky and copious droppings, in some cases blood-stained. Most poultry foods contain anti-coccidiostats (check the packaging), which helps prevent the condition.

- **Newcastle Disease** (*Maladie de Newcastle*) – Commonly known as fowl pest, this disease is unlikely to trouble the average poultry keeper, but as it's one of two 'notifiable' diseases – i.e. you're required to inform your vet of any case (the other is avian influenza – see below), it should be mentioned here. The last major outbreak swept through Denmark in 2003 and there was a small outbreak in pheasants that had been exported to the UK from France in July 2005. Another respiratory infection, its symptoms are typically long, gasping inhalation, mucus from nostrils and greenish-yellow diarrhoea. It's possible to vaccinate birds against this disease.
- **Infectious Bronchitis** (*Bronchite Infectieuse*) – This is a disease more likely to be seen in smaller units, as commercial flocks are generally vaccinated against it. The virus, caused by a coronavirus, is airborne and is transferred from bird to bird via nocturnal coughing and sneezing. Except for very young birds, the mortality rate is quite low, but poultry could succumb to secondary infections. It's possible to protect by vaccination.
- **Marek's Disease** (*Maladie de Marek*) – Sometimes known as fowl paralysis, Marek's disease can occur as a result of stress or an abundance of parasitic worms. It used to be a major contagious disease in domestic poultry but is nowadays less of a problem due to vaccination, although it's thought that there could be a genetic predisposition. Caused by the herpes virus, it can create lesions in birds as young as six weeks. In its 'classical' form, signs show as lameness in one or both legs, which often develops into general paralysis. Affected birds often lie with one leg forwards and the other stretched backwards, but seem otherwise alert and happy to eat food is put within reach. They may later suffer from a bunching of the claws, a gradually worsening wing droop and possibly even a twisted head or paralysed neck. It's invariably fatal. It's unlikely that birds bought from a commercial supplier will be vaccinated against Marek's disease, so it's a precaution worth taking.

Any poultry showing obvious signs of ill health should be taken to the vet – especially with the current threat of avian influenza (see below).

Avian Influenza

Avian influenza (*influenza*, *grippe* or *peste aviaire*), commonly known as bird flu, is the second of the two notifiable diseases (see **Newcastle Disease** above) and is known to be carried by migrating wild birds. Symptoms include drooping wings and tail, fast, laboured breathing and a very high temperature, which drops sharply to subnormal immediately before death. Birds are usually thirsty but refuse food. There's a vaccine, although its effectiveness has yet to be tested – for details contact your vet. By March 2006, the disease had spread to north-east France, and poultry throughout the country must be kept indoors. Additional legislation may be passed if the disease spreads further.

POULTRY CLUBS & EXHIBITIONS

Although the majority of poultry seen in France is of mixed breed – either deliberately crossed by commercial farmers to maximise their egg-laying potential or accidentally inter-bred – it isn't uncommon to discover high quality pure breeds suitable for showing at poultry exhibitions.

Poultry clubs abound – most having the admirable aims of maintaining breeds and quality, distributing leg rings, organising annual shows in their area, and participating in exhibitions elsewhere – and it will pay you to join your local club. Representatives are able to offer beginners advice on such matters as choosing a breed, feeding, and preventing and treating disease. At both shows and sales, you can buy feeders, drinkers, incubators, carrying crates and other accessories. Lists of poultry clubs can be found at 💻 www.chez.com/volaillepoultry, which also has links to many other useful websites.

You may be tempted into exhibiting birds. Obviously, only pure breeds can be considered (see **Pure Breeds & 'Mongrels'** on page 122). Visit a few shows before you enter one and choose a small event to begin with. You cannot just turn up with your prize bird on the day of the show. You will need to submit an entry form, obtained from the relevant club secretary, and then begin to prepare your bird so that it's in tip-top condition. The legs and feet of all breeds require cleaning and smearing with Vaseline, and some breeds need washing in pure soap flakes, their comb and wattles oiled and their ear lobes dusted with baby powder!

All exhibition birds carry leg rings containing an identifying number so that they can be easily traced if lost or stolen. When a bird is sold, it's re-registered to its new owner.

LONGEVITY

A question frequently asked by people wishing to keep poultry is, "How long can I expect my birds to live?" Geese can live a remarkably long time – 20 years or more. Bantams and large fowl can live for 13 to 14 years but are more likely to die at 8 or 9.

As with cats and dogs, if you believe that an old bird is suffering, you may wish to put it out of its misery. A neighbour should be able to help if you want to destroy old or ailing poultry, although – like it or not – it's important that you learn how to do so yourself.

The easiest and most 'humane' method of killing a chicken is the traditional one of 'wringing' its neck. (The word is inappropriate, as the idea is to break the neck.) This is best achieved by holding the bird's legs in one hand (usually your weaker hand) and taking the neck and hackle area in the other, then pulling the head down and twisting it backwards simultaneously; death is instantaneous.

The method for ducks, geese and turkeys is to lay their head on the ground (chin on ground, beak facing forward) while holding their feet, so that you're looking at their back. Place a broom handle over the neck and hold it firmly in place with your feet (one either side of the bird). Then pull up on the legs with both hands. This dislocates the neck. (You cannot use the same method as for chickens unless your arms are exceptionally long.)

8.

OTHER LIVESTOCK

If you're serious about self-sufficiency (some enthusiasts prefer to call it 'self-reliance') you may be considering keeping a cow or a goat in order to have your own supply of milk, but this isn't something to be rushed into without careful thought and planning. Cows are expensive and 'high maintenance', must be registered, and will produce far more milk than you can consume, even with a large family. Goats are easier to manage and goat's milk is particularly beneficial to health – especially if you suffer from skin problems such as eczema – but it's an 'acquired taste'. In any case, you must bear in mind that keeping an animal in milk means having it regularly mated, which in turns means that it will have offspring every year.

You must decide what you're going to do with the offspring that are necessary to the milk supply before buying a cow or a goat for its milk.

If you want to produce your own meat, you may want to keep sheep or pigs (an alternative is poultry – see **Chapter 7**). In this case, you must decide whether you're going to slaughter them yourself (and whether you will be able to bring yourself to do so) or send them to an abattoir – for which you will need suitable transport or fluent French (or both).

Before even entertaining thoughts of keeping animals, you should visit neighbours and gauge their reaction towards your proposed activities. If your cow attracts flies or your goat shed makes an unpleasant smell, they might consider it an 'excessive nuisance' and could apply to the courts to order their removal – definitely not the best way to win friends (see also **Bonfires & Noise** on page 240). In reality, however, living in a rural area, you're unlikely to find much opposition to your plans.

Many of the principles of livestock keeping are the same in any country, so much of this chapter is of a general nature, although there are some details that apply only to France. You're advised to read it **before** committing yourself to keeping livestock, as it will help you decide whether you have the buildings, facilities and dedication to undertake such a project.

SURVIVAL TIP

Whatever animals you decide to buy for your smallholding, it's well worth the effort of getting them used to being tethered or led with a head collar; in cases where this isn't possible (e.g. with some pigs), they should be regularly handled.

A strong post or ring should be installed in animal housing so that it can be tethered with a chain during milking or visits by a vet or farrier.

BUYING LIVESTOCK

When it comes to buying livestock, you should remember that in France, as elsewhere, there are unscrupulous breeders who will seize the chance to offload their poorer stock onto ignorant and unwary newcomers. There have been cases of expatriate Britons buying substandard cattle from resentful French farmers because they didn't know any better. It obviously takes years of experience to become a good judge of stock, but you should find out as much as possible – from neighbours as well as books and the internet – before proceeding. The website of the Institut National Agronomique Paris-Grignon (💻 www.inapg.inra.fr), much of which is written in English, provides information about many breeds of French livestock and offers links to the sites of breed societies and farming organisations, some of which also have an English-language option.

Your next step is to find someone experienced who will 'hold your hand' at the buying stage and be prepared to offer help and advice during the first few months. It's important not to let pride or delusions of knowledge stop you from doing so, as it's the animals that will ultimately suffer if you don't have the necessary experience. If no French neighbours are available to help, you might find fellow expatriates who are prepared to do so by searching the French Entrée website (💻 www.frenchentree.com).

COWS

The idea of having a cow (*vache*) wandering amiably in the garden, keeping the grass down and supplying you with fresh, creamy milk may be part of your rural idyll. The reality may come as something of a shock.

Cows aren't the best animal for the newcomer to rural France and certainly not to be recommended to anyone about to set up a smallholding for the first time.

A single cow produces in the region of 20–25l of milk per day, so you would need a household of a dozen people to drink it all or to be prepared to turn most of it into cheese. Legislation requires that cow's milk for drinking is pasteurised, that the dairy and cooling rooms meet certain standards, especially if you're offering milk for sale to the public – in which case you will also be subject to periodic inspection. You could keep a cow specifically to fatten beef calves, but this is a project fraught with potential difficulties.

In either case, you must comply with the requirements of the 'cow passport' system, which involves obtaining 'holding' numbers (which denote the location of the breeder's premises), herd numbers and ear tags and is a minefield to the French who understand the system, let alone to the newcomer to cattle-keeping and the country.

You must also know how to keep your cow in milk. If you obtain a 'dry' cow (i.e. one that needs to be mated and give birth before she can lactate), you will obviously need to acquire the services of a bull or at least get her impregnated by artificial insemination. Sometimes, for no identifiable reason, a cow is temporarily infertile and so your milk supply can be further delayed.

There are also the costs to consider – not only of the animal itself but also of her food. During the winter, in order for a cow to maintain her weight and health, she must be fed around 30kg of best-quality hay and 8kg of properly balanced 'cake' for every five litres of milk she gives. This should be fed in equal parts, morning and evening – at the same time as milking and cleaning out. **Keeping a cow is therefore not only expensive but also time-consuming – more so than keeping almost any other animal.**

Goats aren't subject to the same rules and regulations and are a much easier proposition for the novice who dreams of his fresh daily pint of milk (see below).

GOATS

In some parts of the country, especially among wealthier farming communities, the goat (*chèvre*) is referred to as the poor man's cow. Despite this apparently derogatory term, goats are widespread throughout France as the providers of the daily litre. In the more prolific farming areas, the Centre-Ouest and the Centre, it's common to see herds of goats (usually of the Saanen breed), whose milk is used to produce cheese. Another commonly seen breed is the Alpine (*Alpine Chamoisée*).

The goat is a mountain animal which can do well on the most unrewarding ground, although the same principles apply to goats as to all farm animals, i.e. they require warm, dry sleeping quarters, and supplementary feeding in winter or in times of drought. Allowed to range freely and given the odd bucket of kitchen waste (and a supply of hay in winter, along with dry bracken or shavings for bedding), a nanny goat will not only provide milk but also clear

▲ © Roger Moss (www.picturefrance.com)

▲ © Vera Bogaerts, photo from istockphoto.com

▼ © Bob Bouwman, photo from istockphoto.com

▲ © Michel Mary, photo from istockphoto.com

▼ © Yanik Chauvin, photo from istockphoto.com

© Clayton Hansen, photo from istockphoto.c

© Frank DiMarco, photo from istockphoto.com

© James Goldsworthy, photo from istockphoto.con

© Jan Tyler, photo from istockphoto.com

© Val Gascoy

© Simon Smith, photo from istockphoto.com

© Guy Stuart, photo from istockphoto.com

© Val Gascoyne

© Tom de Bruyne, photo from istockphoto.com

© Jacques Croizer, photo from istockphoto.com

▲ © Val Gascoyne

▲ © Val Gascoyne

▼ © Val Gascoyne

© Michel Mory, photo from istockphoto.com ▶

▼ © Val Gascoyne

all those unsightly thistles, brambles and weeds from the wildest areas of your plot. Moreover, if correctly milked (see **Milking** on page 148), a nanny will give milk for two years between kiddings. Most importantly for the smallholder, goats are friendly and make good 'pets'.

Housing

Housing should be dry and free of draughts but with an adequate air supply. Goats can withstand heat better than cold and wet, so they should be housed during winter nights or in inclement weather. They do best in a solid, warm building. During the coldest months, goats will practically live in their house, so you must ensure that it's dry, draught-proof and well ventilated. In summer, they should still be allowed access to the building at all times so that they have shelter from the sun and flies.

Fixtures & Fittings

The house should include a wall-mounted hayrack (*râtelier*) – costing around €16 for a light one or €50 for a sturdier version – and a water trough (*abreuvoir*). This should preferably an automatic trough that the goat operates by pressing a plate with her nose, costing around €35 if wall-mounted or twice as much if free-standing. An exterior water trough should also be provided; it's possible to find one that fits through a fence and provides water to two paddocks at once. Expect to pay around €50 for this type. All obviously need connecting to a mains water supply.

A feed trough should also be included in the house and must be securely attached to a wall. Unless it's specifically designed for livestock, a movable food container tends to spend more time upturned than upright, although wedging it into an old tyre usually solves the problem.

SURVIVAL TIP

Feeders and drinkers can be fixed to a wall, but they must be scoured and refilled each day. The temptation is to top up when the water is getting low and not worry about the dirt and parasitic germs that may be breeding there.

All the necessary fixtures and fittings can be bought from any agricultural ironmongers; look under *Elevage: matériel et fournitures*' in the yellow pages.

Milking Bench

A milking bench is a useful accessory, as a goat standing on the ground is too low to be milked comfortably. A bench raises her around 30cm, so you can sit on the edge of the bench or on a stool while milking. Made of wood and around 60cm wide, a bench can be hinged to a wall at one end with two strong legs (also on hinges) at the other end, so that it can be folded flat against the wall when not in use.

Choosing a Goat

Goats are usually pure-bred but there's nothing wrong with buying a cross-bred goat. If you particularly want a pure-bred animal, contact your local goat club; type '*chèvre*' into a French internet search engine and you will find the relevant societies for most breeds. Whichever type of goat you choose, it's essential to check that it's healthy, as follows:

- Look for an animal with an alert expression and bright eyes.
- She should have a small, neat head, a slim neck and shoulders that aren't too heavy.
- Looked at from head to tail, she should be wedge-shaped, getting progressively wider from the shoulders to the rump.
- Seen from the side, she should have a level back with very little slope at the tail; a steep slope here is said to denote a poor milker.
- A young female goat (goatling) should have a lively disposition, a good coat, pink lips and widely-spaced teats.
- Ask to see the mother of any youngster you're considering buying, as she will be a good indicator of the quality of the goatling.

Should you decide to buy a goat that's in milk (known as a milker), which will give you the quickest return on your outlay, you should obviously learn to milk before acquiring her (see **Milking** below). If you're a newcomer to goat keeping, you're advised to buy a goat in kid and still milking from her previous kidding, as animals do better when they've kidded with you than when they're moved soon after coming into milk. A young female which has been mated is probably the best option of all, as she has the whole of her productive life (ten or more years) ahead of her and you will both become used to each other's ways.

Because commercial goat keeping is widespread in France, it's a simple matter to approach a farmer and ask if he's prepared to sell you a youngster from his herd. Alternatively, you might notice a neighbour's goat with kids at foot, and you could offer to buy one of them after it has been weaned. The breed societies (see above) will have a list of breeders in your area. An adult female can cost anything between €200 and €400.

Legislation

All goats must be tagged and registered in accordance with EU regulations, which are the same as for sheep but less complicated than those for cattle. What's known as double-tagging is now coming into force, with one tag (*boucle*) on each ear containing different information, such as the breeders' location and herd reference. Tagging is the responsibility of the breeder, who should give you some spare application forms so that you can register any offspring. After agreeing a sale, the seller writes out a licence containing the ear tag information and should notify the relevant local government office of your purchase within three days. You must keep your newly-acquired animal on your premises for a minimum of six days in case of health problems. In addition, you shouldn't move any of your existing stock (goats or sheep) for the same length of time in case the newcomer is a carrier of disease.

Grazing & Supplementary Feedstuffs

In summer, when they can forage for themselves, goats need little extra feed, but in winter, when they have to be kept in their shed for all or part of the day, some hay prepared from the grass at the edges of your plot or – in accordance with French rural tradition – from the verges of country roads or common land, will be appreciated. (In quiet areas, you could tether your goat on the roadside near your house, but you will have to move the tethering peg at least once a day and be sure that there are no neighbouring dogs that might attack her.)

Goats will thrive on vegetables such as kale, swede, turnip and lucerne and can be given most kitchen scraps, especially stale bread and cabbage leaves. It's possible to buy dry goat food from almost any agricultural supplier, but it's easy to make your own mix of crushed oats, flaked maize, bran and linseed.

Unless you want garden plants devoured and trees stripped of their bark, you will need to tether your goat to confine it to an area where it can eat what it likes. It should be attached by a chain with a wide leather collar and a free-running metal ring to prevent wear and tear on the leather. The tethering peg should have a swivel joint to prevent the chain knotting.

If you're tethering more than one goat, it's important to ensure that they cannot reach each other, or they could choke each other with their chains.

On hot, sunny days, make sure that goats are able to find some shelter but that they cannot get right around trees or bushes, as they always seem to go round in only one direction, shortening the chain with every circuit! Free-range goats need a good paddock fence to prevent their escape, as they're able to jump surprisingly well (see **Fencing** on page 72).

Milking

Goats are easier to milk than cows, and milking is a knack that's quickly acquired – especially if demonstrated by an experienced neighbour – although men should note that the teat of a goat may be too short to accommodate all four fingers of a large hand! Here's how:

1. Grasp a teat lightly in one hand and push it gently upwards towards the base of the udder, so filling the teat with milk.
2. Close the index finger tightly around the neck of the teat, with the hand still pressing gently upwards. This traps the milk in the teat.
3. Close the other fingers in succession tightly round the teat, so forcing the milk down and out.
4. Release your grasp on the teat and relax the upward pressure.
5. Repeat the process with the other hand and the other teat (goats have only two).

As the udder empties, the upward pressure of the hand needs to become firmer and the initial movement of the milking hand a gentle upward punch. When the flow begins to subside, let go of both teats and with both hands gently massage from the top and back of the udder down towards the teats.

Continue milking until the flow subsides again; repeat the massaging movement until no more milk can be drawn.

Failing to extract all the milk at each milking makes a goat think that all the milk isn't required and consequently give progressively less at each milking.

Don't expect milking to be without mishap the first few times – you will be fortunate if you don't end up with the goat lifting her leg in protest at your clumsiness and knocking over the bucket in the process!

Goats need milking twice daily at as near to 12-hourly intervals as possible. It's likely that your goat will give you more milk than you can use, but it's legal to sell un-pasteurised milk from the door or even at your local market (see **Selling Products & Produce** on page 192). Like all milk, goat's milk should be kept in a cool place; once cooled, it can be frozen without detriment.

Equipment

A stainless steel bucket is best for milking into – any other type is likely to taint the milk. A good bucket will cost at least €15. A proper strainer (*tamis*) is rather more expensive at €50 and the filter papers (*filtres*) €4 per 100. Once the milk has cooled, it's possible to store it in a polyurethane churn (*baratte*), which costs around €18. If you want to go into cheese production, however, a cheese pasteurizer will set you back almost €600!

Mating & Breeding

To ensure a continual supply of milk, your nanny will need mating – which must be done during the 'rutting' season, from September until around mid-February. She will come into season every 21 days for most of these five months. If you see a constantly wagging tail, look at the vulva, which is slightly sticky, swollen and pink when she's in season. Either take her to a male (*bouc*) – another advantage of a goat over a cow is easy transportation – obviously having made an appointment beforehand, or arrange this for her next heat, 21 days later. An insemination service is available in the main goat breeding areas. If you've been unable to locate a nearby billy goat, your vet or local breed club will be able to give you the address of the nearest centre.

The nanny should be checked 21 days and 42 days after mating to see that she isn't in season. After this time, she can be assumed to be in kid.

Ailments

Goats can occasionally be affected by parasitic worms, which they pick up when grazing. You should have a regular worming policy and dose your animals with an approved anthelmintic. 'Drenching pistols' (*pistolet doseur*) or dosing syringes (*seringe doseuse*) are available from agricultural suppliers, but the medicine itself may have to be obtained from a vet or chemist – the latter also being knowledgeable about animal diseases and treatment. External parasites such as ticks (*tiques*), maggots (*asticot*) and ringworm (*teignes*) can be controlled by the use of Vetoquinol. It's recommended that goats are treated three or four times annually.

Bloat and scouring can be caused by goats eating too much fresh greenstuffs or wet, frosted or lush grass. Some French goat keepers believe that the white of an egg mixed with water cures scouring, but it's better to seek the advice of a vet if the condition persists for more than a couple of days.

> **SURVIVAL TIP**
> **Since goats are eclectic grazers, they tend to try things that other animals would leave well alone, including poisonous plants such as yew, rhododendron, laurel, laburnum and box, which you should ensure are out of range of your goat.**

Foot Care

The outer horn of a goat's hoof grows continuously to compensate for natural wear and tear. If an animal is deprived of regular exercise on hard ground – and it need be for only a short period each day – its hooves can turn up at the front like Persian slippers. It may therefore occasionally be necessary to trim the outer horn with a paring knife (see **Sheep** on page 151). Hooves that are badly grown may need to be cut with hoof shears (*cisaille à onglons*). It's possible to buy rasps and shears from agricultural suppliers or the '*articles vétérinaires*' section of large hardware shops; a good set will cost around €13. It's best to find an experienced neighbour who's prepared to show you how it's done before you try it yourself. If you cannot, start by taking off very little at a time.

It's also wise to give a goat's hooves regular treatment with linseed oil (*huile de lin*) or a proprietary horse hoof oil or grease (*graisse à pied*), as this will help keep them in good condition, especially during a hot summer, when they may otherwise dry out and crack. A tub of oil or grease costs around €15. As with all such procedures, the earlier you start getting your goats used to having their feet picked up and meddled with, the easier it will be.

SHEEP

Some 7 million sheep (*mouton*) are bred in France for their wool or meat or to provide milk for cheese making. (Perhaps the most famous ewe's milk cheese is Roquefort, prepared with milk from the *Lacaune* sheep.) As well as providing meat, milk and wool, sheep are perfect for grazing orchards and paddocks, as (unlike goats) they cause hardly any damage to pasture, and there's something soothing – perhaps even soporific – in their placid munching. (You may also find their bleating soothing – or maddeningly monotonous!)

Buying

You may think that a sheep is a sheep, but there are no fewer than 47 breeds to choose from. Merinos and several UK breeds such as the Clun-Forest, Dorset Down, Southdown and Suffolk are popular commercially for both their meat and their wool. It's possible to choose a breed specifically for milk production, and a ewe (*brebis*) makes an interesting alternative to a nanny goat. Photographs of all the breeds and information about them can be obtained from the Union de Promotion de la Race (UPRA, ☎ 01 44 08 17 46, 💻 www.upra@inapg.inra.fr). Whichever type you choose (and all types will do equally well in any part of France), it's advisable to start modestly rather than buy a whole flock at once.

It's best to start with in-lamb ewes, which means buying in the autumn or early winter. It's then a matter of finding a breeder with available stock. To find a local breeder, go to 💻 www.upra.inapg.iinfra.fr. Try to purchase from a small flock, as you're more likely to obtain good stock than if you buy from a commercial breeder. The best ewe to buy is one around two or three years old that has already had a couple of lambs. Sheep are more difficult to assess at a glance than goats on account of their long coats, and you should feel through the wool in search of a broad back. As with all animals, look for a bright eye and a clean 'back end'. Again, an experienced neighbour's help and advice is invaluable.

All sheep must have an ear tag, which means that they're registered (to someone – not necessarily you); you will be given all the necessary paperwork by the seller.

Grazing

One hectare of land will support around eight sheep, plus their lambs. If you want to over-winter your animals without too much supplementary feeding, you will need twice as much land. During the summer, sheep need little if any extra feeding, but in some of the drier parts of France it might be necessary to give them hay if the grass burns and loses its nutritional value.

Sheep are quite heavy grazers and should be periodically moved from one paddock to another. Any land you have available for grazing benefits from being split into four plots: sheep, like other grazing animals, appreciate a change of grass. Two of the areas could be used for a hay crop, but in France when grass is likely to be at a premium during the dry summer months, it might be better to buy hay from a neighbour and leave yourself with the extra grazing area. A top dressing of nitrogen fertiliser will improve the resting paddock (see **Fertilising** on page 75).

In the winter, sheep should have access to shelter, and each sheep will need a supplementary daily feed of around 3kg of concentrates plus hay and any surplus root crops from your vegetable patch.

Shearing

Sheep must be sheared annually, in the spring. If you cannot find a neighbour or local farmer to shear your stock for you, it might be possible to hire the services of a contract shearer (*tondeur de moutons*) who's prepared to clip small flocks; the usual means of contact is via word of mouth. Shearers normally charge per sheep (usually around €5) but the price will vary according to the distance he has to travel.

Breeding

Ewes need a dry shed or barn around the time they give birth (21 weeks after mating) and they should have access to a hayrack, water and a trough containing a suitable sheep ration. They will also appreciate some turnips, swedes and cabbage. Each ewe will give birth to one, two or three lambs, which should stay with the mother at least until shearing time (see above).

For lambs in subsequent years, you will obviously need to find a ram. Whether you buy or borrow one depends largely on whether you have friendly, sheep-keeping neighbours, although the problem with relying on a borrowed ram is that its owner won't want to lend it to you until he's sure that it has mated with all the ewes in his own flock – which means that your lambs will be late born, especially if there are other would-be breeders to whom the 'poor', hard working ram has been promised.

If you choose to buy a ram, remember that he will be sexually mature at between 7 and 15 months and that ewes are in season several times a year, so you should keep the ram and ewes separate until you want them to mate. Having decided at what time of year you wish to lamb (usually January or February), work backwards five months (which is the gestation period) and add a further fortnight; that's the time at which you will need to introduce your ram to the ewes.

A ewe is capable of producing two or three lambs each year until around the age of 15, but her fertility will begin to drop (i.e. she will produce fewer lambs and less often) after the age of around eight.

Fattening

It's usual on a smallholding to keep the females or sell them for breeding and to send the males to the abattoir. Unlike pigs (see below), sheep – or rather lambs – require little extra feeding before slaughter. They will fatten quite well simply by having access to good pasture for a few weeks or on a diet of hay, concentrates (*concentrés*, *compléments alimentaires* or *rations supplémentaires*) and, if you have a vegetable garden, any swedes, turnips, cabbages or kale you can spare.

The length of time necessary for fattening varies. Young lambs make the tenderest meat (known as *viande d'agneau de lait*) and are traditionally killed at Easter, when they're only around three months old. More normally, however, lambs are killed at 12 months, when they're mature and the meat has that typical lamb taste – and is known as *viande d'agneau engraissé*.

Castration

To obtain the highest quantity meat, you should have male lambs castrated as early as possible. Castration can be done in two ways. One is using an 'elastrator' (*pince anneaux-gomme*) and rubber rings (*anneaux en cautchouc*). The rings are placed over the scrotum onto the sperm cords, just above the testicles. This should be done when lambs are just one or two days old in order to cause the minimum of discomfort. It's possible to buy an elastrator and boxes of rubber rings from a veterinary chemist or agricultural supplier. The other method is to cut the sperm cords using castrating pliers (*pince à castrer*). This can be done at any time in the first four weeks; after this, it must be attempted only by a vet using an anaesthetic.

Although castration isn't necessary, it will help in producing a better carcass (see above) and allows you to run both young males and females together – an important factor when space is limited.

Health

Unfortunately, sheep suffer from a number of problems, one of the most common being worms (*ténia*), which are picked up when grazing. Worms can live inside a sheep without being noticed and the first sign of infestation is diarrhoea. Most shepherds treat sheep with a wormer (*vermifuge*) at this stage, but the wet, smelly excrement makes them a target for flies during the summer, which then causes another problem. Fly strike results in maggots developing in the anal area, and if untreated they will literally eat the sheep alive! It's therefore essential to use a preventative treatment, such as a gentian violet spray (ask your vet for advice), on a regular basis. It's also advisable to dag your sheep in the spring, i.e. cut away the fleece around the anal area.

There are three types of wormer: benzimidazoles, levamisoles and avermectins. These are generally available in 'pure' form or in solution (known as a drench). A worming drench called Oxfendazole, manufactured by Synanthic, is recommended by many French vets and costs around €34.

External parasites such as ticks (*tiques*), maggots (*asticot*) and ringworm (*teignes*) can be controlled by the use of Vetoquinol. It's recommended that sheep are treated three or four times annually. Sheep dipping isn't required.

Occasionally, sheep go lame due to inflammation of the joints. For mild infections or prevention, use gentian violet spray (*violet gentiane*, either with or without *benzalkonium*) mixed with a 5 per cent iodine solution (*tincture d'iode*). Proprietary brands of spray include Epispray and Negerol, costing around €17. They're essential to the smallholder, as they can be used to treat cuts and wounds on all types of animal.

Like goats and cattle, sheep require a periodic pedicure. This is best done by turning the sheep over into the same position as for shearing. Using a sharp knife (*renette à parer*), pare off a small piece at a time and bring the outer horn flush with the sole of the foot. Neglected hooves may require cutting with shears (*cisaille onglons moutons*).

PIGS

Goats and sheep are easy to keep – apart from the commitment of time. Pigs (*cochon*) are a different matter, so **you should consider the advantages and disadvantages carefully before investing in pigs**.

The benefits include a cheap supply of meat, without the need for specialist feedstuffs (see **Feeding** below), good manure for the garden, and 'free' cultivation equipment! On the downside, pigs are likely to bulldoze parts of your property and, although they're clean animals, their smell can upset members of your family as well as neighbours and any *gîte* or B&B guests. Although they usually make good pets and are generally docile – often being happy to go for a walk with their owners – there are, unfortunately, a number of bad-tempered pigs. Some sows will hardly let you inside the sty when they have piglets and others are prone to bursts of temper under stress.

Choosing a Breed

France has a good selection of pig breeds, each of which has been developed to suit the climate and topography of a particular region and to improve both domesticity and flavour, often resulting in far better quality animals than the 'hybrids' more commonly bred commercially. If you're interested in buying a pure-bred pig, useful information can be found on the website of the Fédération pour Promouvoir l'Elevage des Races Domestiques Menacées (💻 www.chez.com/ferm/principal.html). Breeds to consider include *Basque*, *Bayeux*, *Blanc de l'Ouest*, *Cul noir de Limousin* and *Gasconne*, which originate from Hautes-Pyrénées, Normandy, Brittany/Normandy, the Massif Central and Gers/Gironde respectively; if you happen to live in one of these areas, you may want to select a local breed.

Housing

If, despite the disadvantages (see above), you've decided to keep pigs – whether as a source of meat, to keep a rough area turned over or as a pet – they will need solid housing. **Don't waste your time with a rickety shed, as a pig will have it to bits in no time.**

Many old properties in rural France have a pigsty (*porcherie*) – a legacy of the days when every householder used to keep and butcher his own animals. The traditional stone sty with a yard in front evolved through centuries of study and, according to many people, has never been bettered; if there's one of these on your property, you're already well equipped. Pigs seem to like them, provided there's plenty of bedding in the sleeping quarters, and they're a good way of allowing the animals access to fresh air without letting them root up pasture land. Other buildings can be equally suitable, but the insulation must be good, with no condensation. It helps if the airflow in a pig house can be adjusted, e.g. via windows or a half door.

Pigs are greedy and messy eaters and movable troughs are seldom satisfactory, as they will have them over in no time and much of the food will be trodden into the ground. If you have a permanent pig house, you should build a concrete trough into one wall, preferably so that it can be filled from outside. Alternatively, there's a plentiful supply of old kitchen sinks in France, which can be bought cheaply from *vide-greniers*, *dépôt-ventes* and the building material yards of Emmaüs centres, etc. They make good feed troughs, as they're too heavy for even the hungriest pig to upset.

The perfect pig run would be a small copse or a patch of rough ground containing a few trees for shade and shelter. Wet or boggy land is unsuitable, as is a patch that's too small and so gets churned up and becomes foul smelling.

Feeding

Commercially-bred pigs are generally fed on pignuts, which can be bought from an agricultural merchant (*alimentation animale*). If your pigs are allowed to roam about outside, however, they will pick up some of their own food, including vegetation. A natural diet may take longer to produce meat, as it isn't as efficient as specialist pig foods and the pigs will use up energy snuffling about and keeping warm, but it means less work for you and a much better life for the pigs, and it can be supplemented by surplus milk from a goat and left-over food. Provided you're rearing and producing for your own consumption, it's legal to feed them certain kitchen waste in the time-honoured way.

Legislation designed to prevent foot and mouth disease makes it illegal in France (and elsewhere in Europe) for a diet made up of 'scraps' to include meat waste.

Unless your pig is completely free ranging, you should give it medicated mash or meal (*pâtée*), which can be bought from an agricultural supplier or vet. A young pig weighing 18kg needs around 1kg of medicated feed per day, increasing as it gets heavier to a maximum of around 3kg. Medicated feed must be kept separate from ordinary food and should be clearly labelled.

Breeding

As with sheep and goats, you will find it easiest to start your pig-breeding empire by buying a pregnant sow. (A sow can start producing at just six months.) Subsequently, you can mate her with a neighbour's boar or use artificial insemination. (Boar licensing has been abandoned, which means that anybody can keep one for breeding.)

Boars are aggressive and have dangerous tusks; they must be treated with the utmost respect, as people are occasionally killed or maimed by them.

Signs that a sow is in season – which can be at any time of year – include standing perfectly still, a deep grunt and reddening of the vulva. If you can find a boar owner who is willing to keep your sow for a few days when she's in season, so much the better, as you may make the journey only to find that she isn't quite ready and must wait another day or two.

The gestation period is nearly four months – three months, three weeks and three days, to be exact – and you should allow a sow two months for suckling her litter, which comprises an average of 14 piglets. After weaning, she can be in pig again within a week or two so you could, in theory, have two litters – and up to 30 piglets – per year.

Fattening

A medium pork pig will take around five or six months to produce on the 'backyard system' (see **Feeding** above), but some French traditionalists keep their animals a full year, despite the fact that they're likely to be too fat by modern standards and the joints very big.

If you're fond of pigs but still want to breed, kill and eat (or sell) them, a compromise might be to keep a sow for life and use only her offspring for meat. So that you don't know you're eating a particular pig, you can send several away together (see page 166), asking for the meat of only one to be returned and the rest sold.

HORSES, PONIES & DONKEYS

No one without experience should take on a horse (*cheval*) or pony (*poney*) without a great deal of consideration. They need constant care and attention and must be registered and possess a veterinary passport. This document contains information regarding the age, size, sex and distinguishing marks of the animal and must be handed to the new owner if you sell it. A record of what medicines and other treatment have been applied is also required. Although the main purpose of these documents is to protect against theft and provide proof of breeding, there are other occasions when they must be produced – not least when an animal must be put down and the carcass removed for disposal. (see page 165).

Donkeys

Donkeys (*âne*) are, unfortunately, often regarded as pets and are very popular in France. It's tempting for the newcomer to rural living to buy one, thinking that it will be a less demanding alternative to a horse and will help keep the grass down. They're definitely less work and will keep small paddocks, orchards and scrubby areas grazed, but they cannot be neglected and **you mustn't buy a donkey on the whim of a grandchild or because it looks appealing**.

One donkey can be kept on half a hectare if you're prepared to keep the paddock in good condition by removing the dung, mowing the rough parts and plying fertiliser. It will be even more successful if the paddock is divided in half and grazed in alternate months. Donkeys will happily graze where intended but, if food becomes scarce, will make short work of stripping the bark from fruit trees and aren't averse to gnawing at fences. As well as good grazing, in winter they also need a supplement of hay and pony cubes or a mixture of bran and oats.

They're sociable animals and a single donkey will often prove to be noisy, bad-tempered and depressed (remember Eeyore in the Winnie-the-Pooh stories?), although they can be happy with a goat or even sheep as well as with another donkey.

Although they will sleep outdoors in the coldest of weather, donkeys are like horses in needing shelter as well as good feeding and regular worming and hoof care (see **Farriers** below). Also like horses, they're long lived, having a lifespan of 20 to 30 years. They should be handled regularly so that they won't bite or kick you or a vet or farrier when they need to be checked or have their hooves trimmed.

Farriers

Donkeys need their feet checked and trimmed every 12 weeks or so – even if you don't ride, drive or work them. Likewise, horses not ridden or driven will need their feet attending to regularly, in order to keep them in good shape and prevent 'sand cracks' developing. Although some horses can be left unshod, it's important to keep their hooves in shape.

Horseshoes, nails and general farriery equipment can be bought at many hardware shops (*quincailleries*) but, unless you know what you're doing, you should use a farrier. A good farrier (*maréchal-ferrant*) is important and isn't cheap – nor, in some parts of France, easy to find. Nailing a shoe isn't a DIY job, as the shoe must be the right size and shape for the hoof, and a misplaced nail can lame an animal.

Whereas in the UK farriers must be qualified to standards set by the Worshipful Company of Farriers, in France anyone can set up in the business and so it's extremely important that you don't simply employ the first one listed in the yellow pages.

The cost of employing a farrier varies – you should be paying for his skill and advice as well as the cost of his materials and transport. To have a donkey's hooves trimmed, expect to pay around €65.

BEES

You may be tempted to keep bees (*abeille*) in France, and there are good reasons for doing so. The predictable climate and profusion of flowering plants in most regions make bee keeping a reliable and therefore popular hobby, which can generate a substantial financial return if you sell the honey (see **Selling Products & Produce** on page 192), although it can be expensive in the initial stages.

Even wearing a protective suit, you will occasionally be stung, so you should take anti-histamines in case you have a violent reaction.

Before throwing yourself into bee keeping, it's wise to seek out as much information and advice as you can. Consider joining a local beekeeping group or make the acquaintance of a local beekeeper. There are numerous associations in each region and your local bee inspector (see below) will be able to put you in touch with their secretaries. The national beekeeping association is the Syndicat National d'Apiculteurs (5 Rue de Copenhague, 75008 Paris, ☎ 01 45 22 48 42, ✉ abeille-de-france@wanadoo.fr, 💻 www.apiculture.com/sna).

> **SURVIVAL TIP**
> **Don't even think about keeping bees if you're nervous about being stung, as the bees are likely to detect your fear and attack you.**

Hives

Although size and dimensions vary from type to type (but French hives tend to be bigger than British or American hives), all beehives (*ruche*) work on a common principle. They consist of a series of boxes containing a number of removable frames, upon which the bees draw out their wax combs to contain their young and a store of honey. With care, it's possible to remove honey without harming the bees and leave them with sufficient stores to feed themselves during the autumn and winter.

There are no problems associated with bringing hives with you from another country – provided they're clean and properly sterilised. It's important to ensure that you also bring plenty of spare parts, however, as they may not be available in France. It might be possible to have a hive made for you. Look under *Elevage: matériel et fournitures* in the yellow pages and you may find a builder of livestock equipment (goat houses, aviaries, etc) who's prepared to do so.

New hives are expensive, but second-hand equipment is sometimes available and usually advertised in local newspapers. Alternatively, it's worthwhile advertising in the 'wanted' section of the British community website (💻 http://ukgrapevine.monsite.wanadoo.fr), part of which is dedicated to smallholders and French rural living enthusiasts.

If you buy second-hand equipment from non-professionals, there's a high risk of its containing disease. As with equipment for livestock, ensure that everything is thoroughly cleaned and disinfected before use.

For details of all the equipment you're likely to need and suppliers, go to the online World's Bee-keeping Directory (🖳 www.beehoo.com), which has pages in English and French.

Location

It's worth taking some time to consider the location of a hive, as, once positioned, it's difficult to move without confusing and perhaps even losing the bees. A hive must be positioned well away from paths and roads; when the bees are working hard, the last thing you (or they) want is humans blundering through their flight path. You should choose a firm, level area, preferably sheltered from the prevailing wind and not underneath trees. Ideally, the bees should be able to approach it from any direction without obstruction. The stand on which the hive sits should be solid and level so that you won't have to prop it up when the bees are working.

Stocking

The movement of bees throughout Europe is regulated and it's best to avoid the difficulties involved in transferring a nucleus (*noyau*) to France from another country. In any case, bees don't travel well, even within France: stocks of bees brought from the Paris area to southern France, for example, won't thrive, as they won't be able to adapt to the different flowering seasons. Your best bet is to buy a nucleus (i.e. a collection of bees without a queen) or a small colony containing a young queen (*reine*) from a reputable local supplier, as this will be the most suitable for the environment. Although this may take a year to enlarge into a productive unit, it will give you much better results in the long term.

You also need to find out about the bees you're thinking of buying. Some colonies can be quite aggressive, others docile as long as you have a young queen; but for some reason, once certain queens are more than a couple of years old, they can turn the hive into a vicious colony. Harder working and more productive bees can be somewhat bad tempered; more amiable bees may produce less honey but are better for the beginner.

SURVIVAL TIP
Don't ever be tempted to collect a swarm of bees, as it will always be untrustworthy.

Calendar

The best time to stock bees is early spring, and the following is a summary of the tasks to be carried out in each season.

Spring

As spring approaches, you will start to notice worker bees congregating on the flight board and making short flights on mild, sunny days. They're assessing the available food, removing waste and fetching water.

Soon, they will start returning with pollen; the hair 'baskets' on their back legs will be packed full of pollen grains varying in colour from white through yellows and oranges to brown. When pollen is being brought in, it's a sign that youngsters are being raised in anticipation of the honey flow. When honey is being produced (generally from May), you will notice that there are vast numbers of bees coming and going, arriving fully laden and landing heavily, and you should be able to detect the smell of honey. (It isn't mere coincidence that the expression 'busy as a bee' is used in languages worldwide.)

Choose a fine sunny day and open the hive to note progress. The hive should be clean and there should be many cells containing eggs, which indicates that the queen is laying well. Eggs will be found in the centre of a frame, whereas honey and pollen are generally in the corners and around the edges. This ensures that the eggs are protected from a drop in temperature. Other positive signs include worker bees 'drawing' out new combs in readiness for an influx of honey.

Summer

Once all the frames in the brood box are full of honey, it's time to add a 'honey-super' – if you don't, the bees will swarm. A honey-super is a shallow box containing frames in the form of wax sheets, which the bees will fill with honey. You can buy the sheets ready-made or in kit form (in packs of ten), and it's important to ensure that you have some spares – fellow beekeepers may not be able to help you if they've also run out.

Once a honey-super is completed and full of honey, the bees will 'cap' it by sealing it with wax (suitable for candle-making or polishing the dining room table!). Remove it and replace it with another. In southern areas of France, you might need to do this two or three times, but in the most northern regions one 'super' will be sufficient for the whole season. Exactly when to add it (or them) obviously depends on where you are, how good the 'crop' is and how productive your bees are.

A wire mesh frame, the 'queen excluder', is set between the honey-super and the brood box, allowing the worker bees access to fill the frames but preventing the slightly larger queen from laying her eggs in them, thus spoiling the honey.

By the end of summer, the honey will be ready to harvest. When the honey flow is slowing, but before the season is fully over, remove the honey from the comb using an 'extractor', which works by centrifugal force. Extractors can often be bought second-hand and are available via the internet (e.g. 💻 www.beehoo.com and 💻 www.agriseek.com/buy-sell/bee keeping/equipment). The frames should then be returned to the hives; the bees will eat the residue left on them.

SURVIVAL TIP

Make sure you have all the tools you need before opening a hive; leaving it open while you go back to the house to fetch something won't endear you to your bees.

Autumn

In a normal season, bees will find the residue sufficient to keep them going through the autumn and winter, but a good bee keeper will offer additional winter feed. Gently lift the rear of the hive at regular intervals to check that there's a sufficient food store inside. Hungry bees are lighter than well-fed ones and, with experience, it's possible to assess whether feeding is required. This is via a sugar-based mix, which is laid on a tray. It should consist of around 2.5kg of sugar per litre of water. After a couple of feeds, the bees will want no more and the mixture should be removed, as a water-based mix left in a hive can cause mould.

Winter

If you haven't checked or have failed to correctly assess the food store, you will need to feed your bees during the winter, but this should be avoided if possible, as bees can become aggressive at this time of year. If you have to feed them, give them blocks of 'sugar candy', which is dry and so cannot cause mould in the hive.

Even if your bees don't need feeding, a weekly visit is necessary to ensure that your hives are secure and undamaged and that there are no signs of mice entering.

Queens

At certain times, it's necessary to locate the queen in order to check that she's fit and active and to eradicate queen cells. You may not find the queen immediately, as she's elusive and will slip out of sight. You should see combs with eggs in them (the sealed ones containing young) and honey stored in a corner. You may also see sealed cells with slightly raised tops; these contain drones or males and are a normal part of hive life. The queen cells, which are usually larger and therefore easily distinguished, contain young queens and must be eradicated; otherwise, these virgin queens will hatch and the hive will swarm alongside the old queen, leaving you with a much-depleted hive. If your queen is inactive, she needs to be killed, by squeezing her between your thumb and forefinger.

Diseases

A number of diseases can affect bees, including Acarine Disease, American Foul Brood and Nosema; if your hives become infected, they will probably have to be destroyed.

A recent threat to bees, now widespread in Europe, is the Varroa mite, which invades a colony and weakens the young at the brood stage. If not controlled, it can ravage a hive in a season; the bees become weakened and stunted and the colony cannot produce sufficient food. Apistan strips (which are treated with an acaricide) should be inserted between the frames in late summer or early autumn. The chemical is passed around the colony and kills the mite. The strips are then removed, leaving a clean hive ready for the following season.

TRANSPORT

It's essential that you have a means of transport suitable for collecting sacks of feed and bales of hay as well as for moving livestock or beehives around. The family saloon is probably not the best vehicle in which to take your nanny goat to the billy down the road every time she needs mating. It might be possible to buy a second-hand van – and the classic Renault 4 ('*quatrelle*') or Citroën 2CV (*deux-chevaux*) would be ideal. They're the ultimate small farmer's vehicle, designed with high clearance and good load bearing for duties such as the above. Unfortunately, French farmers know this and hold onto them until they literally fall to pieces, so they're almost impossible to find in usable condition.

An alternative is to buy a trailer (*remorque*) and build a cover to protect feedbags from the rain and to prevent your nanny goat, anxious to arrive at her appointment with the billy, from making an unscheduled exit. Remember that in France, trailers must conform to strict regulations and, over a certain size, must have their own *carte grise* (see **Tractors & Trailers** on page 171). To load animals into the trailer, you might need a ramp and possibly some sort of holding pen. The ramp should have fenced sides to avoid accidents to yourself or your livestock.

DEATH & DISPOSAL

Even if not intended for the abattoir (see below), no livestock can be expected to live for ever. Some will pass away peacefully during the night; for others, the end can be a gradual decline until the services of a veterinary surgeon are required. Either way, there will be the problem of disposing of the body.

It's illegal in France to bury (*enterrer*) animals weighing over 35kg on your land. A dead animal weighing more than this must therefore be disposed of.

Incineration (*crémation*) is the usual method. Neighbouring farmers, a vet or your *mairie* will tell you where to find the nearest incinerator (*incinérateur*), and you can either take the animal there yourself or ask for it to be collected. You will be charged around €1 per kilo, plus a collection fee (if appropriate), which varies according to the distance to be covered.

Killing for Meat

Provided the meat is for your own consumption, it's legal to have sheep and pigs killed on your premises. Otherwise, you can take them to an abattoir. One advantage of having animals killed at home is that it reduces stress, which isn't good for the meat (or the animal): too much adrenalin forms a chemical reaction that makes the meat less tender. Some small abattoir owners will allow you to take animals in the night before they're slaughtered, in order to give them time to calm down.

Taking a single animal to slaughter isn't easy. If it's a youngster that has never been away from its mother, it's doubly difficult and so, if your situation allows, it's better to wean any youngsters some time before they're due to be sent away.

An appointment is necessary and you will be charged for killing the animal and for having the carcass cut into joints. Current prices are €20 for killing and €20 for jointing a pig; €12 for killing and €20 for jointing a sheep. In addition, every animal must be inspected by a resident vet, for which the abattoir will charge around €30.

At an abattoir, animals are stunned by an electric shock from a pair of 'stunning tongs' before being hoisted up by their back legs. Carried along on a moving belt, they then have their throats cut and bleed to death. Pigs are then dropped into a vat of scalding water in order to remove the bristles; cattle and sheep are skinned. Next, the belly is cut open and the innards removed. If you wish to keep any of the edible parts (heart, kidneys, liver etc), you should ask for them to be returned along with the carcass. After being washed down, the carcass is transferred to a pre-chilling section and then on to a cold room before being jointed and packed ready for collection.

9.

Machinery & Tools

If you're intending to work your land, you will obviously need some machinery. Some basic tools and their maintenance are described later in this chapter, but it begins with machinery, as serious work necessitates serious boys' toys! Before making any major purchases – tempting though it may be – estimate the amount of work that will be required. A neighbour might be prepared to carry out some cultivation or other tasks, such as haymaking, which will save you the expense of buying equipment. On the other hand, he will want to carry out his own work first and, when you need him, he may be busy. Another option is to hire equipment when you need it (see **Plant Hire** on page 174).

SURVIVAL TIP

Before using major machinery or tools in France, observe a French professional at work – he doesn't appear to hurry, isn't stressed, and works smoothly and efficiently; his tools are clean and cherished and he's able to work all day without apparent strain.

GENERATORS

One expensive item that it might make sense to buy rather than hire is a generator (*groupe électrogène*). A generator will have a multitude of uses around your property and, if you're planning a complete renovation, it may be essential when the electricity has to be disconnected for re-wiring.

Bearing in mind the initial outlay (prices start at around €850), it's important to buy a generator that's suitable for the job you have in mind. Petrol- and diesel-powered generators are available. A petrol generator is generally cheaper and quieter and is adequate for most jobs, while diesel has the advantage of being economical in prolonged use, and most models have a larger fuel tank than petrol generators. Most generators are single phase (*monophasé*) but the most powerful ones are three phase (*triphasé*).

- For light work, such as DIY and powering garden tools, a 1.8–4kW/2.25–5kVA model should be sufficient. A three-phase generator would give 4kW/5kVA.
- For lighting and some heating you require a 6.0–8.6kW/7.5–10.7kVA or three-phase 5.6–9.2kW/7–11.5kVA model.

- For prolonged use and/or heavy duty work (mostly diesel-driven) a 3.4–5.2kW/4.25–6.5kVA or three-phase 4.8–5.2kW/6–6.5kVA is required.

ROTARY TILLERS

If you have a small amount of land to cultivate, you may want to buy or hire a rotary tiller (*motobineuse* or *rotofraise*) – commonly known in English as a Rotovator, although this is a trade name – which is a petrol or diesel engine coupled through a drive shaft to a set of rotating digging tines (*fraises*). They're activated by a pair of handles, and the tilling depth can be altered by handle-mounted controls.

There are many makes and sizes of tiller. The smaller machines usually have just a single set of tines and require a certain amount of effort on the part of the operator, who must guide and partly drive them. Although they're adequate for small plots, the novelty will soon wear off if you have to work with one all day, especially if it has only a single forward gear.

Larger tillers are obviously more expensive but have wheels that are driven by the engine and are therefore easier to use, as it's simply a matter of adjusting the forward speed and walking behind while the machine does the hard work. They usually have two forward gears and one reverse. There are generally two sets of three tines or, if back-mounted, a block of four. Some models have removable tines, which can be replaced by a single-furrow plough to enable you to break up particularly heavy ground – such as an old pasture. It's possible to purchase other attachments, such as a disc cultivator, to further break down the soil.

Rotary tillers vary in width: plough attachments (*brabants*) give a cultivating width of 80-90cm, while a tiller with a single set of tines may have a working width of only 30cm. **Don't even consider a rotary tiller with smaller than a 5hp engine.** Prices start at around €250 for the smallest and most basic types.

Tillers are flexible and compact (they can be stored in a standard shed or garage) and, properly looked after, should serve you for many years. However, they aren't suitable for cultivating large areas, for which you will need a tractor.

TRACTORS & TRAILERS

Few things are more evocative of the French rural scene than tractors trundling along country roads at 25kph (15mph), and it seems as if everyone has a trailer of some sort – not without good reason.

Mini-tractors

The next step up from a rotary tiller is a compact tractor or mini-tractor (*petit tracteur*), which has a two-, three- or four-cylinder engine (usually diesel), and is usually equipped with hydraulic arms at the rear to carry and lift implements such as ploughs, tines and disc cultivators, as well as a tow hitch for small trailers. Some mini-tractors are equipped with 'power take-off shafts' (PTOs) to drive cultivators (*cultivateurs/fraises rotatives*) and mowers (*tondeuses*).

As with any machinery, you need to assess the work a mini-tractor is expected to do before buying or hiring one. In addition to considering whether the engine has sufficient power for your needs and whether the attachments are solid and sensibly designed for constant work, you should find out whether spares are readily available and whether the dealer will be able to service and repair it. Ask your neighbours and other acquaintances about their experience and opinions of the various models available.

Tractors

If you have a large area to work, it might be worth considering a small second-hand agricultural tractor (a new tractor will be astronomically expensive). An old tractor may bear the scars of a working life and not be quite as powerful as a newer model, but its advantages are many. It will be more powerful and probably less expensive than a new mini-tractor and require only a little tender loving care before it's capable of some hard work. You will also be able to use it with implements common to all tractors, which can often also be bought quite cheaply from local second-hand dealers or at sales and auctions (see **Attachments** below) – or you may be able to borrow them from a neighbour in return for some help when he's busy. The biggest advantage is that the depreciation on a new model is huge, whereas on a second-hand tractor most of the depreciation will have already occurred and, should you ever wish to sell it, you will lose very little. The only disadvantage is that with an old tractor there's unlikely to be a warranty.

In rural France, small farmers routinely use models that elsewhere would have been lovingly restored for the show circuit or as part of a heritage collection. Even those who normally use a modern machine for ploughing and heavy-duty farming prefer to use their trusty old workhorse for lighter jobs, such as fertilising and spraying, and, as a consequence, there are plenty to choose from in the second-hand market. Models to look out for include Deutz, Massey-Ferguson, Someca, Zetor and, of course, Renault.

Because of the sudden interest in old tractors among foreigners in France, the price of '50s and '60s models has escalated in recent years to such an extent that even a non-runner bought from an agricultural agent will cost you in the region of €1,000, while one in full working order will command well over double that price.

For a list of websites where new and used tractors can be found, see **Appendix C**.

Attachments

It's possible to purchase many attachments specifically designed for each type of tractor, including general-purpose cutters fitted either with blades (*tondeuses de finition*), rotating cutting chains (*gyrobroyeurs*) or grasscutters (*broyeurs à herbe*).

Using a box (*benne*) which attaches to the three-point linkage is a better way of carrying fertilisers and food than hooking up a trailer, especially when only small quantities need to be transported. A sprayer (*pulvérisateur*) and a watering unit (*cuve d'arrosage*) are also invaluable.

To find the prices of agricultural equipment, you will need to visit a dealer, as most don't provide a printed list, although some information can be found via the internet (see **Appendix C**).

Road Use

If you purchase a tractor for use on your land and don't drive it on the road, it doesn't need to have number plates or go through a mechanical inspection (*contrôle technique*), but if you're going to travel on even a few metres of public highway – perhaps to go from one plot to another or to fill up at the local garage – both are required. You will need to take the *carte grise*, the *certificat de cession* from the sale and your identity paper to the local *préfecture*. When buying new from an authorised dealer, he should complete the paperwork on your behalf.

Trailers

Unless you have a van or lorry, a trailer (*remorque*) will be indispensable. Note, however, that a *carte grise* is required for a trailer with a carrying capacity of over 500kg and that brakes are obligatory on trailers capable of carrying over 750kg. If you tow a trailer behind your car, a normal driving licence (*permis B*) is sufficient, provided the combined weight of the car and the trailer doesn't exceed 3.5 tonnes; if it does, you will need a *permis E(B)*.

PLANT HIRE

If you're planning any serious DIY projects in your new home, it's likely that you will need to hire tools or machinery. Tool hire shops are found in or near most towns – they're often located ontrading and industrial estates (*zone industrielle* or *artisanale*, abbreviated to *ZI* and *ZA* on signs).

Always bear in mind, however, that hiring plant isn't always the cheapest option. It may be possible to buy second-hand equipment, and it's certainly worth your while checking the classified advertisements in local newspapers. You may, for example, be able to pick up a concrete mixer in good working order for around a third of the new price – equivalent to hiring one for just five or six weeks (or less if you sell it afterwards). This way, you won't have to worry about escalating hire costs if your concreting work is unexpectedly delayed.

Hire Companies

Many tool hire companies, such as EPAGRI, Loca Ser and Loxam, have branches throughout France and the contact numbers and addresses can be found under '*Location de matériel pour entrepreneurs*' in the yellow pages or in local newspaper advertisements. You can hire almost anything from a shovel (*pelle*) to a JCB. If you need to cut a large hole through masonry or concrete in order to route cables or pipes, you can hire an industrial drill (*perceuse pneumatique*) that will make light work of it. You may wish to excavate an area of land to put in a patio or parking spaces: hire companies can supply a machine that will dig the area, another to compact the hard core for the base and a third to mix the cement to lay the slabs.

Larger items can be delivered and collected at the end of the hire period, but compare charges between companies as they may vary significantly. If you own a large car or have access to a small trailer, you may be able to collect and return, say, a small concrete mixer yourself and do so at a time convenient to you.

As well as the hire fee, you will be required to leave a damage deposit, which is refunded on return of the equipment in a satisfactory condition. Careful planning is required to ensure that all preliminary work is completed beforehand and, if possible, doing several jobs requiring the same tool at the same time. This will not only minimise your hire costs but will also save time collecting and returning equipment.

Checks & Safety

European regulations require you to have a certificate of competence before hiring certain tools. The hire company concerned will demonstrate how the tool should be used but won't issue a certificate, for which you must undergo a course, e.g. at an agricultural college. Hire shops should supply safety equipment if it's required, but you might prefer to purchase it, as it's likely you'll need it for other tasks at a later date and it may be preferable to use new safety equipment. For most jobs, safety goggles (*lunettes de protection*) and ear defenders (*protecteur auditif*) are the minimum that should be worn.

Before accepting delivery of a tool, check it for damage or malfunction – or you may find yourself liable for a repair necessitated by someone else's negligence. Refuse to accept any mechanical or electrical equipment that you consider unsafe.

If the item to be hired is powered by an internal combustion engine, the hire company should tell you what type of fuel to use. Most will also offer to sell you fuel, although it may be cheaper elsewhere.

It's essential that you use only the fuel specified; failure to do so could result in serious engine damage and the loss of all or part of your damage deposit.

Tools powered by electricity may require a transformer (*transformateur*) to reduce the voltage to 110V; the hire company should advise you of this and also hire you a transformer if you don't own one. **Never connect a 110V machine to the mains, as this will almost certainly result in serious damage to you and the machine.**

In the case of sanders, which require replacement sanding discs or belts, the hire company will advise you how many and what type you need (a discount is usually given for any unused belts returned with the tool, but it's as well to check this when signing the hire agreement). It's better to have too many than run out and have to return for more – and possibly find the company closed for a two-hour lunch break, *le week-end* or a public holiday.

Electric or petrol-powered disc cutters for cement blocks or paving slabs will be offered with a diamond-impregnated cutting disc. These are very efficient, causing less dust and lasting longer than fibre discs. The hire company should measure the diameter when you collect the tool and again when you return – they will then charge you on the basis of the amount of disc you've used. Diamond discs are expensive, but, if you're planning to do a lot of work, it may work out cheaper to buy one.

Advice

Before hiring (or indeed buying) a tool, you must be sure that it's sufficiently powerful and robust for the task in hand. There's no satisfaction in hiring a cheap machine that isn't up to the job – both you and the machine will struggle and you will soon get tired and frustrated. Injury can result, the machine may become damaged, and you certainly won't get a satisfactory result – leading to more work later. A larger, industrial machine will be easier to use and give a much better result.

Obtain advice, either from the hire company or from someone with experience of using the tool. If you explain what you want to do, the hire company should recommend the most suitable tool for the purpose. If you don't know the French word for the tool you wish to hire, ask for the catalogue (*catalogue*) and find the relevant picture.

Avoid wasting valuable hire time by ensuring that you know exactly how to use a tool – you wouldn't be the first person to spend the whole of your first day's hire getting the hang of operating a mini-digger (*pelle chargeur*) without achieving any of the desired results!

Using Hired Tools

When using a hire tool, treat it as you would your own. Let the machine do the work at the speed it's designed to and don't force it. Keep it clean and change filters or cutters when advised. At the end of each day's work, clean, lubricate and adjust it as required ready for the next day. In the case of a cement mixer, rinse the drum and stand after each batch unless you plan to mix another immediately; leaving it while you lay your cement and perhaps have your lunch will result in your returning to a solid encrustation, which will be difficult, if not impossible, to remove. If you return it in this state, you will be penalised.

Secure all hired tools before going off site, as you will be held responsible for any loss. (This applies to your own tools as well, including a generator if you have one, which should be kept in a secure shed or outhouse.) At the end of the hire period and before returning an item, thoroughly clean, lubricate, adjust and test it.

BUYING TOOLS

If you're coming to rural France from an urban or suburban environment, where you had only a small garden (or none at all) and had never carried out major DIY work, you may have only the most basic items, such as hammers, screwdrivers and pliers, and perhaps a spade (*bêche*), fork (*fourche*) and rake (*râteau*). When you start working your plot, however, you will probably find that you need more specialised items, such as a three-pronged cultivator (*griffe trios dents*) and a post-hole digger (*bêche-tarière*), although you needn't rush out and buy these as soon as you arrive.

Tool designs can vary greatly from country to country. For example, many professional workmen prefer to use traditional, straight-handled spades, shovels and rakes, which will be familiar to Americans but which Britons may find almost impossible to use.

Prices compare favourably with those in the UK. For example, a spade costing around £12 in the UK can be bought in France for around €12, and whereas a long-handled 'slasher' (*croissant débroussailleur*) costs around £35 from a UK agricultural supplier, while its French equivalent is priced at just €35. A wide range of tools are available in France and, as when hiring, you should consider the size of the job and the suitability of your intended purchase before buying anything. You may be able to get away with using cheap, disposable equipment for a one-off project, but if you're likely to need similar tools in the near future, it pays to invest in quality (see below).

Hand Tools

If you've arrived in France without even basic tools, you will need to visit your local ironmonger's (*quincaillerie*) and stock up. For a small garden or light usage, you might consider a multi-function tool, which consists of a handle with clip-on tool heads. These are sold at most supermarkets and garden centres. For occasional use, they're excellent, as they take up little storage space, are light and comfortable to use, and are simple to operate. For more serious use, it's wise to buy individual tools.

SURVIVAL TIP

When it comes to tools it's advisable to buy the best you can afford, as you will be repaid by years of satisfactory service. The saying that 'you get what you pay for' has never been truer than with tools.

Pick them up, compare them, test their weight and balance, and examine the handles. Cheap tools often have thin handles, which bend easily and seem designed to break as soon as the tool is used. Look for hickory or ash handles and don't be impressed by paint or varnish coatings, which are usually applied to disguise poor-quality wood. Tools are expensive and good tools more so, but if looked after they're a good investment – and a pleasure to use.

Consider stainless steel garden forks and spades – they're a joy to use, easy to keep clean and, although initially expensive, an extremely good investment. At the very least, buy a spade with a forged steel blade, as cheaper spades have a blade made from pressed steel sheet, which will often buckle and bend under strain.

Power Tools

Power tools are expensive, so it's unlikely that you will buy more specialised items until you need them. A good chainsaw costs in the region of €400 to €600, a petrol-driven strimmer from €300. For a one-off project, it might be possible to hire (see page 174) or to borrow from a neighbour. However, most rural dwellers will sooner or later find certain items essential. These include the following:

- **Backpack Sprayer (*pulvérisateur à dos*)** – Although perhaps not technically a power tool, a backpack or knapsack sprayer is an extremely useful item and has several general uses, such as watering, weed-killing (be sure to clean it well after use), fertilising and fumigating livestock sheds.
- **Brush-cutter or Strimmer (*débroussailleuse*)** – An electric strimmer is one tool you can safely leave behind when you move to rural France, as you will almost certainly need a more powerful, petrol-driven machine to keep weeds and undergrowth at bay.

- **Chainsaw (*tronçonneuse*)** – An electric chainsaw will be of limited usefulness, and you should buy a petrol-driven saw for anything other than occasional light tasks. (See also **Using a Chainsaw** on page 182.)
- **Hedge-trimmer (*taille-haies*)** – Again, there's a choice between electric (*à moteur électrique*) and petrol (*thermique*) models, which will depend on the amount of cutting you have to do.
- **Tractor-mower (*tondeuse auto-portée*)** – A ride-on lawnmower may seem a luxury but it becomes a necessity if you have more than a few hundred square metres of lawn.

SURVIVAL TIP

Always wear protective overalls when using power tools, especially hedge-trimmers and strimmers, when a face and ear protector (*protecteur auditif avec écran facial*) should also be worn.

Wheelbarrows

An ordinary garden wheelbarrow (*brouette*) is unsuitable for moving large quantities of earth, hardcore or concrete: not only is it too small, but it probably won't withstand the weight it will be asked to carry. You can buy a more substantial builder's barrow (costing around €55 from any building retail outlet), but you may be able to find a good second-hand one at one of the many *foires à tout* or *vide-greniers* that are held almost weekly in spring and autumn throughout rural France. Emmaüs (charity) shops yards are also worth checking, as they often yield barrows and sack trolleys (*diable*) at bargain prices (a new sack trolley can cost over €100). Don't be tempted to buy an old-fashioned wooden wheelbarrow – they may be pretty but they're heavy and cumbersome. If you need a heavy-duty wheelbarrow for a one-off job, you might be better off hiring one or, better still, using your car and trailer.

Sales & Promotions

In the early part of the year, most hardware shops have sales, during which all kinds of tools are on offer. Initially they may seem like bargains, but a word of warning. Whereas in the UK, for example, goods offered at a discount must normally have been offered at a higher price for a number of weeks beforehand, in France such sales are more accurately promotions (*promotions*) and the goods are bought in specially. Some are undoubtedly good value, but many are cheap imports and not always suitable for the task they claim to be designed for.

MAINTENANCE

Five minutes' tedious work is preferable to having to replace an expensive machine. If you own any machinery, a little maintenance at the end of the season will ensure that it will work properly when you wish to use it the following year. Petrol or a petrol-and-oil mixture left throughout the winter in a strimmer or chainsaw becomes stale and the delicate mechanism of carburettors can become clogged with deposits. Hand tools also benefit from a few minutes' regular maintenance.

Cleaning

Tools such as lawnmowers and rotary cultivators should always be inverted and cleaned thoroughly each time they're used. Compacted grass cuttings and weeds release acid that can corrode cutting decks and blades. If possible, scrape the underside clean, brush thoroughly and then rinse with a hose. Allow to dry before storing. The simple application of an oily rag will keep surfaces bright and shiny until you next use the tool. The following tips apply to all engines:

- Having thoroughly cleaned your machine, start the engine and allow it to warm up. Stop it and then empty the fuel tank. Restart, and allow the engine to idle until it runs out of fuel, which empties the carburettor.
- Remove the spark plug or plugs and inject a small amount (around 10ml) of light oil into each cylinder before gently turning the engine over by hand to spread the oil around the cylinder walls.
- Clean and replace the spark plugs (*bougies d'allumage*), but **don't re-connect the leads**. Your engine is now safe for the winter.
- When next required, the engine should be filled with fresh fuel and the plug leads re-connected. Expect to see a little smoke from the exhaust when you start it.

- The fuel removed from your machines may be disposed of at your local public tip (*déchetterie*).

Don't ever be tempted to pour petrol or engine oil into a watercourse or on any ground where it may eventually be washed into a watercourse. Burning it isn't an option either, as oil can be as explosive as petrol and result in serious injury.

Winter is a good time to get all your mowers, strimmers and rotary tillers serviced. Look under *Motoculture de plaisance* for the telephone number of your nearest garden machinery mechanic. A *mécanique agricole*, who normally repairs farm and vine-growing implements, may also service and repair garden equipment.

Hand Tools

Hand tools that have been used for digging or other dirty jobs should first have any soil or dirt removed. Next, clean with a good stiff brush and water, before allowing it to dry thoroughly. Finally, a wipe with a rag dipped in oil will ensure that rust is kept at bay (rust not only makes the next use of the tool more difficult but in extreme cases can alter the nature of the steel and damage it irrevocably).

Wooden handles are frequently neglected on hand tools and shouldn't ever be left in wet conditions. You should occasionally rub them down with fine sandpaper and apply a light coat of suitable oil such as linseed oil (*huile de lin*), which will soak into the wood and protect it against wood-boring insects as well as moisture damage.

SURVIVAL TIP

Never paint wooden handles, as paint seals in moisture and makes a tool less comfortable to use.

Sharpening is another task that's frequently neglected. Statistics support the belief that more injuries result from the use of blunt tools than sharp ones, as an inefficient blade or cutting edge causes excessive force to be applied, which often results in injury. When using cutting tools, take a break occasionally to change or sharpen the blade(s) – the task will be quicker and more bearable and the machine will last longer.

USING A CHAINSAW

It goes without saying that a chainsaw is an extremely dangerous piece of equipment. If you've any serious cutting to do it's advisable to call in an expert, who will probably use a heavy-duty professional chainsaw (*tronçonneuse professionelle*). He will charge a reasonable fee and may even do the job in return for the wood.

> **SURVIVAL TIP**
> **If you pay someone to work on your property, particularly using a chainsaw, you must ensure that he's insured against injury. This can be done using the *chèque emploi service* system, of which your bank can provide details.**

If you choose to use a chainsaw yourself, note the following safety advice. (If you want to hire one, you may also be required to provide a certificate of competence – see page 175.)

- If possible, use a good pruning saw (*scie turbocut*), which makes a cleaner cut and is much safer!
- Read the safety and operating instructions and practise at ground level until you feel confident.
- Always wear a helmet (*casque de protection*), ear defenders (*protecteur auditif*) and goggles (*lunettes de protection*).
- **Never** attempt to cut down a mature tree unless you fully understand the science of when and where to cut and the likely trajectory of fall.
- No matter how competent you are with a saw, **never** attempt to cut anything above shoulder height.
- Always position yourself safely so that the branch to be cut is at waist level.
- Always take off the whole branch close to the tree trunk, leaving a stump around an inch long.

- To ensure that your cuts line up, tie string or stick insulating tape around the branch.
- Take the weight off the branch by either propping it safely or tying it to a strong branch above.
- Start by cutting approximately half an inch into the wood under the branch and at least half the way around it. This will prevent the falling branch tearing an unsightly strip of bark as it falls.
- Then cut from the top, following the line of string or tape.
- Take your time and make sure that you will be able to move out of harm's way when the branch falls – even if it's tied to a branch above, there's still a danger of kickback from the butt-end.

10.

Making Money

Even if you manage to produce most of your own food and are therefore largely 'self-sufficient', you will still need an income to cover your production costs and other living expenses, such as utilities, taxes and insurance. Many people think of running a *gîte* or bed and breakfast, and these options are covered briefly in this chapter (for more detail, refer to *Earning Money from Your French Home* by Survival Books – see page 287), but there are other ways of making money from your rural property, which are also considered here. For further general information about making money in France, refer to *Making a Living in France* (Survival Books – see page 287).

SURVIVAL TIP

Whatever venture you decide upon, you should obey the first rule of living in France and visit your local *mairie* to ensure that your ideas won't cause problems with neighbours or that, through ignorance, you aren't about to break the law.

REGISTRATION

Many people will advise keeping all transactions cash-based and not declaring any earnings to the tax office but, needless to say, this is illegal and penalties can be severe if you're found out. In any case, if you're making your home in France, it's only right that you should contribute to the country's running costs by paying income tax, and you should register with the authorities before even starting any money-making scheme.

In some countries, including the UK, you're entitled to earn a certain amount before your earnings are taxed; the French system is more complicated. Much depends on how you're registered. If, for instance, you have visions of becoming a sheep farmer and breed them for their meat, you need to register as an *agriculteur* and declare your earnings to the Impôt sur le Revenu. If, however, you plan to sell the wool, you would be classed as *commerce* and need to declare your earnings to the Bénéfice Industriel et Commercial.

Small businesses are slightly less complicated but it's impossible to state exactly how much you're allowed to earn before being subject to tax, as much depends on individual circumstances. Some allowances are available (usually between 10 and 20 per cent) and you may also be able to claim a deduction for using your home as business premises – to be entitled to do so, you must be non-salaried and must own (not rent) your house.

Don't forget that you will also have to make 'contributions' for health cover, which is a variable percentage based on your turnover (*chiffre d'affaires*). For the first two years, it's a fixed amount and it's adjusted thereafter.

Note also that, if you have two or more unrelated jobs such as selling farm produce, running a B&B and writing books, you may need not only to register three businesses but also to pay three lots of social security.

SURVIVAL TIP

Registration and taxation is a complex area and you're advised to take expert advice before committing yourself to a particular business regime.

BED & BREAKFAST & GITES

Nearly everyone buying a home in rural France has the idea of renovating a barn and providing some form of holiday accommodation without perhaps realising how saturated this market has become in recent years. It's also very hard work and, during the summer months, may not leave you much time to develop the smallholding that you fondly hoped to create as a result of moving to rural France. B&B in particular creates an enormous amount of work due to the almost daily bed changes, preparation of breakfast (and often an evening meal) and the need to be on standby 24 hours a day. At least with *gîtes*, you need only change linen on a weekly basis and guests are self-sufficient regarding meals.

There's always a temptation to overestimate the length of the season and the number of bookings you will be able to attract.

Nevertheless, letting part or all of your property for part of the year can bring in some useful income without contravening any French laws. If you let your property for less than half the year and/or the property is your principal residence, you may be granted exemption from *taxe professionelle.*

Swimming Pools

A property with a swimming pool is bound to attract more bookings but all pools must now have at least one of the following safety devices fitted.

- **Alarm** – An approved alarm installed in such a way that children cannot switch it off.
- **Barrier** – A 1m-high barrier (e.g. a fence) with an approved gate-locking system.
- **Cover** – An approved safety cover that supports the weight of a child and is strong enough for an adult to walk across it.
- **Shelter** – A fixed or sliding cover that prevents access to the pool.

Marketing

It's no good thinking that your home is so desirable that you won't need to spend time and money to attract clients. Marketing is a very important and time-consuming part of running B&B and *gîte* accommodation – without it, your hopes of a constant stream of happy holidaymakers won't materialise. However, there are many ways of marketing your property other than advertising, which can be both expensive and ineffective, and it pays to try every free method available, including PR and, especially, word of mouth. As someone once said, "Half of advertising is wasted but, unfortunately, no one knows which half." You can set up your own website and link it to other holiday letting schemes. And it always pays to work with other local people in the same business and send any surplus guests to competitors in the hope that they will reciprocate.

> **SURVIVAL TIP**
>
> **It may pay to ask a friend in the UK to act as your booking agent, as some potential holidaymakers think that calling France costs a fortune and worry that they will have to speak French.**

You can advertise your property in magazines and on websites where you pay for the advertisement but handle bookings yourself. Some companies publish holiday rental brochures and will advertise your property, but they may insist on handling all the bookings, on which they take a percentage. Brittany Ferries is unusual in offering a choice between its Holiday Homes (including handling) and Owners in France (advertising only) schemes. Advertisements in most annual brochures need to be submitted by the end of August for the following year's holiday season.

CAMPING & CARAVAN SITES

Another money-making venture popular among those moving to rural France is to develop an area of land for camping and caravans; most people think that all they have to do is provide a tap and toilet facilities, then sit back and collect the rental money. As with most things in life, it's rarely that simple and there are several things to consider before embarking on such a scheme.

Needless to say, the first thing to do is to check with your *mairie* that your proposed campsite won't cause a nuisance. If you want to have more than half a dozen pitches, you must supply at least two showers, two WCs and two wash basins, as well as installing a *fosse septique* with a capacity of at least 5,000 litres. In addition, you must register your business with the Chamber of Commerce and the French Tourist Board, which will then make periodic inspections. You will also need to check what insurance is required.

If you're content to offer half a dozen pitches, a letter of consent from the *mairie* may be all that's required, as the French government is encouraging diversification from normal farming practices. At this level, it's up to you whether you supply any facilities, and ordinary household insurance should provide sufficient cover, although it's wise to check, as requirements vary with the region and locality. Bear in mind, however, that France has some of the best campsites in the world, so it's unlikely that many people will want to stay on a site with few facilities.

It pays to have been a camper or caravanner yourself, as you will know what prospective clients are looking for and the best places to advertise. How much to charge per night depends on the facilities offered and your location. For the first year you should be prepared for a certain amount of trial and error.

KENNELS & CATTERIES

Although the French are less inclined to board their pets when they go away than the British, for example, and usually either leave them to fend for themselves or take them along, with more and more expats living permanently in France, there's a growing demand in some areas for kennels and catteries run by English-speaking proprietors. However, there are currently more kennels available than catteries and you should check the local competition before committing yourself.

Restrictions

Generally, provided you don't change the exterior appearance of your buildings and any extensions won't be larger than 20m², you don't require planning permission. However, you may need permission to change the use of a building, e.g. converting a barn into a cattery, and there are other legal restrictions. **Always check with the *mairie* first.**

Under Articles R214-25 and R214-26 of the *code rural*, it's necessary to obtain a *certificat de capacité* recognised by the Direction Départementale de l'Agriculture et des Forêts (DDAF). Those who have been drawing income for at least three years and can show invoices and income tax returns or, in the case of kennels, have recognition from the Société Centrale Canine (155, avenue Jean Jaurès, 93535 Aubervilliers Cedex, ☎ 01 49 37 54 00) as a trainer or possess a registered kennel name are exempt; others must attend a short course and take an examination. This applies to anyone drawing an income from cats and dogs, whether they're running a kennel/cattery or a training or breeding establishment. Details of the process are available from the Département des Services Vétérinaires (DSV) or your *préfecture*.

PET-SITTING

If you cannot or don't wish to set up kennels, it's possible to make some money by offering to board dogs in your home. If you do so, you must make it clear that you cannot be held liable for anything untoward happening to someone's dog while it's in your care – and preferably get the owner to sign a form to that effect. Nevertheless, you must take all reasonable steps to ensure the animal's well-being, making sure your property is fenced and that any gates are self-shutting. Remember to ask owners for the name of their regular vet; if he isn't located near your home look for one in your area and tell owners that you intend to consult him if necessary. Obtain an emergency number – accidents with animals always happen late at night or at weekends! To advertise your services, place a notice in your vet's surgery or in the local supermarket. Try to obtain testimonials, as recommendations are highly valued in France.

Increasingly popular is home sitting, whereby you stay at the animal owner's house, caring for his pets as well as his home and garden. For this service, you should be paid around €150 per week.

DOG BREEDING

If you have a pedigree bitch and would like to breed from her at home and sell the puppies, you're exempt from the *certificat de capacité* (see above) provided you don't rear more than one litter per year. If you advertise the resultant offspring in a newspaper, you must, by law, mention the puppies' or the mother's vaccination number(s). In addition, you should mention the number of animals in the litter. It's important that your puppies have a birth certificate (*certificat de naissance*) within 15 days of birth, detailing the name, sex and colour of each animal, and they should have an identifying tattoo or microchip within six months. The puppies' pedigree must be certified by the Société Centrale Canine. With some breeds, it's possible obtain a pedigree without a birth certificate (*sans généalogie attestée*).

LIVERY STABLES

Experienced horse owners may be tempted to convert outbuildings into stables and offer a livery service. To do so, you need to register the business with your regional Chambre d'Agriculture. If you intend to offer riding activities you will also need to apply to the Direction Départementale de la Jeunesse et des Sports and take out public liability insurance. If owners keep their horses with you on a DIY basis, you may also have to insure against them injuring themselves on your property.

SURVIVAL TIP

You must insist that the owners of horses kept on your property insure against the animal causing injury to other livestock and humans.

It's also necessary to register with the Service Vétérinaire; although your premises won't be inspected regularly, there may be spot checks and, if you're giving lessons to the public, an initial inspection. Full identifying documentation for each horse must be available for inspection at all times.

Even if you're already in possession of a BHSII or equivalent qualification, you must be qualified and licensed in France before establishing any sort of equestrian business, including training or breeding. Breeding stock is also regulated and you may be unable to sell any offspring unless you've obtained certification from the relevant breed society for the mare and registered the foal. Horses without recognised breed papers cannot compete in most disciplines and can be sold only for 'leisure' riding or driving. From 2008, the electronic chipping of horses will be compulsory.

In areas where riding is most popular, it should be easy to find a local farrier, feed supplier or saddler, although in others it may prove difficult, so check in advance.

SELLING PRODUCTS & PRODUCE

If you're a keen gardener, egg producer, cider maker, landscape painter or wood turner (see page 196) or have simply decided that you have too much stuff in the house and want to get rid of some of it, you may wish to offer your wares or surplus belongings for sale to an eagerly awaiting public. If you're in an area where the public passes on a regular basis, it's possible to sell garden produce from the gate without obtaining permission or notifying anyone, although (as ever) it's advisable to check with the *mairie*. If you're off the beaten track, the *mairie* will probably give you permission to erect signs around the village directing potential customers to your property. If you want to sell in the village street, you must have permission from the *mairie*, which may charge you a small fee for the privilege. You should also check whether you're allowed to sell the type of produce you intend to, e.g. unpasteurised milk.

Registering with the MSA

If you aim to earn a living from your smallholding, there are a number of things to consider, the first of which is whether to register with the Mutualité Sociale Agricole (MSA). The MSA is a kind of combined Department of Social Security and Farmers' Union, which represents the interests of French farmers and pays them a pension when they retire, as well as organising training and providing subsidies.

The cost and financial implications of registration vary from person to person. For example, if you're under 40, you could qualify as a *jeune agriculteur* and benefit from rebates on your outgoings and general taxes. Be aware, however, that to receive a pension at the end of your farming career you will need to have made a certain amount of contributions, which won't be possible if you either don't earn enough and/or are too old to make the necessary number of years' contributions.

The MSA is very helpful to newcomers to farming and will explain the benefits and implications of membership. You can opt into a part-time system and even opt out after a year, but if you're then found selling produce on a regular basis you may end up with a hefty fine. You can also be fined if you market crops that you haven't listed on your application form.

Market Stalls

Your village or local town will undoubtedly hold a weekly market, at which you may wish to set up a stall. Once again, your first move must be to go to the *mairie* and inform them of your intentions. They will tell you the size of pitch you can have and the costs involved. A pitch with a 2m frontage is unlikely to cost more than €5 per day and, in many cases, will be much less, although there may be a higher rate for using a vehicle as your stall.

When you go to book a pitch, it's a wise precaution to take your passport and at least one utility bill to prove you are who you say you are and that you're resident in France. Not all *mairies* ask for this information, but it's as well to be prepared. Make your plans well in advance, as many markets have a waiting list. Larger markets require newcomers to arrive early in the morning in order to queue for any unoccupied pitches.

Once you've set up your stall, a market inspector will ascertain that your stall complies with any relevant regulations and advise you of any problems. He will also collect the rent and issue you with a receipt. Once you've become established at a market, it's important to attend every week – your pitch will quickly be re-let if you fail to attend.

Foires à Tout & Vide-greniers

If you want to get rid of some of the things you brought with you – which you thought would come in handy one day but which you've never managed to find a use for – it might be possible to take a table at a *Foire à tout* or *vide-grenier* (France's equivalent to a car boot or jumble sale). Ask at the *mairie* when these are held in your area and contact the organisers to reserve a space.

Holding a sale on your own property is a different matter and you will need to obtain permission to do so. If it occupies less than 300m², the *mairie* can give authorisation, otherwise you must obtain permission from the *préfecture*. In both cases, you must wait at least two weeks while your application is considered. When first making contact with either office, you will need to take with you some identification, details of the date, times, location and likely area of the sale, and also a list of the things to be sold.

Selling food and drink at a *vide-grenier* involves strict controls and, once again, you shouldn't neglect to inform the authorities of your intentions. If you're the organiser, you must have a bound book in which are entered the names and addresses of vendors. A loose file isn't normally accepted, as there's the obvious opportunity to insert or remove pages at a later date. The book must be signed by the *commissaire de police* or the *maire* of the *commune* in which the event is being held and be given a serial number.

Those taking part in a *vide-grenier* on a one-off or occasional basis aren't normally expected to declare their earnings from the event to the tax authorities.

Firewood

Most of your French neighbours will have their own supply of firewood, but you may find a market in the surrounding towns for cut and seasoned logs from your property – even when they have central heating, most French houses feature an open fire.

Any wood will burn if it's dry enough but there's no doubt that some woods burn better than others. (Which wood burns best of all is a matter of opinion, but ash is often cited.) Usually, it's a question of offering what's available rather than being selective but, given a choice, you might offer a mixture of woods, which will allow a base of fast-burning woods (e.g. poplar) to generate enough heat to allow slow-burning woods (such as oak) to burn properly. Oak burns well when dry and cut into small pieces if it's given a good base on which to get going, but otherwise it tends to smoulder. If you're living in a vine-growing area and can get hold of the stumps of old vines that have been removed in the autumn in preparation for new planting, these burn exceptionally well and give a lot of heat.

Apple wood – and fruit wood generally – smells good, although it's a shame to burn it as it's soft enough to carve and has an attractive grain. It might be better to cut the base into sections and make a little extra money by selling it to a craftsman or turning it yourself (see **Wood Turning** on page 196).

If you plan to sell logs, you should cut trees and branches in the winter when the sap is 'dormant'. Timber should be left for at least a season in order to dry out. Even when left standing in heavy rain, seasoned wood doesn't absorb much moisture or retain much of the sap it originally contained and any moisture soon dries out. Coppicing and pollarding (see pages 68 and 67) produces good firewood and has the advantage of sustainability.

Wood in France is usually sold by the *stère*. The trouble is that the definition of a *stère* varies widely (even among 'authorities' on the subject) – it's anything between 0.55 and 1m³ – and in any case wood is rarely measured but merely estimated, so the amount of wood you end up selling could be rather different from the amount you thought you were quoting for! Price varies according to a number of factors, not least the type of wood. For fast-burning wood such as poplar you may be able to charge no more than €15 per *stère*, whereas you may get two or three times as much for oak. Normally, logs are cut into 1m or 1.20m lengths, and you should charge extra for cutting logs into shorter lengths – an extra €10 per load is usual.

If you want to offer a delivery service (which will greatly increase your chance of selling firewood), you will of course need suitable transport (see **Tractors & Trailers** on page 171).

Poultry

Unless you intend to become a commercial poultry farmer, you will be breeding poultry only to replace old stock and ensure a continual supply of eggs. Nevertheless, it's unlikely that all the chicks will be female and you will left with the question of what to do with the males. If you're going to succeed in your enterprise, you will have to harden your heart, as the French do, and fatten unwanted birds for the table.

If you don't think you can eat your own stock, there will be no shortage of locals willing to buy them from you and you should be able to charge an oven-ready price of between €2 and €3 per kilo for chickens and at least €3 to €5 per kilo for ducks and geese. To get the best price – which vary according to the region and quality, as well as supply and demand – you should separate the cockerels, ganders and drakes from their female counterparts as soon as you can tell their sex (sexing chickens and ducks is easy enough, but geese are more of a problem and you may need to ask a neighbour to help). The females, which you're intending to keep until they can join your laying poultry, can be kept in a separate house until they're mature, while the males should be penned elsewhere, preferably in a fold unit (see page 121).

You should feed the male birds with the usual proprietary poultry feeds (see **Food & Drink** on page 123) until the age of around 12 weeks and then use a good-quality, cereal-based fattening ration – often labelled simply '*céreales*'. A 20kg bag, which you may have to buy from a more specialised outlet than a supermarket, costs around €10. If your land adjoins fields that are left as stubble for a few weeks after harvesting, you could ask the farmer if he minds your birds being penned there in fold units. The French believe that the best chicken meat results from young birds being left to forage on natural food such as worms, insects and snails – an organic diet supplemented by wheat and maize!

At the age of 16 to 20 weeks, cockerels should be fat enough to make a good *coq au vin*. Ducks and geese mature slightly more quickly and should be ready for market at around 16 weeks. The best way to dispatch birds is by wringing their necks (see **Longevity** on page 138).

Table Birds

If you're interested in selling poultry as a means of making money from your smallholding rather than merely as a practical use for unwanted stock, you might consider purchasing specially bred 'table birds'. The best known of these is the white *poulet de Bresse*, which can sometimes be found at small markets and command a better price than the more common poultry types. Although they cost you more – perhaps €7 to €10 at six weeks old – you can expect a return of at least €4 per kilo oven-ready as opposed to the usual €2 to €3 for an ordinary chicken.

WOOD TURNING

A property in rural France is a good place to consider wood turning, either for pleasure or with a view to selling the results of your work – or both. Dead fruit trees can provide some beautiful turning material after a suitable seasoning period. You will also gain much pleasure in sourcing wood yourself, but even if the wood you find on your own land isn't suitable, you will no doubt find a sawmill within easy reach.

> SURVIVAL TIP
>
> **Often pieces suitable for turning are treated as waste by sawmills, and burrs on the sides of trees, although difficult to turn, produce wonderful bowls and boxes.**

Most large tool shops stock an assortment of lathes (*tour à bois*), which incidentally are generally compatible with UK fittings such as chucks and faceplates. Alternatively, many British companies will deliver lathes and fittings to France surprisingly inexpensively.

There are many types of lathe, but some of the cheaper models are made from relatively soft metal, and stripped threads cannot be repaired. Look out for solid models with substantial main bearings on the headstock, as these will take a lot of wear, and avoid fiddly plastic locking screws on things such as the tool rest, as they take a lot of punishment. Power isn't as important as quality of construction, as motors may have to run for long periods and there's a danger of overheating. The speed changes on lathes can be manual (via pulleys or gears) or electronic, which are easier to use and therefore recommended for novices.

The turning tools you need depend largely on what you wish to achieve, but the best quality are made from carbon steel. They lose their edge quite quickly and therefore require frequent attention, particularly when you're turning hard or abrasive woods, but they're easy to re-sharpen.

It pays to invest in good-quality chisels (*ciseau bois*), which will cost you €12 to €15 each. Expect to pay €8 for a small file (*lime*) and €35 for a plane (*rabot*).

Ensure that wood is well seasoned before attempting to work it, as it tends to change shape and split during the drying process. Timber should be stored out of direct sun and rain, with spacers or 'stickers' between each length. The drying time varies, but a general rule is a year for every inch of thickness. Beware of boring insects, as they can riddle timber with unsightly holes, although some can look decorative in larger pieces. If wood already has holes in it, squirt a little turpentine into each hole to ensure that the past residents aren't still at home!

In some areas of France, it's possible to attend a residential wood turning course, but to fully understand what's being taught you will need a reasonable command of the language. Ask for further details at your nearest agricultural college (*lycée agricole*).

WINE SELLING

If your property has a wine cellar (*cave*), which is likely, you will probably want to keep it well stocked – but possibly not only for your own consumption. If you choose your labels and years sensibly, you could make a little money by reselling wine after a suitable maturation period. One of the main attractions of this line of business is that wine isn't taxable, as it's defined as a 'wasting asset' – i.e. the longer you have it, the less it's worth – although in practice it can appreciate. Also, if you're dealing only with small amounts and selling privately, either by word of mouth or via small ads in specialised magazines, there's no need to register as a retailer.

Generally, it isn't worth stocking anything but the best wines, although this doesn't necessarily mean that you cannot contemplate such a project unless you live in Médoc or the Côte Rôtie, as outstanding wines are produced throughout France. An alternative may be to buy large quantities and sell to friends and acquaintances. Many *gîte* owners and others involved in the holiday trade include a bottle of locally produced wine in their 'welcome package' and find that their clients are often keen to buy a case or two to take home.

Among the classic wines, Bordeaux generally mature faster than Burgundies (which are also less predictable in quality) and so offer a quicker turnover. Whatever you stock, you will need to look after your wine and it's likely that you will need to make minor alterations to an existing *cave*, as it may have been put to other uses by the previous owners of your property.

SURVIVAL TIP
If any wine fails to sell, you may end up drinking it yourself – so make sure that whatever you buy is to your taste!

WRITING & PHOTOGRAPHY

If all else fails, you can try writing or taking photographs to supplement your income. Although many people have written of their experiences in rural France, all hoping to become the next Peter Mayle, you may be able to find a publisher if you have a particular interest or knowledge and can write interestingly. The editors of the ever-increasing number of newspapers and magazines aimed at readers either already living in France or dreaming of doing so are continually seeking new writers, as are publishers with an annual catalogue to fill.

It's important that you select the right publishers and approach them in the appropriate manner. Some are happy to consider unsolicited manuscripts while others wish to see only a synopsis. In most cases, a letter or email of introduction is appreciated. Their details and preferred method of approach can be found in either the *Writer's & Artist's Yearbook* or the *Writer's Handbook*, both of which are published annually (in the late autumn) and contain invaluable advice on getting your work published.

Articles usually sell better when accompanied by photographs. With the advent of digital cameras, these are easy to take (although taking good photos is another matter) and to send as an email attachment, but make sure that they're of high enough quality (use the 'high' setting on your camera for maximum resolution). Magazine and book publishers vary greatly in what they consider to be the ideal size, so ask them for details of their requirements.

SURVIVAL TIP

Don't expect to take professional quality photos if you have little experience – buy a good book and learn about composition and light. Study the work of the experts in photography and other magazines; practise at every opportunity and never venture out without your camera (if you do, it's bound to be the day you see the perfect shot!).

Photographs of rural France are also sought after by some magazine publishers, although not all are willing to pay for them! After seeing your work, they may commission you to supply pictures for a particular article they plan to run, but they're more likely buy your work 'on spec'. Before selling any pictures, check whether the magazine is also buying the copyright to them – if they are you will be unable to use the same photograph again commercially and should therefore demand a much higher fee (usually the fee is for single use only). Wildlife and country-orientated publications that don't deal specifically with French life may also be interested in photographs of the country's flora and fauna, as might those aimed at farmers and smallholders.

11.

Rural Pursuits

Part of the pleasure of living in rural France is the opportunity to take part in rural pursuits, whether these be the traditional pastimes of hunting, shooting and fishing or simply walking in the countryside. Rural pursuits are a good way of meeting local people, they're generally cheap or even free and the different seasons offer a wealth of possibilities.

HUNTING, SHOOTING & FISHING

The general term for hunting and shooting is *la chasse*, which encompasses many field sports practised in the UK and other countries, as well as several that have rightly been outlawed for many years. For example, badger digging, known either as *déterrage* or *vénerie sous terre*, has a large following among terrier owners, and the shooting of thrushes and larks is an opportunity not to be missed by the majority of shooters, giving rise to the myth that continental 'sportsmen' will shoot anything that moves. Nothing is further from the truth and the enthusiasm for *la chasse* has, in most cases, little to do with the number of animals shot but a lot to do with camaraderie and tradition. Because of the widespread love of hunting and shooting, the government, local authorities, hunting organisations and individuals ensure that the environment for wild game is as good as it can be to ensure that the relevant species continue to thrive.

The freedom to hunt and shoot animals may be the reason you're moving to rural France, – where some 2 million guns are possessed for sporting purposes – or you may find the pastime abhorrent. Whatever your feelings and opinions about hunting and shooting, you must accept that they're part of the rural life you've chosen to adopt.

It would certainly not go down well with your neighbours if you were to move in and immediately start voicing your disapproval of traditional rural sports.

Bear in mind that hunting, shooting and fishing are an important aspect of self-sufficiency, which is itself part of country living.

Although game shooters have no right to enter private land (*propriété privée*) without permission, when land has been used for this purpose for many years, they may not bother to ask. Moreover, banning hunters from your land won't endear you to your French neighbours!

Hunting with Hounds

France is the only country in the world to have almost 40 breeds of hunting hounds and terriers. The majority of these are kept in almost 300 packs – comprising around 10,000 dogs in total and supported by some 500,000 hunting enthusiasts.

Hares, foxes, rabbits, deer and wild boar are hunted with hounds; the hunting of deer and boar is known more specifically as *la grande vénerie*. Only six of the 40 departments, the Aisne (02), Indre (36), Indre-et-Loire (37), Loir-et-Cher (41), Orne (61) and the Vienne (86) have packs hunting fallow deer, roe deer and boar, although others contain packs hunting one or two of the three.

Further information on hunting with hounds can be obtained from the Société de Vénerie, 32 rue Chevert, 75007 Paris (☎ 01 47 53 93 93).

On Horseback

Hunting on horseback is known as *la vénerie à cheval* and is extremely popular. Deer and wild boar are the main quarry, although on occasions, hare and fox are hunted on horseback. (Unlike in the UK – at least officially – no packs of hounds are kept specifically to hunt foxes.)

All 'mounted packs' are structured organisations, whose members must pay a subscription of between €1,500 and €2,800 per year. Until recently, you needed to contact hunt committees directly before joining a hunt, which is still the best approach where possible. You can also use local contacts or visit one of the summer hound shows advertised in local newspapers or on posters fixed to trees and buildings. With the increasing number of English-speaking hunting agencies, arrangements can sometimes be made via the internet; enter 'hunting in France' into a search engine such as Google and you will find useful contact details, including organisations which provide horses.

Although the French hunting uniform is different from those in the UK or US, attire normally worn in those countries – black jacket, fawn breeches, black butcher boots and a hunting tie (stock) – is acceptable 'visitor' wear. Those who can read French can find more information on the French hunting website (💻 www.venerie.org).

On Foot

Beaglers are also well catered for in France, where packs are used for *vénerie à pied* (literally 'hunting on foot'), also known as *petite vénerie*. It's a popular sport, not least because it's inexpensive, although it includes all the ceremony usually observed by practitioners of *grande vénerie*. The quarry is generally hare or rabbit. For further information, contact the Club Français du Beagle, Beagle Harrier et Harrier (15 rue Turgot, 22000 Saint-Brieuc, ☎ 02 96 61 82 88).

Creating a Pack

You may have fond ideas of starting your own pack (*meute*) of hounds in the hope of encouraging paying guests from the UK or elsewhere. To do so, you must apply for an *attestation de meute* to the Direction Départementale de l'Agriculture et de la Forêt (DDAF) in the department where your kennels are (or will be) situated. The application must also be approved by both the Association Française des Equipages de Vénerie (AFEV) – the nearest body corresponding to the UK's Association of Masters of Hounds – and the Fédération Départementale des Chasseurs. You must specify the number of hounds you plan to keep, the land that will be crossed and the exact species of quarry. Permission is granted for one year at a time and must be renewed annually.

Hawking

Hunting with hawks is popular in certain parts of France. The generic term is *la chasse au vol*, and there are various sub-sections, including *vol d'amont* (using a bird and pointer or setter dog) and *gibier chasse* (in which hares, rabbits, pheasants, partridges, quail and even woodcock may be killed). For information, contact the Association Nationale de Fauconniers et Autoursiers Français (Belligan, 49130 Saint Gemmes-sur-Loire, 💻 www.anfa.net).

Shooting

The majority of rural shooters would rather face the challenge of game shooting than indulge in the more artificial forms of shooting, such as target (*tir au fusil*), ball-trap (*tir à balle*) and clay pigeon (*tir aux pigeons d'argile*), although these all have their followers. Contact the Fédération Française de Tir (268–270 rue de Brément, 93561 Rosny-sur-Bois Cedex, ☎ 01 48 12 12 20) or the Fédération Française de Ball-trap et de Tir à Balle (20 rue Thiers, 92100 Boulogne Billancourt, ☎ 01 41 41 05 05). The addresses of local target and clay pigeon shooting groups can be obtained from *L'Almanach du*

Chasseur, which is published annually in the autumn and is available from all main newsagents' and book shops.

Shooting usually takes place on Sunday mornings from the end of September until February. The season varies from region to region and from year to year; the dates are usually posted at *mairies* or you can contact the Direction Départementale de l'Agriculture (DDA), whose number is listed at the beginning of phone books. There are plans to shorten the season (to the end of January) to protect migrating birds during their return to breeding grounds.

Importing Guns

If you're a keen hunter, you're likely to want to bring your guns with you to France. If you're moving from the UK, however, this may not be a simple matter. The UK Department of Trade and Industry (DTI) doesn't normally permit the export of firearms without a licence it has issued but may not be able to supply you with the requisite forms! Depending on the purpose for which firearms are intended and their calibre, it's possible – at least, theoretically – to take guns from one European Union (EU) country to another by acquiring a European Firearms Pass (EFP). This was intended to facilitate the free movement of hunters and marksmen (and their weapons) within the EU, but the EFP isn't always recognised by the DTI.

Depending upon the type of weapons being transferred, French Customs may require you to present an import permit (*autorisation d'importation de matériels de guerre-armes et munitions*), which consists of form CERFA 11192*01, obtainable from the Direction Générale des Douanes et Droits Indirects (23 bis rue de l'Université, 75700 Paris) or from Customs (*Douanes*) border posts.

You may need to pay import duty and tax. The amount payable varies but is normally between 4.5 and 5.5 per cent of the value of the gun(s), but also depends on the type of firearms being imported. If the guns have been in your possession for the six months preceding your departure from your home country, they may be exempt, provided they're itemised among your household possessions. You should also notify your local *préfecture*, telling them that you possess Category 5 firearms (e.g. shotguns – see below). Category 7 weapons (e.g. airguns – see below) don't require an import permit, but you should still declare them to Customs.

Buying & Keeping Guns

Although French firearm laws were tightened some years ago, legislation is still more relaxed than in the UK, for example, and some guns can be owned without restriction. However, a shooting permit is required before any can be used to hunt game (see below).

Firearms are divided into categories according to how dangerous they are. Category 5 weapons, which include shotguns, centre-fire sporting rifles and rifle/shotgun combinations, can be purchased freely on production of proof of your address and identity, and must be registered at the place of purchase. Category 7 weapons, such as rim-fire rifles, airguns and starter pistols, can be bought on production of identity but don't need to be registered. To buy pistols and military rifles you require a permit from your local police station or *préfecture*, although applicants belonging to a gun club should have no problem in obtaining one (see below).

Some military weapons, such as a .308 rifles, are forbidden in France, despite being permitted in the UK and elsewhere.

For target shooting weapons, it's also necessary to join the Fédération Française de Tir. Membership usually includes affiliation to a local group and costs €100. If you want to buy a pistol, you can ask your club for a log book (*carte de tir*), which must be stamped by a club official every two months. Once you've obtained three stamps, a green 'preliminary notice' (*avis préalable*) is issued and signed by the regional club president. You send this along with your log book, a copy of your Fédération Française de Tir membership card and a photograph of your gun cabinet (see below), to your *préfecture*, informing them that you wish to buy a pistol.

There's a possibility that shooters will soon have to obtain a medical certificate, renewable every three to five years, so check the latest regulations.

Pistols cannot be stored at home but must be kept at a gun club. A cabinet (*armoire de sécurité*) for sporting shotguns must be bolted to a wall and locked by an internal mechanism so that it cannot be broken open with a 'jemmy'. Gun cabinets cost between around €80 and €450 depending on the number of guns accommodated. Ammunition should be stored in a separate locked container. There's also a variety of locking devices that can be attached to a gun – generally trigger locks (*verrou d'arme à clé*), which cost around €15.

Obtaining a Shooting Permit

A shooting permit (*permis de chasse*) allows you to shoot certain species during prescribed seasons. It isn't necessary if you only plan to do target or clay pigeon shooting, although you require affiliation to a local gun club (see **Buying Guns** above). To obtain a permit, you must pass a two-part exam (*examen du permis de chasser*) involving practical and written tests. The process is quite straightforward but (not surprisingly for France) involves a lot of paperwork and 'running around' from one office to another.

Several departments and bodies are involved in the acquiring of a *permis*. The Office Nationale de la Chasse et de la Faune Sauvage (💻 www.oncfs.gouv.fr/permis/index.php) oversees the training and examination process, while its implementation is the responsibility to the Fédération Nationale des Chasseurs (💻 www.chasseursdefrance.com), which delegates to departmental organisations, although the exam is standard throughout the country. You can approach any of these organisations or your *préfecture* to start the application process.

> **SURVIVAL TIP**
> **When taking the exam, you're expected to know the rules, regulations and likely quarry in all parts of France, not just the area in which you live.**

Once you've completed the paperwork and paid a fee (currently €16), you will receive a date and time for the first of three half-day theory sessions at a training centre. Only one is obligatory but it's best to attend all three, unless you're fluent in the language and will understand everything at the first hearing. You're taught the regulations governing shooting, basic ballistics and how to recognise quarry and protected species. You can buy a 200-page book (including mock questions) and videos to help you learn the required information. The sessions end with the exam, consisting of 21 multiple choice questions – of which you must answer 16 (76 per cent) correctly, including the two 'eliminatory' questions (generally to do with gun security and/or protected species identification); if you answer either of these incorrectly, you fail. Once you've passed the theory exam, you're given a date for a half-day practical training session, which consists of the following three parts:

- **Part One** – This covers safety. For example, you learn how to carry a shotgun and when to 'break' it, to decide when and where it's safe to shoot at clay pigeons, which are colour coded into 'shootable' and 'protected' species, and in what situations you mustn't shoot, e.g. when facing a road or woodland.

- **Part Two** – This is carried out using live ammunition and tests your ability to react in a more realistic situation.
- **Part Three** – The third part of the test specifically relates to larger game such as deer and wild boar.

If you're considered competent after training, you're given a date for the practical exam, which follows the same procedure and isn't difficult provided you take your time, think what you're doing and always give priority to safety. During the examination you must load and unload a rifle and shoot at a moving target, whilst at all times ensuring that it's safe to do so. Like the theory test (see above), the exam carries 21 points with a pass mark of 16.

Assuming that you pass, you will receive a certificate entitling you to apply to the *préfet* for your licence. Once this arrives, you must validate it for the season by buying the departmental federation stamps (€50), the government stamp (€50) and obligatory third-party insurance (€20). It's advisable to insure your gun (and dog if you have one) at the same time. Annual validation for the *permis* is via the Fédération Départementale des Chasseurs and the *préfecture*.

Temporary Permits: It's possible to buy a day's shooting permit through an agency. Many advertise in the UK sporting press and can supply permits to shoot anything from game to wild boar. Some companies, such as Chasse de la Loire (Massif du Graffard, 49490 Genneteil, 💻 www.chasseloire.com), can provide guns and ammunition and will arrange hunting insurance and a temporary permit. Safety training, range practice and the company of an experienced guide is insisted upon by most agencies. If you're a member of a UK shooting organisation, such as the British Association for Shooting and Conservation (BASC), your membership will cover insurance; otherwise comprehensive accident insurance is necessary.

If you're visiting France from the UK, you're permitted to bring your own guns, but note that the Civil Aviation Authority has strict rules concerning the transportation of firearms and some airlines refuse to carry them; therefore you must check before booking. On checking in at an airport, you must declare them so that security officers can take them and stow them on the plane. There's a 5kg net weight limit on ammunition. On arrival at the French airport, your gun and ammunition can be collected upon production of the appropriate documentation; confirm all the requirements well in advance. On your return to your home country, you must declare your guns at Customs; if you don't you may be liable to prosecution for illegally importing firearms.

Locals may offer you a day's shooting with them. If so, ask at your *mairie* regarding the legal situation. Some *mairies* can grant permission for the odd day, while others will refer you to your local *préfecture*. Permits for non-residents are also available from the *préfecture*, for which you must provide two passport-size photographs, your passport and a shotgun certificate (with a French translation).

In areas where shooting is banned, it's usually shown by a sign (chasse interdite/gardée). Shooting within 150m of a house is strictly forbidden.

Fishing

French anglers generally prefer coarse fishing to game fishing, although France offers some of the best of both categories in Europe. Some 75 species of fish live and breed in France's innumerable lakes (*lac*), rivers (*rivière*), ponds (*étang*), reservoirs (*réservoir*) and canals (*canal*). Almost all waters are protected – signs such as *pêche réservée/gardée* are commonplace – and a fishing licence is required to fish anywhere. Fishing rights may be owned by a club, private landowner or the local community. Many of the best fishing waters are in private hands, although it may be possible to obtain permission from the owner. Often stretches of a river are divided between local clubs, which anglers must join in order to fish there.

Regulations & Licences

Fishing rights for waters on public land are the property of the state and a fishing tax (*taxe piscicole*) is levied. It's usually also necessary to purchase a national angling licence (*carte de pêche*) before fishing anywhere, which automatically makes you a member of the Association de Pêche et de Pisciculture (APP). In addition, a number of stamps are required, depending on what type of fish you're planning to catch.

The *carte de pêche* and the basic stamp (*timbre fiscal de base/à la ligne*), which shows you've paid the fishing tax for one *department,* currently costs €55 and entitles you to fish all the public lakes and rivers within the area. You can also buy an extra stamp, known as the *Entente Haliautique et Grand*

Ouest, which allows fishing in over 50 *départements* throughout southern, central and north-west France. You can, however, only buy this stamp after you've purchased permits for first and second category waters (see below). Expect to pay around €75 for this additional stamp, although buying it at the same time as the basic stamp can save you up to 50 percent. The cost of additional stamps varies according to the type of fishing you plan to do and whether you will be coarse or game fishing or both. Further details regarding the *carte de pêche* can be obtained from the website of the Conseil Supérieur de la Pêche (💻 www.csp.environnement.gouv.fr).

Categories & Seasons

Waters are divided into two categories: first (*première*) and second (*2ème*). In the first, you can fish for trout (and, in some cases, salmon), but despite only having paid to fish for game, it's also possible to fish for carp, perch, pike and zander on many of these waters. As in the UK, there's a 'close' season for game fishing, which runs from 20th September to 12th March. Second category waters are for coarse fishing and generally allow fishing all year round, although there are exceptions, e.g. a spring close season exists for pike and zander in some first and second category waters.

Holiday Permits

Casual or visiting anglers can purchase a *carte de pêche vacances* that allows a fortnight's fishing on both categories of water between June and September. It costs €30 and can be bought from tackle shops, *bar/tabacs*, regional angling associations and the national sports equipment chain, Décathlon. You will need a passport-size photograph and some form of identification. Day tickets (*carte journalière*) and a pass for anglers under 16 (*carte jeune*) are also available. Under 12s can often fish for free, but it's still necessary for them to carry a *carte de pêche*.

Always carry your permit when fishing, as wardens (who patrol many of the waters) may ask to see it and you can be fined if you don't have one.

If you're visiting France on a fishing holiday and returning home to the UK, you're advised to sterilise your equipment before fishing in British rivers. Britain is currently free of the *Gyrodactylus salis* parasite that attacks the skin, fins and gills of salmon, trout and some other freshwater fish. If it was imported into the UK, the only means of eradication would be the complete destruction of whole catchments of fish; cleaning your equipment is therefore essential.

Night Fishing

Night fishing areas (*parcours de pêche de nuit*) are identified by 'lots', which are simply a way of dividing rivers into manageable sections and are numbered sequentially. *Parcours* are clearly signposted on river banks.

When night fishing (or at any other time, for that matter), look out for Electricité de France's danger signs: '*Sous les lignes prudence – restons à distance*'. The use of graphite in the manufacture of continental fishing rods has greatly increased the chance of death by electrocution from contact with overhead power lines.

Sea Fishing

Boats for deep-sea fishing expeditions can be hired from ports and harbours. Sea fishing off the Atlantic coast is better than in the Mediterranean. Fishing in ports isn't permitted but you can fish anywhere else along the sea front. You can use a normal fishing rod and basic gear such as a bucket and net. Your catch must be of a minimum size, which varies with the region. Gathering shellfish is also strictly controlled, especially sea urchins and oysters, which are seasonal. To avoid potential misunderstandings, it's advisable to visit the maritime affairs office in the area where you plan to fish.

RAMBLING & HIKING

If you're living in or visiting a rural area, you're likely to want to use the network of local footpaths (*sentiers*). Generally, French farmers and landowners object less to walkers on their land than their counterparts in the UK, for example, but you still need to take care not to damage standing crops, leave gates open or risk setting fire to woodland or dried grass by carelessly discarding cigarette ends. If you're approached by an irate farmer, you will simply have to plead ignorance and apologise.

Some landowners don't take kindly to your picking their mushrooms, as the harvesting of certain varieties is much anticipated and highly prized by locals. If you do pick any fungi, ensure that you know what you're picking, as many varieties are fatally poisonous. Pharmacists sometimes open at weekends during the mushroom season for the express purpose of identifying what's edible and what isn't. **If you're in any doubt, show him what you've picked before even thinking about eating them.**

It's inadvisable to deviate from marked paths on shooting days, unless you want to risk ending up in a local *chasseur*'s game bag!

Footpaths & Maps

There are many miles of footpaths in the country, most (but not all) of which are signposted. Official walking trails include routes that are part of the *Grande Randonnée* (GR) network, established in 1947 and under the control of the Fédération Française de la Randonnée Pédestre (FFRP), which issues permits and provides insurance (neither of which are obligatory). Routes are marked by white/red or yellow/red bars on trees, rocks, walls and posts.

The organisation also publishes a series of topographical guides covering all of the country's long-distance footpaths. Many maps are written in English and include information such as where to park your car, what you might see *en route*, the location of restaurants and overnight accommodation. The Michelin 1,100 Orange Series of maps are also good, but the ultimate is the IGN Blue Series, which is detailed enough to show individual buildings. The French Rambling Association (FFRP, 💻 www.ffrp.asso.fr) also produces maps and information regarding national footpaths and rights of way.

Mountain Hiking

For more serious walkers, France has some of the finest areas for hiking (*tourisme pédestre*) in Western Europe. Spring and autumn are the best seasons for hiking, although in mountainous regions the best time for identifying flowers is between May and August. When considering mountain hiking it's necessary to prepare thoroughly and observe the following guidelines:

- Take local maps and make sure that you know how to read them.
- Wear appropriate clothing (especially footwear) for the weather and the area – even in summer you can suffer hypothermia if you're caught in a rainstorm followed by a cool period.
- Acquaint yourself with any refuge huts on your route (they're shown on walking maps). There's a small charge for their use, so make sure that you take some money with you.
- Don't walk on your own – it's easy to slip and injure yourself and not be able to summon help.
- Take a mobile phone – although generally frowned upon in the countryside, it's essential when hiking. Make sure it's fully charged and, if it's a 'pay-as-you-go' phone, that you have plenty of credit.
- You should take food and, more importantly, several litres of water, as you may be out longer than intended (it's easy to get lost) or that the place where you planned to stop for lunch is closed.

Don't over-exert yourself, particularly at high altitudes, where the air is thinner. If you aren't fit, take it easy and set a slow pace. It's easy to underestimate the duration or difficulty of a hike.

Organised Walks

You will often see posters and advertisements in your village and local newspapers giving details of forthcoming walks (*randonnées*), which are usually community or charity events. Although they're usually intended just for walkers (*à pied*), some allow cyclists (*en vélo*), horse riders (*équestres*) and even ponies and traps (*en attelage*). Some larger villages organise 10-15km (6-11mi) walking trips throughout the year. They're great fun and an excellent way to meet locals – and improve your command of French at the same time.

CANOEING & KAYAKING

With so many miles of waterways throughout the country, hiring a canoe (*canoë*), kayak (*kayak*) or small boat is a good way of seeing much of rural

France, but take particular care when canoeing, as even the most benign of rivers can have dangerous 'white water' patches. **On some rivers, there are quicksand-like banks of silt and shingle where people have been drowned.**

Leisurely touring that avoids 'thrills' but has the added interest of occasional gentle rapids is popular in France. The hire cost usually includes the price of a downstream pick-up and return to base. Some operators offer guided river tours at set times, where you normally travel in a group with two or three experienced canoeists leading the way. If you're really keen and want to buy a canoe or kayak, retail sports outlets such as Décathlon stock a good variety. There are many local canoeing clubs, most of which are affiliated to the Fédération Française de Canoë-Kayak (FFCK, 87 quai de la Marne, 94340 Joinville-le-Pont, ☎ 01 45 11 08 50).

CYCLING

Racing cyclists are a common sight in most areas on Sunday mornings, as road racing is a popular sport amongst the French. Most towns have their own clubs and keen cyclists may wish to join the Fédération Française de Cyclo-tourisme/FFCT (8 rue Jean-Marie Jégo, 75013 Paris, ☎ 01 44 16 88 88).

Rural regions are perfect for off-road and mountain biking, as there are many cycle paths (*piste cyclable*) to follow. Some areas have a network of tracks that will take you through beautiful countryside and along riverbanks. Some *GR* trails (see **Rambling & Hiking** on page 211) are open to mountain bikes, but check before using one. You can hire a mountain bike (*vélo tout-terrain/VTT*) from many outlets. Didier-Richard produces a series of guides for mountain bike enthusiasts, and each *département* also has a Comité Départemental du Cyclo-tourisme to promote all aspects of cycling.

Generally, the French look favourably upon cyclists, even if you accidentally end up on private land. On the road, most motorists give cyclists a wide berth when overtaking, but it pays to be cautious on rural roads due to the recklessness of some French drivers, who blithely assume that there's nothing but clear road around every blind corner.

HORSE RIDING

Horse riding is popular throughout the country. In many parts of France riders are well catered for by bridleways (*randonnées équestres*), riding schools and livery stables, where you can hire horses for lessons or hacking. You should be insured (even to join a hack) and you may be asked to show your *Galop Stages* (similar to UK Riding Club levels), which show your competence and can be gained at any authorised riding school (*centre équestre/hippique*). In fact, a reputable establishment should enquire about your riding experience and also your height and weight when you book, so that you can be matched with a horse appropriate for your skill and size. Don't exaggerate your capabilities or you may be put on an animal that's too strong for you. For more information contact the Association Nationale pour le Tourisme Équestre et l'Équitation de Loisirs (15 rue de Bruxelles, 75009 Paris, ☎ 01 42 81 42 82). To find your nearest riding school look under *Equitation et centres hippiques* in the yellow pages.

There are many horse shows in France, ranging from local events to international competitions, such as those staged at the Cadre Noir headquarters at Saumur in the Western Loire. If you're keen to compete, both you and your horse must be licensed and suitably qualified. Generally, competition horses must be registered with the relevant breed society and the same applies to dressage horses, even if they have *Grand Prix* status elsewhere. (The reason that horses from other countries can compete in France is that they do so under international rules, which are entirely different from those that apply to horses resident in France.)

BOULES & OTHER GAMES

Although by no means restricted to rural living – indeed it would be rare to wander through any town on a warm summer's evening and not witness a game – *boules* (and its variations) is an essential part of the French way of life and deserves a mention here.

The main difference between *boules* and *pétanque* is that in *boules* you release the ball when moving up to the 'launch' spot, whereas in *pétanque*, you stand still with both feet together as you throw. It's usually thought that of the two variations, *pétanque* is the easier game to play as it requires no special playing area, the pitch is smaller and the rules are simpler. In *pétanque*, the thrower stands in a circle just large enough to contain both feet and throws his or her ball from a stationary crouching position.

The pitch required for *boules* varies in size but is usually around 3m x 12m. It's normally played between two teams comprising two (*doublettes*), three (*triplettes*) or four (*quadrettes*) players. Singles matches (*tête à tête*) are also possible. In a singles or doubles game, each player has three *boules* (two each in triples). A member of the starting team throws a small marker ball up the pitch. Ideally, it should land somewhere between 6m and 10m from the throwing point, and the object is for the remaining players to lob their *boules* as close to the target ball as possible.

After one player from each team has thrown, the next person to throw is decided by whose *boule* finished closest to the marker. The team furthest away continues to throw until they get a closer *boule* than the other team or until they run out of balls. The team whose *boule* (or *boules*) eventually lies closest wins what is known as the 'end'. When the *boules* are too close to decide the nearest, a piece of string is used to measure the distance between them and the marker ball (called the *cochonnet* in some parts of France). A match continues until a team scores 11 points (*la partie*). A second or return match in a series of three is called *la revanche* and, if each side has won one match, the deciding game is called *la belle*.

Mostly seen in rural areas, *palet sur planche* is played with a plank of poplar wood and discs of metal around 5cm (2in) in diameter and weighing around 140g (3oz). *Le lancer du fer à cheval* (horseshoe pitching) requires used horseshoes and five pointed wooden stakes. The stakes, of differing heights, are hammered into the ground and the point of the exercise is to throw the shoes around the base of the stakes. Rules and regulations for most of these pastimes can be downloaded from the Fédération Gallèse des Jeux et Sports website (💻 www.jeuxbretons.org).

CLOTHING & EQUIPMENT

The French enthusiasm for the Great Outdoors in general, and field sports in particular, means that there's a vast array of specialist clothing and equipment available. Most is of good quality and some, such as Le Chameau boots, are sought after worldwide but, being French made, are much cheaper in France than elsewhere. A visit to a *fête de chasse* is often worthwhile, as boots and clothing are sold at special show prices, resulting in some great bargains. In August and early September, some French supermarkets in rural areas change their 'promotions' from school clothing and equipment to field sports gear in readiness for the forthcoming shooting season. Décathlon, France's premier sports equipment outlet, is well worth a visit, as it caters for every conceivable field sport and rural pursuit, including walking, cycling, running, rowing and riding.

DOG

12.

Wildlife

France has a wealth of unique flora and fauna and its wildlife is unusually abundant and varied due to its diverse topography and traditional farming practices. Some parts of the country are vast, featureless prairies with not a tree in sight, but in most areas it's possible to find small fields of mixed crops, vineyards, hedgerows and ditches, which provide a habitat for many animals and birds and protection from predators, natural food and a perfect breeding environment.

Cattle are regularly moved from field to field, providing natural fertiliser and creating small troughs and ridges with their hooves – an ideal growing medium for countless tiny plants. Wild flowers (including rare orchids and fritillaries) benefit from the headlands and ditches surrounding fields, and the diversity of plants provides an ideal habitat for the butterflies and insects that are necessary for pollination. Some types of butterfly can survive in woodland, but there isn't enough nectar available for most butterflies, which rely on wild flowers. These seem to flourish in what are, agriculturally speaking, poorer soils, such as roadside verges and the neglected corners of small fields: the more impoverished the soil, the greater the diversity of plants; where fertiliser is applied to the ground, coarser and more vigorous species begin to dominate, choking most of the more delicate varieties (see **Meadows** on page 70).

This chapter investigates some of the common – and not so common – wildlife to be found in France.

INSECTS

If you're moving from the UK, you will almost certainly be struck by the variety and size of insects in France. Fortunately, few of them are harmful.

Spiders

Probably the spiders (*araignée*) you will have most contact with house spiders, whose untidy, dusty webs infest attics and barns. Some common house spiders (*Tegenaria gigantean*) grow a little larger than those seen in the UK but, like all house spiders, they're harmless. Although it's often tempting to get rid of them, they reduce the fly population and the old adage 'If you wish to live and thrive, let a spider stay alive' generally applies. If they're where you don't wish them to be, trap them in a container and deposit them gently outside.

Male spiders are often much smaller than females and you can often see them acting out an elaborate courtship display.

There are some very pretty orb web-weaving spiders, such as the garden spider (*Araneus diadematus*), found on fences and hedges between August and October. Their brown body has a white cross on its abdomen. Of the various wolf spiders, the nursery-web (*Pisaura mirabilis*) is abundant in dense vegetation, often roaming in search of likely prey. Two strange characteristics of the nursery-web are the fact that it generally rests with its front pair of legs pointing forward and angled away from its body, and that the female carries her egg cocoon in her fangs, only attaching it to a plant just before the eggs are due to hatch.

Some spiders can give a nasty bite, which can be sore for a few days, but they're generally more interested in small insects than large humans. The more dangerous species are often strikingly coloured or marked; scarlet or yellow and black, for example, is a warning sign to predators to stay away. The only spider likely to cause harm from its bite is the tarantula (*Lycosa narbonensis*). It's rare in France but is sometimes seen in southern regions. At 25cm (10in) long, this member of the wolf spider family lives in burrows and hunts on the ground and, although its bite may be troublesome, it isn't life-threatening. (Mythology claimed that the cure for its bite was to carry out a complicated dance to disperse the venom – hence the Tarantella.)

Centipedes & Crickets

Not strictly an insect because of its 15 pairs of legs but included in this section for convenience is a centipede (*mille-pattes* – literally meaning 1,000 legs and also the word for millipedes, despite the French reputation for logic) that has very long legs and antennae. Often seen in France, it can move over walls at incredible speed and seems impressively large, although this is an illusion caused by the length of its legs. In any case, it's harmless to all but the small insects it eats. Mainly active in warm weather, it hibernates in cracks and crannies when winter approaches. If disturbed in the winter, e.g. among debris in an outbuilding, it moves very slowly and appears hunched up and unwell.

Amongst the cricket (*grillon*) family is a very large variety known informally as '*cri-cri*' by many French rural dwellers owing to the sound it makes. Similar to a North American cicada, it spends some time underground as a grub before pupating into a 3cm-long green or brown creature. It's flightless, with stumps for wings, which it rubs together to produce the sound that gives it its name. Unlike most bush crickets, it's active throughout the day and calls to its mate repeatedly in hot weather. Well camouflaged amongst the shrubs it inhabits, it may be hard to spot but is well worth looking out for.

Hornets, Flies, Wasps & Mosquitoes

Quite common in France is the hornet (*frelon*). It looks like an oversize wasp, though its brown and yellow rather than black and yellow. It can give a very painful sting if disturbed and is best avoided; if left alone it won't harm you. If you have a hornet's or wasp's (*guèpe*) nest in your garden that's causing problems, the fire service (*sapeur-pompiers*) will deal with it, as both are classed as a danger to the public. However, the *sapeur-pompiers* are no longer allowed to destroy bees' nests, as they're a protected species, and so will offer to send out a private pest control company. Another member of this family that can be disconcerting is the carpenter bee (*Xylocopa violacea*), a large, solitary insect that flies noisily from flower to flower. It nests in burrows, but its habit of burrowing in decayed wood gives it its name Unlike the 'common-or-garden' bee, it's shiny black, with iridescent, smoky blue-black wings. Despite its alarming appearance, it's totally harmless to humans (the only danger it poses is from collapsing beams and arbours!).

The common housefly (*mouche*) is probably the biggest cause of annoyance and harm to human health. Its unsavoury eating habits cause germs to infect uncovered food, sometimes causing digestive upsets. You should therefore cover all foodstuffs, avoid purchasing confectionery or cakes from open market stalls and wash all vegetables and salads before use. You can buy window stickers from supermarkets and ironmongers' (*quincailleries*) which give off an odour that seems to repel flies. The stickers are usually sold in batches of two or four and have a flower head design. They cost anywhere between €2 and €7, the most expensive usually being the most effective.

Mosquitoes (*moustiques*) in France don't carry the malaria bacterium and therefore, although their bite can be annoying and cause a histamine reaction in some people, they won't threaten your life. They can, however, seriously spoil your enjoyment of French rural life (especially if your home is situated near water).

Simple precautions can minimise the risk of inconvenience from insects. For example, most supermarkets and ironmongers carry stocks of various anti-mosquito products for both indoor and outdoor use. Alternatively, it's possible to buy rolls of fine plastic mesh in various colours and staple it to simple homemade timber frames, with which your windows can be covered during the summer months. Because the majority of French windows open inwards, the window can be left open for ventilation and the insects remain outside. Bead or tape curtains over frequently-used doorways will deter flies from entering.

Ants & Stick Insects

There are some interesting ants (*fourmi*) in France, possibly the most fascinating being the four-spotted (*fourmi à quatre taches*). It's unique in the ant world, being the only one to possess an abdomen decorated with four cream-coloured spots. It nests in trees rather than on the ground and is thought to feed on honeydew 'milked' from tree-dwelling aphids. Ordinary ants found around the house can be controlled by tubes of *anti-fourmis* gels that are active for three months or by small plastic traps baited with a poisonous substance. Both are available from supermarkets.

The praying mantis (*mante religieuse*) is also common and is often seen flying from bush to bush preying on smaller insects such as grasshoppers (*sauterelle*) and crickets, which it seizes with its front legs before proceeding to eat them rather like a human with a cob of sweetcorn! The praying mantis is a valuable garden insect, as it also grazes on aphids; if you find a mantis egg case, which looks like a shrivelled walnut, put it under a rose bush. Being green, they're difficult to spot amongst the foliage, but they're fascinating to watch. Another common resident, but difficult to spot, is the stick insect (*phasme*). Confined to pet shops in the UK, they're present all summer in France. Green or brown, they're usually motionless, but when mobile they move in a slow, jerky motion to dupe birds and other predators into thinking that they're twigs shaken by the wind rather than a tasty morsel.

Finally – and particularly for those previously living in northern parts of the UK, especially Scotland – there are midges (*moucheron*) in France, but they don't bite with the same ferocity as their counterparts north of the border!

MOTHS & BUTTERFLIES

There are many beautiful butterflies (*papillon*) and moths (*papillon de nuit*) in France, where there are still many large areas of uncultivated land, which are a haven for them. For further information on this fascinating subject, refer to *Butterflies & Moths in Britain and Europe* by David Carter (Pan) and *Wildlife of Britain and Europe* by Michael Chinery (Harper Collins).

Moths

There are too many moths to list here but four are worth mentioning.

- **Giant Peacock Moth (*Saturnia pyri*)** – This is thought to be Europe's largest moth, with a wingspan of 7cm (3in). It flies at night in early summer and is often mistaken for a bat.
- **Hummingbird Hawk Moth (*Macroglosssum stellatarum*)** – This moth is unusual in flying by day. Its name is apt, as it hovers like a hummingbird while feeding on nectar from flowers, particularly lavender, bedstraws and honeysuckle. It also loves the nectar of ivy-leafed pelargoniums, so if you've planted these in tubs or pots you have a good chance of seeing this moth feeding.
- **Pine Processional Moth (*Thaumotepoea pityocampa*)** – If you have pine trees in your area, you may well see one of the most fascinating of moths. The adult pine processional moth is a dull brown and not very interesting; it's the caterpillars (*chenille*) that are worth watching. Protected by a 'nest' or ball of gossamer, they feed high in the tops of pine trees (to which they can cause considerable damage), and in the spring or early summer they leave the nest *en masse* in a nose-to-tail procession, seeking an alternative food source. The line of caterpillars can reach 7m (23ft) in length, the individual at the head of the column doing the 'steering' and the tail-ender doing the pushing. At night, they form a tight coil, which unwinds again at first light.

Be careful not to touch pine processional moth caterpillars, as the secretion from their bristles can cause severe skin irritation. They can prove fatal to cats and dogs; even the frass from their nests can cause animals respiratory problems.

- **Oak Processional Moth (*Thaumotepoea procesionea*)** – Similar to the pine processional moth, this species – as its name implies – feeds on oak leaves; the two can easily be distinguished in caterpillar form by the fact that the oak processional marches in pairs.

Butterflies

Some butterfly species are highly mobile and don't remain in a particular area for long, while others live in colonies and require a balanced, long-term environment. If you're living in an area of France where there's an equal amount of woodland and arable land, these are ideal conditions and you should be able to spot many varieties, including chequered skippers (*Carterocephalus palaemon*), pearl-bordered fritillaries (*Clossiana euphrosyne*) and duke of burgundy fritillaries (*Hamearis lucina*).

Open ground provides shelter, sun, larval feeding-sites and plants such as brambles, thistles and knapweed, all of which produce nectar for the adult meadow brown (*Maniola jurina*) and ringlet (*Aphantopus hyperantus*). Even species such as the purple emperor (*Apatura iris*), usually thought of as preferring a woodland canopy, need ridge-edge sallows on which to breed and are quite common on farmland.

Swallowtails (*Papilio machaon*), queen of Spain fritillaries (*Issoria lathonia*), adonis blues (*Lysandra bellargus*) and large blues (*Maculiea arion*) are common throughout France, while other varieties are mostly found in specific areas. The two-tailed pasha (*Charaxes jasius*) of the Mediterranean coast and the apollo (*Parnassius apollo*) found in the Alps and Pyrenees are just two examples. Look out in particular for the famous Camberwell beauty (*Nymphalis antiopa*), which, although found throughout the country, isn't common anywhere.

MAMMALS

Like the rest of this chapter, this section is concerned only with creatures not normally encountered in rural parts of the UK. Foxes, badgers, moles, mice, voles and squirrels abound in France, although the last named are predominantly of the red variety – one of the most stunning creatures to look out for if you've only ever seen grey squirrels. However, if you've never been alert or quiet enough to see them in the UK, you're unlikely to see them in France either, as – unlike the semi-tame foxes that live an unnatural life in urban areas or grey squirrels emboldened by office workers' lunchtime sandwiches – they're truly wild, shy and secretive creatures that shun human company and generally pose no threat.

Wild Boar

With the exception of the European bison found in the Dordogne and recently re-introduced into the area south of Vire on the Orne/Calvados border, the largest mammal you're likely to see is the wild boar (*sanglier*). Both males and females can be aggressive in defence of their family but tales of people being pursued for miles by an enraged animal are vastly exaggerated. Wild boar live in the plentiful forests and wooded regions across most of France but are less widespread in the north. They need rivers or lakes for water but their diet varies according to the region, resulting in specific types that may be larger or smaller than the national average. They vary in colour from black to russet, often going grey with age. If you're fortunate enough to spot one in woodland, take a quick look, then change your direction and leave it well alone. Don't walk towards it and, if you have a dog with you, keep it on a leash.

Deer

All species of deer found in the UK, including red (*cerf*), roe (*chevreuil*), fallow (*daim*) and sika (*cerf sika*), are present in France, where their numbers are maintained for sporting reasons. Stalkers and hunters class them as 'big game' (*le grand gibier*), although in some commercial forest regions the roe deer is considered more of a nuisance than a prized prey. In wooded, mountainous *départements* such as Alpes-Maritimes, Cantal, Gard and Lozère, you may be fortunate enough to spot a mouflon, a large animal with thick, backward curving horns, like a cross between a deer and a sheep. Certain *départements*, including Hautes-Alpes, Haute-Savoie and Vosges, are home to the chamois, a small, shy delicate deer with short, upright horns. Hunted nearly to extinction for its famously soft skin, which was tanned and used for fine leatherwork, it's now a rare species and, although some shooting is permitted, a special licence is required. To see chamois you will need to be prepared for some serious and energetic climbing in the mountains!

Coypu & Mink

Both coypu (*ragondin*) and mink (*vison*) are quite common in France, particularly around lakes and waterways. The coypu is a large rodent – around 60cm (24in) long – with a 40cm (16in) tail and a beaver-like appearance. In France, most drainage ditches are kept working by the combined efforts of farmers and *communes* and facilitate the coypu's movement. Verdant hedgerows and a variety of crops provide good grazing, and it isn't unusual to see a family of five or more feeding in the middle of a field. Like those of rats, their regular runs are easy to spot, being muddy and greasy. Considering the size of the animal, its holes are relatively small but the damage they cause to banks, waterways and crops make them a serious pest. Indeed, there have been fatal accidents such as when the edge of a field, undermined by coypu, gave way under the weight of a working tractor, causing the machine to turn over into a water-filled ditch.

There's great concern throughout France that coypu are as much a cause of the spread of leptospiral jaundice among domestic animals and humans as rats. One study of 540 specimens found that over 50 per cent had been in contact with more than one form of leptospirosis.

The local shooting club (*fédération des chasseurs*) is permitted to trap and shoot coypu at certain times of the year and should be contacted via the *mairie* if they cause a nuisance on your land.

Also present throughout France is the European mink, which differs from the mink found in the UK (descended from escaped American imports) in that the patch of white fur on its muzzle doesn't extend around the eye. A similar shape to a weasel or stoat but larger, it's mainly nocturnal, feeding on water voles, rats, mice, young birds, frogs and fish.

Bats

There are around 30 species of bat (*chauve-souris*) in France. The most common is the pipistrelle (*Pipistrellus pipistrellus*). Unfortunately, the bat population is decreasing as a result of pesticide use. Being long-living insectivores, bats accumulate pesticides in their fat tissue and gradually become sterile.

To protect bats, you shouldn't over-use pesticides in the garden or termite or woodwork treatments in roofs. Alternative products made from natural substances and based on triazoles and pyrethroides are available.

Any water-based product and products marked as suitable for use around farm animals and foodstuffs are generally safe. If you have bats in your house, contact the Société Française pour l'Étude et la Protection des Mammifères (SFEPM, ☎ 02 48 70 40 03, 🖳 www.museum-bourges.net or 🖳 http://sfepm.ciril.fr or 🖳 http://aptcs.ciril.fr) for a local contact.

Unusual Mammals

Many knowledgeable country people go a lifetime without seeing certain species; if you see the following, count yourself fortunate

- **Genet (*genette*)** – About the size of a small cat, the genet is beautifully marked in cream and black with a long, barred tail. It's nocturnal and usually solitary, feeding mainly on rodents and young birds. It can climb well, but may also set up home in a disused fox (*renard*) or badger (*blaireau*) earth. You may be fortunate enough to see one in scrub and woodland, especially near the Loire or Rhône or in the Pyrenees.
- **Garden Dormouse (*Eliomys quercinus*)** – This animal is totally different from the common dormouse (*loir*). It has a black mask on its face and its long, slender tail has a flattened black and white tuft at the tip. Cat owners may see the garden dormouse if their pets chance upon one in the early autumn as it becomes dormant after a period of summer fattening.
- **Highland Cattle** – Of interest to rural dwellers in the regional parks of Alsace and Moselle is the possibility of coming across highland cattle on a Sunday afternoon perambulation! In an effort to limit the increasing risk of fire due to the decline in grazing and forestry activity, these long-horned and extremely shaggy creatures are used to control the vegetation.

REPTILES & AMPHIBIANS

Being cold-blooded, reptiles and amphibians are inactive at low temperatures and, with the exception of a few Mediterranean species, hibernate during the colder months of the year, so you're obviously more likely to see them on hot summer days. Most south-facing walls are home to a lizard or two and they can give you quite a start as they suddenly scuttle away.

Snakes

Among the most emotive of subjects is that of snakes (*serpent*). Normally harmless creatures, they're neither slimy nor aggressive. Snakes are merely cold-blooded reptiles, usually going about the business of survival, seeking food and shelter and wishing to do so without interference. There are poisonous snakes in rural France (see below), just as there are in most other countries, but it's necessary to put the danger they constitute in perspective. As with sharks, the number of human deaths caused by snakes is tiny compared with that resulting from man-made dangers such as cars and electrical appliances. On the other hand, the number of harmless snakes killed through fear or ignorance is staggering and unnecessary.

Due to the warm climate and large areas of undisturbed land, there are more snakes in France per hectare than in the UK, for example, but the majority are harmless. Even those that can cause harm will do so only if threatened, but you should take the following precautions to minimise your chance of being bitten (and of harming a snake):

- Snakes often take shelter in outbuildings, where you should take care not to disturb them.
- If you're venturing on foot into areas of scrub or woodland, wear sensible shoes or boots, don't let children run barefoot and keep dogs on a leash.
- If you're preparing to work on an untended or overgrown area of garden, once again wear boots or shoes and enter the area first in a positive fashion with heavy footsteps and perhaps beating the undergrowth with a heavy stick.

Snakes have no ears but they can feel vibration and, on sensing your approach, will slip away unnoticed. Being relatively slow moving, however, they will be forced to defend themselves if children or animals run into their territory. The French believe that keeping free-ranging poultry in the garden deters snakes, which are frightened of the pattering of chickens' feet! If you see a snake, avoid it and let it go on its way or change your direction. A good book on snakes will help you identify them.

Poisonous Snakes

The only really dangerous snake found throughout France is the adder or viper (*Vipera berus*). The danger is that, as it's slow moving, you can come upon it before it can slip way, and it may strike in self-defence.

SURVIVAL TIP

A zigzag pattern on a snake's back usually identifies it as an adder, but be aware that adders' colouration and patterning varies enormously and that there are harmless grass snakes with similar markings to the adder.

The vertical pupil of the adder, as distinct from the round pupil of the grass snake, is a more reliable identifier.

The asp (*Vipera aspis*) is more venomous than the adder but is found only in certain parts of the country. It can be distinguished from the adder by its upturned snout, but you may not choose to get that close!

Other venomous snakes have their fangs inside their jaws and can inject venom into prey only once it's inside the mouth. **Therefore they're harmless to humans**. This group includes the cat snake (*Telescopus fallax*), which lives mainly on lizards, and the rarely seen Montpelier snake (*Malpolon monspessulanus*).

According to statistics, no venom is injected in around 40 per cent of snakebites. Nevertheless, you should know what to do if you or someone else is bitten by an adder or asp. Some symptoms of a venomous bite appear quickly, while others – such as vomiting, thirst, hypotension and abdominal pain – may affect a victim hours later. As snake venom is allergenic and can induce heart attacks, it's important not to move the patient, as this can cause the venom to spread through the bloodstream. Call an ambulance or other medical help and get the victim to a hospital as quickly as possible. Although chemists and doctors won't have the necessary antidote, the former sell a small box called *aspivenin*, which contains nozzles for sucking out the poison. If one of these or anti-histamine cream is applied immediately, it can help in reducing the venom's effectiveness.

Non-poisonous Snakes

Of the non-venomous snakes, the most common are the familiar grass or smooth snake (*Natrix natrix*). There are various types, colours and sizes, up to 2m in length, and they can be found both in and out of water. The grass snake is recognisable by its yellow collar. The viperine (*Natrix maura*) is smaller, measuring no more than 1m, and is grey-green with irregular black markings.

Another beautiful French resident is the western whip snake (*Coluber viridiflavus*), which can be up to 1.5m long. Unlike most other snakes, it's very fast, as it preys upon lizards and other snakes.

On the Mediterranean coast you may be fortunate enough to see the ladder snake (*Elaphe scalaris*), named after the ladder-like pattern on the back of its young. It can grow up to 1.6m in length and lives mainly on small mammals.

Lizards

Commonly mistaken for snakes but in fact classified as lizards (*lézard*) are the slowworm (*Anguis fragilis*) and the scarcer three-toed skink (*Chalcides chalcides*). The slowworm, which can grow up to 50cm (20in) long, is a beautiful golden colour with very smooth, shiny skin and distinguishable from snakes by its eyelids. You might find it under stones or boards lying on the ground and, when disturbed, it will often feign death and appear stiff. Be careful if you handle it as, like all lizards, it has a tail that's easily broken off and will hardly grow again (see below). The slowworm is valued by gardeners, as it lives on slugs. Much smaller than the slowworm is the three-toed skink, which, as its name suggests, has three toes on each leg. Although its legs are short, it can move very quickly.

You're much more likely to encounter the common wall lizard (*Podarcis muralis*). Active throughout the warmer months, it can be seen climbing on the walls of houses and outbuildings and sunbathing on garden walls and fences. Up to 8cm (3in) long with a tail up to two and half times its body length, it feeds on flies and other small insects. It varies in colour from brown to grey, usually with a dark line along its back. It can be difficult to identify, as it resembles its close cousin, the viviparous lizard (*Lacerta vivipara*). The only sure way of telling them apart is to count the scales – if you can get close enough! If there are over 40 across its back, it's a wall lizard; if there are fewer than 36, it's a viviparous.

Less common, but worth looking out for, is the green lizard (*Lacerta viridis*), which grows up to 13cm (5in) and has a tail twice its body length. It prefers denser vegetation and is therefore not so easily seen. Usually feeding on a diet of small insects, it also takes birds' eggs and fruit. The male is all green with a beautiful blue throat when mature, while the female is green or brown blotched and less impressive.

Lizards are commonly found with no tail or one that has re-grown. The tail snaps off very easily if grabbed by a predator, leaving the lizard free to escape. They seem to come to no harm after such an encounter, probably because the blood vessels at each vertebral joint contract to ensure that there's no bleeding. A final, interesting curiosity of all lizards is that the males have two penises!

Frogs, Toads & Newts

Probably your first encounter with frogs (*grenouille*) will be hearing rather than seeing them (unless you include edible frogs), as during the early evening and throughout the night from April/May onwards, they will serenade you with their calls. Go looking for them quietly during daylight and you may wonder where the noise comes from. Though mostly active during the day, they prefer to shelter from the hot sun and seek moist, shady places.

The largest frog you will encounter is the marsh frog (*Rana ridibunda*). At up to 15cm (6in) in length, it's around twice the size of the common frog (*Rana temoraria*). Apart from its size, it's recognisable by its colour – dull brown with black blotches. Like most frogs, it feeds on insects and small fish. Smaller and more colourful is the famous edible frog (*Rana esculenta*), which is green and around 12cm (5in) long. Large vocal sacs under the throat expand when it 'croaks'. Like snails, edible frogs are now farmed in order to satisfy the French appetite! Much smaller, at 5cm (2in), is the green tree frog (*Hyla arborea*). As the name implies, it climbs into trees and shrubs with the help of suckers on its feet, which allow purchase on shiny leaves. Like the edible frog, it's green and is rarely seen by day (but most certainly heard at night, its call alsobeing produced via an enormous vocal sac under the chin).

Toads (*crapauds*) tend to live in drier places than frogs, and they have better developed lungs. The common toad (*Bufo bufo*)is frequently seen in most regions. In certain areas, you may also spot the much smaller midwife toad (*Alytes obstetricans*), so named because of the habit the male has of carrying the eggs on his back legs until they're ready to hatch, when he enters the water. The natterjack toad (*Bufo calamita*) inhabits sandy places, usually near to brackish water and coastal marshes.

There are several newts (*tritons*) to be found in France. The fire salamander (*Salamandra salamandra*) is the largest, growing up to 25cm (10in). Identification is easy thanks to its vivid skin colours: yellow/orange and black. These serve as a warning to predators and, in a further effort to deter them, the fire salamander resorts to unpleasant skin secretions. Its breeding habits are different from those of other newts: the female retains the fertilised eggs in her body until they hatch or even, in some areas, until they've become miniature adults.

Of the tortoise family, only the European pond terrapin (*Emys orbicularis*) is common in France. At 30cm (12in) long, this pond-dwelling creature lives on fish, water insects and crustaceans. Often seen basking on exposed logs or rocks at the water's edge, they will quickly disappear when disturbed.

BIRDS

Where France really comes into its own is in its huge variety of birds. There are at least 25 breeds of daytime hunting raptors (*les rapaces diurnes*), either resident or migratory, some of which are quite rare. The honey buzzard is probably the most common and can often be seen perched on telephone posts and dead trees. Montague and marsh harriers, and red and black kites are also common; unusually for birds of prey, they're sometimes seen in groups.

In the south-west and east, stork numbers have been increasing in recent years. Storks, which like low marshy ground with trees, are often confused with cranes, but one way of telling them apart in flight is by their noise: if they're silent, they're storks; noisy and they're almost certainly cranes. The hoopoe is only an infrequent and rarely seen visitor to the UK but is common in France. It has bright brown plumage, an orange breast and a magnificent crest on its head, which it raises to attract a mate. Look out for it, as it can often be spotted on lawns and grassland searching for insects. The golden oriole, about the size of a song thrush, is another spectacular bird, which lives high in woods and orchards. The male has a bright golden plumage and dark brown wings. A few pairs have recently colonised southern Britain but they're fairly common throughout France.

Both black- and grey-headed woodpeckers are also seen in France despite being rare in the UK. Like the hoopoe, the black woodpecker can often be seen searching for worms and grubs on lawns and grassland. Nightingales are rarely seen but their spectacular song fills the warm spring nights with an unforgettable melody – they also sing during the day, but you're less likely to hear them because of the distractions of other bird song. Kingfishers can be regularly seen if you take the time to sit quietly by even the smallest of streams or ponds with shrubs and bushes along their banks: concentrate on dead branches and fence posts, as the kingfisher will often use these as vantage points before diving into the water after small fish. A bird that's surprisingly no longer common in the UK is the cheeky house sparrow. Its demise there is cause for much concern and research, but in rural France its presence is, thankfully, unavoidable.

Owls

Of the owl species (*les rapaces nocturnes*), nine are commonly seen. Europe's largest owl is the eagle owl. Recognisable by its size and tufted ears, it's found in most of France and can prey upon animals as large as the hare. At the other end of the scale is the scops owl, found in the southern regions. Although not Europe's smallest (that honour goes to the pygmy, which isn't seen in France), it's only 19cm (8in) high. Depending on the type, owls are known as either *chouettes* or *hiboux* in French. Generally, *chouettes* have a rounded head, while *hiboux* have 'ears' or a horned appearance. Typically, however, there's an exception: the short-eared owl (*hibou des marais*), which has no visible protrusions.

The barn owl (*chouette effraie*), in gradual decline in the UK, is common in all parts of France, although in some areas it's regarded as a bad omen (see **Beliefs & Superstitions** on page 239). Unlike other owls, the little owl is active during the day and can often be seen sitting on fences and telegraph posts. Unfortunately, it likes to nest in hollow trees, which are becoming increasingly rare, and is mainly an insectivore and therefore, like bats, has suffered from the increasing use of pesticides. In certain parts of France, the little owl has disappeared completely.

Bird Watching

Some regions of France are suited to certain species of bird. Obviously, the coastlines and estuaries provide the perfect habitat for waders and waterfowl, while the Pyrenees are home to the griffon vulture, the alpine chough, white-backed woodpeckers and bonelli's warbler. Gavarnie is the primary 'birding' site in this area but, overall, the Carmargue is the most famous part of France for bird watching due to the wealth of species and the diversity of its topography. Other excellent locations include Sept Iles off the coast of Brittany, the Baie d'Aiguillon on the west coast, the densely forested hills of the Argonne in the north-east, the lakes and agricultural areas of La Brenne in the centre, and Dombes, north of Lyons. Fontainebleau, Sologne and the Lac du Der Chantecoq, all south-east of Paris, are also popular sites with twitchers.

WILD FLOWERS & FUNGI

France has an abundance of wild flowers, and many roadside verges and ditches contain rare plants. The *commune* is responsible for cutting the verges of even the quietest roads, usually once in spring and again in late summer. This second cutting is extremely important to the wellbeing of many plant species, as it's done after the flowers have set seeds for the following year. The seeds fall to the ground and either germinate or lie dormant until the spring. In addition, the lack of exhaust fumes and, in most parts, of the need for salt to be spread on the roads in winter, give wild flowers the best possible chance of survival.

In fields and hedgerows, bio-diversity allows for a tremendous variety of flower types that are rare elsewhere. Rare plants are protected by law (i.e. it's illegal to pick or collect them), although the extent and effectiveness of legislation varies greatly. Considering the vast number of varieties to be found, surprisingly few are legally protected. Nevertheless, you should resist the temptation to transplant 'wild' flowers to your garden.

Fungi

A popular pastime throughout France is collecting and eating wild mushrooms and fungi. Equipped with a good book, you can spend many hours in this pursuit.

Illustrations in books can be very deceptive, with the result that both edible and poisonous fungi can appear similar. Some varieties are deadly poisonous.

Arm yourself with a strong basket and a number of paper bags; each type of mushroom that you believe to be edible should be put in a separate bag to avoid contamination. In order to determine whether they're edible you should take them to your local pharmacist, who is trained to identify them – he may even advise you on the best way to cook them! The use of wild mushrooms is central to rural cooking and the results can be exquisite.

Truffles

It's doubtful whether you will come across truffles, even in the southern areas where they grow well. Because of the high prices paid for the best specimens – in excess of €1,000 per kilo – there's a great deal of illegal activity surrounding what are called 'black diamonds'. Truffle theft is on the increase, and tales of armed robbers in trucks stealing 30kg of truffles in one night from protected oak forests aren't unknown. Truffle-hunting dogs, which, fully trained, can fetch as much as €4,000, are occasionally stolen from their kennels by desperate truffle smugglers.

13.

RURAL LIFE

To make the most of life in rural France, it's useful to know a little about the local culture and to obtain a few 'insider' tips. It isn't enough to simply to 'live' in rural France; if you want to thrive you must immerse yourself in every aspect of country life. The allure of rural living isn't confined to the freedom of open spaces, the pleasures of keeping animals and the beauty of the flora and fauna; it's also about becoming an active member of the community and achieving a sense of belonging – and you can only hope to do this by integrating fully with the French and understanding their culture and way of life (and mysterious foibles). Creating a colony of expatriates and having little or nothing to do with the real world outside it won't endear you to the locals, but more importantly you will be the loser by missing out on so much of what the country has to offer.

Rural idiosyncrasies include the fact that you can pay cheques, but not cash, into a bank on a Saturday morning. Christmas is celebrated mainly on Christmas Eve, and Boxing Day isn't a public holiday; for most French people it means a return to work. Christmas cards are exchanged, but more popular is the tradition of sending New Year cards – another little habit well worth getting into.

This chapter might equally have been titled 'Miscellaneous' or 'Other Considerations' and includes information, organised alphabetically (but otherwise in no particular order), which didn't belong in any previous chapter.

AGRICULTURAL SHOWS

Agricultural shows aren't usually open to 'amateurs' and some events are exclusive to members of specific breed societies (there's strong rivalry between licensed farmers for the prizes at the regular cattle and livestock shows held throughout France). Probably the nearest thing to an agricultural show of the type common in the UK is the *comice agricole*, at which displays include themed floats, cattle (*vaches*), horses (*chevaux*), donkeys (*ânes*) and ponies (*poneys*), as well as other animals in the alarming-sounding '*parc à bestiaux*'! In addition, human obstacle races are included, together with displays of traditional rural crafts such as threshing (*battage à l'ancienne*). Flower shows are also quite popular, despite the fact that most rural inhabitants see little point in growing anything that cannot be eaten!

Many *communes* organise a *concours de labours* – similar to a UK ploughing match – in which old tractors, cultivators and other agricultural machinery are pressed into competition. A *concours* usually begins with a procession of implements before the competition proper commences, but sometimes the competitive element will have been completed the day before. However it's run, there's usually a large lunch included, for which you can buy tickets from your local baker or butcher. Afterwards, there's usually a game of *boules* or *palet* (see page 215) and a dance (*bal*) in the evening.

BELIEFS & SUPERSTITIONS

Like all countries, France has a wealth of traditional beliefs and superstitions – and nowhere more so than in the country. Some, such as planting and harvesting according to the phases of the moon (see **Planting by the Moon** on page 101), have a scientific background. Others, like the belief that sighting a barn owl in or around your house is a bad omen (often signifying a forthcoming bereavement), are superstitions based on the experience of a local family generations ago – which was then taken as 'gospel' by neighbouring villagers. In some areas, '*ganipotes*' are said to wander near ponds and rivers. They're variously believed to be the souls of dead, unbaptised children or young, spell-bound girls, forced into running through the countryside late at night – the only way to release them from their spell being to catch one, hold it tight and force it into divulging its name. The *ganipote* is friendly compared to other creatures, such as the malevolent *beurdasse* and *bigourne* ... If animals fall ill, some farmers still believe that a spell has been cast over them, while others think that if you have a skin problem, such as psoriasis, eczema or even a burn, you should visit a faith healer.

Most traditions and superstitions fall some way between these extremes. There's circumstantial evidence, for example, that planting vegetables, trees and flowers between 'lay-lines' can improve their growth, and if you were to ask a neighbour why half your cabbages have done better than the others, he may cite lay-lines as the reason. It could be due to nothing more mysterious than a change in the soil or the underlying rock strata, but it's worth taking a look around you and seeing whether **all** the plants and trees in one part of your land have done better than those in another before jumping to any conclusions.

There's also a widely held belief that mosquitoes are more active and troublesome on or around a full moon and that crickets are noisier during the same period. As there's more likelihood of rain immediately after a full moon and mosquitoes prefer a moist atmosphere, there's probably some truth in the observation. Crickets may take advantage of the extra light provided by a full moon to extend their wing-rubbing activities, which is how they produce their distinctive sound, and subsequent mating habits.

A particularly widespread 'superstition' is the one regarding beginning a job on a Friday. According to rural inhabitants, if you start any new work or project on a Friday, the job will never be finished (foreigners could be forgiven for thinking that this applies to every day of the week when it come to builders!) – therefore, it's better to leave it until the following Monday!

BONFIRES & NOISE

In many *départements* and *communes*, it's illegal to light a bonfire during the summer months because of the danger of starting a fire in the surrounding fields and hedgerows. Generally, this ban is imposed between the months of May and October, but the dates vary with the area.

Mowing your lawn on a Sunday may contravene noise abatement laws in some areas, which, in any case, is a matter of courtesy as most French people spend their Sundays relaxing (and, of course, eating) with family and friends. Similarly, you shouldn't cause any disturbance after 10pm if you wish to avoid upsetting your neighbours, although the commonly held belief that it's illegal to make noise above a certain level after this time is a myth.

Unfortunately, the mere fact of having a neighbour can bring inconvenience – his dog may bark and his cockerel crow at some unearthly hour – but as you've chosen to live in the country, such inconveniences should be considered normal. If the same dog barks all day, however, this can be classed as a nuisance and you may have cause to complain (initially to the neighbour and subsequently to the *mairie*); persistent offenders can be taken to a tribunal and, if found guilty, must pay a fine of €450!

If you believe that you're suffering from 'excessive neighbourhood inconvenience' (*trouble excessif du voisinage*), you should do your utmost to resolve it with your neighbour (perhaps by asking the *maire* to intervene) before involving a lawyer (*avocat*). If you've bought a house next to a farm that has been there for years, you will probably be fighting a losing battle as it will be assumed that you bought it with full knowledge and acceptance of the existing nuisance. If on the other hand, the farm alters or extends its original activities, you have a good chance of convincing a judge to rule in your favour. It's important not to forget, however, that the noise and nuisance problem can work both ways, and you must ensure that your activities don't cause your neighbours similar inconvenience.

CHRISTMAS TIPS

It's usual to give certain 'public servants' an end-of-year tip – especially the *sapeurs-pompiers*, who are held in high regard (see page 247). A few days or weeks before Christmas, you will receive a visit from uniformed representatives of not only the *pompiers*, but also the postal service and sometimes the refuse collectors. (Thankfully, the last arrives in his car rather than his lorry!) Rather than just expecting you to give them money, some come to the door armed with calendars (*almanach*); although these are technically a present and you can give as much or as little as you think appropriate, a sum of €7 to €10 is usually suggested. (It's wise to have a plentiful supply of €10 notes in readiness for these visits.) The calendars may not be the kind you would choose to adorn your home, but they provide all the essential information you're likely to need throughout the coming year – recipes, maps, what months to buy what cheeses and DIY tips – as well as all the latest gossip on newly-canonised Saints!

Anyone who has helped you during the year – whether it's the secretary at the local *mairie* or the garage mechanic who fixed a minor problem with your car free of charge – will be pleased to receive a small gift of appreciation at Christmas and your kind thoughts will undoubtedly reap dividends during the following year.

CRIME

Statistically, France has a similar crime rate to the rest of Europe, but in rural areas, crime is generally low and limited to minor theft. Even in small towns, the many street celebrations beloved of the French invariably pass off without mishap and often without sight or sound of a single policeman. Brushing shoulder-to-shoulder in Bastille Day crowds, you're more likely to be greeted by a smile than a drunken leer and you could hold your wallet out in invitation and know it wouldn't be given a second glance. Binge drinking, which seems to cause the politicians so much heartache in the UK, is rare in France – tables on the pavement and outside bars are full to overflowing with youths and beer bottles, but you rarely encounter aggressive drunks.

In some areas of France, the situation is different – especially along the Mediterranean coast, where drug trafficking and other social ills can lead to crime even in relatively remote parts. Elsewhere, rural inhabitants are content to leave their doors unlocked and suffer no theft or burglary as a result. Nevertheless, it's unwise to have the same careless attitude if you go away for an extended period or you use your property only for occasional holidays, in which case you must take all reasonable steps to secure your home. Otherwise, if you're burgled, your insurance company won't reimburse you. If you're unfortunate enough to suffer a break-in, you should report it in person at the nearest police station, where you must complete a form (*déclaration de vol/plainte*), which must be done within 24 hours if you plan to make a claim on your insurance.

Police

When you're new to France, the different types of police can be confusing. There are four main forces. The *police nationale* are most commonly seen in towns and deal with all crime occurring in the area under the jurisdiction of the town's police station (*commissariat de police*). The *gendarmerie nationale* is part of the army and deals with serious crime on a nationwide scale. *Gendarmes* are recognisable by the gold buttons on their blue uniforms and traditional cap (*képi*). Members of the *Compagnie Républicaine de la Sécurité* (CRS) are often referred to as riot police, as they're responsible for crowd control and public disturbances, although they also have other duties. In rural areas, you're most likely to encounter the *police municipale*, who deal mainly with petty crime, traffic offences and road accidents. Unlike the other forces, which are all armed, the *police municiple* are provided only with rubber bullets – not that they're much less effective at close quarters!

FETES & SAINTS' DAYS

The French are noted for their love of a good time and the opportunity to turn any occasion into an event. Almost every village or *commune* organises an annual *fête* of some description, and there's bound to be one in your area every weekend during the summer months and several on public holidays. In keeping with the average Frenchman's priorities, every possible form of food is saluted, honoured and celebrated. Even the humble omelette and mushroom are 'feted' with street parties, which often necessitate closing the roads leading to and from everywhere with the remotest affiliation to any local produce.

With over 80 of France's 95 *départements* producing wine, it plays an important part in the local economy, and merrymaking begins in January on the Day of St Vincent, the patron saint of wine growers. Throughout the country, brotherhoods dress in their official regalia and parade through the towns. Vines are glorified in April (when they're in bud) and May (as they're flowering), September sees the reading of the banns for the harvest, October includes thanks for the harvest and November sees the arrival of the '*vin nouveau*'. Needless to say, each occasion involves some form of eating, drinking and celebration. In Burgundy, home of some of the world's premier wines, days (and sometimes people) are lost during the annual tastings and subsequent auctions.

The National Pig Squealing Championships is a unique celebration of overindulgence. On the second Sunday of August, visitors flock to Tric-sur-Baisc in Hautes-Pyrénées to watch contestants line up on stage and imitate specific pig noises in front of a panel of judges. The Black Pudding (*boudin noir*) Championships are held at the same time, and the rules are even simpler: to consume as much *boudin noir* as possible in four minutes (currently, the record stands at 1.4m!).

The custom of the *Feux de la Saint Jean* is upheld in many rural areas as a celebration of summer. A great wooden tower is erected and then burnt; various superstitions are attached to this event, including the belief that whoever can recover a piece of charred wood without burning himself will have good luck in the coming year.

France is proud of its history and heritage and celebrates them annually on the second weekend of September (*le Week-end* or *Les Journées du Patrimoine*). Many events are held to commemorate the country's architecture, countryside, art and culture. All grand public buildings and sites of historical interest offer free entry on this weekend, and exhibitions, demonstrations and guided tours are organised to remind both young and old of their heritage. (The tradition started in 1984, when it was called the *Journée Portes Ouvertes*. Other European countries subsequently joined in, but it's the French who still lead the way: during the September 2005 weekend, an estimated 12 million people visited some 17,000 sites.) An list of events can be found at 💻 www.journeesdupatrimoine.culture.fr.

Looking at your calendar – bought from your friendly *facteur* (see page 240) – you will notice that every day, with the exception of religious holidays, May Day (*Fête du Travail*), Mothers' and Fathers' Days (*Fêtes des Mères et Pères*), Bastille Day (*Fête Nationale*) and Armistice Day (*Armistice 1918*), is devoted to a Saint. To some older rural inhabitants, 'their' Saint's Day is more important than their birthday and it isn't unknown for greetings to be sent on that day while a birthday is ignored!

MARKETS

Nothing is more evocative of French life than the local market. It's a fascinating place that sells everything from *fromage* to *fraises*, *rillette* to *ratatouille*. In most rural markets, it's possible to buy fresh eels skinned before your eyes and cooked on a barbeque, chickens alive and chickens spit-roasted, 20 varieties of olives and almost as many of honey. The market trader's produce is always beautifully presented – radishes are displayed in perfect rows, with the tips of their roots not a centimetre out of line. *Barquettes* of summer fruit form patchwork quilts of mouth-watering colours, and the smells of cooking mix with the inevitable sound of accordion music from the man who sells cheap CDs and DVDs. (Anywhere else, this music would make you cringe with embarrassment, but in a market it seems part of the ambience.)

Stalls are mostly family-run and, during school holidays, even the youngest children are expected to help. It's a hard life for the traders but an even harder one for the unsold poultry that have to be taken home, uncrated, fed and watered, before being captured again the next day in the hope of being sold at the next market venue. If you plan to buy livestock from a market, it's therefore important to check its condition thoroughly (see **Choosing Stock** on page 121).

Most casual visitors to a market make the mistake of arriving too late. The majority of stallholders have begun to pack up by 12.30pm, and by 1.30 the refuse collectors have been, the square is washed down and there's hardly any evidence that a market has taken place. To buy the best produce, you shouldn't arrive any later than 9am, when most stalls will be up and running and produce fresh and plentiful. There are also fewer crowds at this time – mostly locals who use the market as a weekly meeting place as well as a place to shop, rather than tourists who mainly come to look.

Although a market isn't usually the cheapest place to shop, you will have the opportunity to buy fresh local produce rather than food that has been frozen and flown halfway around the world. You can also buy cheeses and meats that you cannot find in even the best stocked supermarkets. If buying organic food is important to you, the market is usually the place to go, although organic food is becoming widely available throughout France and most supermarkets now have an organic section in both their vegetable and grocery departments. (All food sold as organic must come from growers, processors and importers who are registered and approved by organic certification bodies. These bodies appoint inspectors to visit farms and check that no fertilisers or pesticides have been used that aren't approved for organic production, and that the land has been farmed organically for at least two years.)

NEWSPAPERS & HOME DELIVERIES

Most *départements* and large towns have their own free newspapers, usually published weekly (*hebdomadaire*) and distributed via *bar/tabacs* and *maisons de la presse*, or possibly dropped through your letterbox. They're an excellent way of discovering what's on in your locality and usually have a comprehensive classified section where it's possible to find employment, tradesmen, equipment and advertisements for animals, cars, furniture and houses. There may also be a regional or sub-regional edition of a national newspaper for your area. It's possible to have newspapers delivered to your home; in most cases it's simply a matter of buying one and completing a form.

French News (SARL Brussac, 225 route d'Angoulème, BP4042, 24004 Périgueux Cedex, ☎ 05 53 06 84 40, 💻 www.french-news.com) is a monthly paper written in English and printed in France, which includes a round-up of news from most of the regions and also contains a comprehensive classified section. It's obtainable from most newsagents and on subscription. *The Connexion* (BP25, 06480 La Colle sur Loup, ☎ 04 93 32 16 59, 💻 www.connexionfrance.com) is another locally-published English-language newspaper widely distributed in France or available on subscription.

Other items that can be delivered to your door include bread from your local bakery. (You may be lucky and be in the catchment area of two or more village *boulangeries*, allowing you the luxury of choosing your supplier.) Mobile butchers', fishmongers' and general stores often make weekly trips to local villages, as do suppliers of frozen foods. They're unlikely, however, to call on you unless asked. It isn't unknown for shoe and even clothes salesmen to turn up unannounced at your door; although there never appears to be any pressure to buy, once you've done so don't be surprised if your home becomes a regular calling point every two or three months!

Many of the major supermarkets employ people to deliver handouts and brochures announcing their weekly promotions, and the post office is paid to deliver publicity from other sources. There's strong objection in some areas to the ever-increasing amount of 'junk mail' and it's now possible to obtain stickers to affix to your letterbox stating that you don't wish to receive unsolicited printed matter. Alternatively, you can write your own '*pas de publicité*' sign in the hope that the relevant deliverers will take heed.

POSTAL SERVICES

The French Post Office (La Poste) is a state-owned company, but its monopoly on the handling of letters is due to end in 2006. In addition to the usual postal services, you can make domestic and international cash transfers, and pay utility bills at post offices, as well as using their internet facilities (including free and permanent email addresses) and banking and mortgage services. Larger post offices usually have a photocopy machine and other facilities, but don't expect such luxuries in your local office. Over 60 per cent of La Poste's 17,000 offices are in towns and villages with fewer than 2,000 inhabitants, but they don't always open all day or even every day. It's becoming increasingly common for the post office in one village to be open from, say, 9 until 11.30am and then for the counter staff (usually consisting of one person) to move to the office in the next village for afternoon trading between 2 and 4.30pm!

Post boxes in each village and hamlet are emptied daily from Mondays to Fridays, but you may have to make a trip to the local town to post a letter on a Saturday, although in most areas it's possible to hand post to the *facteur* when he delivers to your house and even buy stamps from him. (This service is provided in rural *communes* mainly to assist the elderly, who often have no transport and would otherwise find it difficult to post letters.)

Few if any rural houses have letterboxes in the door, and most have a box at the end of the drive, by the gatepost or attached to a garden wall. Although it's lockable, the postman has a master key and therefore can deliver even bulky parcels without disturbing you – provided your box is the official size and shape.

RECYCLING

The French are quite keen on recycling, and most villages have at least one collection point where you can leave things to be recycled. Normally, there are three bins: one for bottles and glass; one for plastics, tins and cardboard; and one for newspapers, brochures and catalogues. In some villages, it's also possible to leave clothes for the French Red Cross (Croix Rouge Française). You may be able to leave your recyclable waste in colour-coded bags, baskets or boxes for collection by refuse collectors (*éboueurs*).

Most rural areas are well equipped with rubbish dumps (*déchetterie*). They aren't open every day, but opening times are usually listed in local newspapers and village news bulletins, and on a sign at the tip itself. It's possible to dispose of most things, but check with the person in charge which skip (*benne*) is for which kind of waste, as each one is for certain materials only, such as metals, wood, garden refuse, cardboard and non-recyclable waste.

SURVIVAL TIP

Old engine oil and car batteries can be discarded, but they must be deposited in the receptacles provided.

SAPEURS-POMPIERS

In France, the fire brigade (*sapeurs-pompiers*) deals with much more than fires and is highly respected. Firemen are trained to deal with many emergencies and are often first on the scene of accidents, equipped to deal with life-threatening injuries as well as heart attacks and similar crises. In rural areas, they're in great demand at the height of summer, when the tinder-dry conditions encourage field and woodland fires. Known by the French as 'the soldiers of fire' (*les soldats du feu*), they use spotter planes and volunteer patrols during the most dangerous months.

There are almost a quarter of a million firemen in France, over three-quarters of whom are volunteer part-timers, paid only when they respond to a call. Paid firemen and volunteers are often seen in uniform at village celebrations, such as those held on 14th July and at the annual Armistice Day service, where they're inspected by local dignitaries and take part in a parade alongside children from the local school.

AGRICULTURAL SHOW
1ST PRIZE

APPENDICES

Appendix A: Useful Addresses

Embassies & Consulates

Australia: 4 rue Jean Rey, 75015 Paris (☎ 01 40 59 33 00).

Canada: 35 avenue Montaigne, 75008 Paris (☎ 01 44 43 29 00).

Ireland: 41 rue Rude, 75016 Paris (☎ 01 44 17 67 00).

New Zealand: 7ter rue Léonard de Vinci, 75016 Paris (☎ 01 45 01 43 43).

United Kingdom: 35 rue Faubourg St Honoré, 75008 Paris (see below) and 18bis rue Anjou, 75008 Paris (☎ 01 44 51 31 02).

United States of America: 2 rue St Florentin, 75001 Paris (☎ 01 43 12 22 22) and 2 avenue Gabriel, 75001 Paris (☎ 08 10 26 46 26).

British Consulates-General

Bordeaux: 353 boulevard du Président Wilson, BP 91, 33073 Bordeaux (☎ 05 57 22 21 10). Covers departments 9, 12, 16, 17, 19, 23, 24, 31, 32, 33, 40, 46, 47, 64, 65, 79, 81, 82, 86, 87.

Lille: 11 square Dutilleul, 59800 Lille (☎ 03 20 12 82 72). Covers departments 2, 8, 59, 62, 80.

Lyon: 24 rue Childebert, 69288 Lyon Cedex 1 (☎ 04 72 77 81 70). Covers departments 1, 3, 7, 15, 21, 25, 26, 38, 39, 42, 43, 63, 69, 70, 71, 73, 74,90.

Marseille: 24 avenue du Prado, 13006 Marseille (☎ 04 91 15 72 10). Covers departments 4, 5, 6, 11, 13, 30, 34, 48, 66, 83, 84 (also the island of Corsica).

Paris: 35 rue du Faubourg Saint Honoré, 75008 Paris (☎ 01 44 51 31 02). Covers departments 10, 14, 18, 22, 27, 28, 29, 35, 36, 37, 41, 44, 45, 49, 50, 51, 52, 53, 54, 55, 56, 57, 58, 60, 67, 72, 75, 77, 78, 88, 91, 92, 93, 94, 95 and the overseas territories and departments.

Miscellaneous

British Association of Removers (BAR) Overseas, 3 Churchill Court, 58 Station Road, North Harrow, London HA2 7SA, UK (☎ 020-8861 3331).

Centre des Impôts de Non-Résidents, 9 rue d'Uzès, 75094 Paris Cedex 02 (☎ 01 44 76 18 00).

Chambre des Notaires, 1 boulevard de Sébastopol, 75005 Paris (☎ 01 44 82 24 00).

Compagnie Nationale des Experts Immobiliers, 18 rue Volney, 75002 Paris 💻 www.expert-cnei.com).

Department for Environment, Food & Rural Affairs (DEFRA), 1A Page Street, London SW1P 4PQ, UK (☎ 020-7904 6000, 💻 www.defra.gov.uk).

Department of Work and Pensions, Overseas Branch, Room TC001, Longbenton, Newcastle-upon-Tyne, NE98 1YX (☎ 0191-218 7547).

Electricité de France/Gaz de France, 5 rue Mander, 75002 Paris (☎ 01 42 33 64 68).

Fédération Française de l'UPRA et Livres Généalogiques, 16 rue Claude Bernard, 75231 Paris Cedex 05 (☎ 01 44 08 17 46).

Fédération Nationale de l'Immobilier (FNAIM), 129 rue du Faubourg St Honoré, 75008 Paris 💻 www.fnaim.fr).

Fédération Nationale des Gites de France, 59 rue St Lazare, Paris 75439 (☎ 01 49 70 75 75, 💻 www.gites-de-France.fr).

Fédération Nationale des Sociétés d'Aménagement Foncier et d'Etablissement Rural (FNSAFER), 3 rue de Turin, 75008 Paris (☎ 01 44 69 86 00, 💻 www.safer-fr.com).

French Chamber of Commerce, 21 Dartmouth Street, London SW1H 9BP, UK (☎ 020-7304 4040, 💻 www.ccfgb.co.uk).

Groupement pour la Promotion dur Tir Cynégétique et Sportif, Ker Maria, 35450 Val d'Ize (☎ 02 99 49 84 61).

Institut de Botanique, 163 rue Auguste Broussonnet, 34000 Montpellier (☎ 04 99 23 21 80).

International Council on Monuments and Sites (ICOMOS), 49–51 rue de la Fédération, 75015 Paris (☎ 01 45 67 67 70)

Société Centrale Canine, 115 avenue Jean Jaurès, 93535 Aubervilliers Cedex (☎ 01 49 37 54 00, 💻 www.scc.asso.fr).

Société Nationale d'Horticulture de France, 84 rue de Grenelle, 75007 Paris (☎01 44 39 78 78, 💻 www.snhf.org).

Union Nationale des Fédérations Départementales de Chasseurs, 48 rue d'Alésia, 75014 Paris (☎ 01 43 27 85 76).

Veterinary Medicines Directorate, Woodham Lane, New Haw, Addlestone, Surrey KT15 3LS, UK (☎ 01932-336911, 💻 www.vmd.gov.uk).

APPENDIX B: FURTHER READING

The books and magazines mentioned in this section are only a very small part of what is available. Some relate directly to living in rural France, while others are of general interest to those hoping to get the best from their French rural property.

Books

Note that some titles may now be out of print but could still be obtainable through libraries or the internet. Second-hand book shops often include sections of value to the smallholder and self-sufficiency enthusiast. The publication title is followed by the author's name and the publisher's name (in brackets). Titles in italics indicate books in French. Other books about living and working in France published by Survival Books are listed (and can be ordered) on the pages at the end of this book.

Poultry & Livestock

The Agricultural Notebook, Ed. R.J. Halley (Butterworth Scientific).

Bantams: A Guide to Keeping, Breeding & Showing, J.C. Jeremy Hobson (Crowood).

The Bee Craftsman, H.J. Wadey (Bee Craft).

The Complete Book of Self-Sufficiency, John Seymour (Faber).

Domestic & Ornamental Fowl, Valerie Porter (Pelham).

Goat Husbandry, David Mackenzie (Faber & Faber).

Hens in the Garden, Eggs in the Kitchen, Charlotte Popescu (Cavalier Paperbacks).

Home Poultry Keeping, Dr Geoffrey Eley (A & C Black).

How Goes the Plough, Philip Rant (Hobson-Hall Publications).

Les Moutons, Helmut Kuhnemann (Ulmar).

Les Poules, Beate et Leopold Peitz (Ulmar).

Practical Poultry Keeping, David Bland (Crowood).

Flower & Vegetable Gardening

Calendrier Lunaire de l'Agriculteur, P. Cadorin (Editions de Vecchi).

Créer un Petit Potager (Editions Rustica).

Cultiver les Petits Fruits (Editions Rustica).

The Fruit Expert, Dr D.G. Hessayon (Transworld).

Glossary of Gardening and Horticultural Terms: French-English & English- French, Alan S. Lindsey (Hadley Pager).

Les Légumes, Helmut Kuhnemann (Ulmar).

The No-Work Garden, Bob Flowerdew (Kyle Cathie).

The Vegetable & Herb Expert, Dr D.G. Hessayon (Transworld).

Year in Your Garden, Geoff Hamilton (Headline).

Trees & Shrubs

Arbres et Arbustes du Soleil (Editions Rustica).

La Culture des Agrumes, A Colombo (Editions de Vecchi). Deals with growing citrus fruits.

Encylopédie des Arbres de France et d'Europe, B. Ticli (Editions de Vecchi).

Wildlife & Natural History

Bons ou Mauvais Champignons?, Ewald Gerhardt (Delachaux et Niestlé). Distinguishing edible from inedible mushrooms.

Butterflies and Moths, Ed. Michael Chinery (Harper Collins).

Butterflies and Moths in Britain and Europe, David Carter (Pan).

The Concise Guide to Mushrooms & Toadstools, Gordon Dickson (New Holland).

Oiseaux de France et d'Europe, Rob Hume, (Larousse).

La Taupe, Guy Degrand (Editions de Vecchi). All you ever need to know about moles!

Where to Watch Birds in Britain and Europe, John Gooders (Helm).

Wildflowers of Britain and Europe, Thomas Schauer (Collins).

Wildlife of Britain and Europe, Ed. Michael Chinery (Kingfisher Publications).

Country Sports & Pursuits

L'Almanach du Chasseur (Communication-Presse-Edition).

Angling in France, Philip Pembroke (Phil Pembroke).

La Chasse, Jean-Pierre Villenave (Larousse).

Classic Walks in France, Rob Hunter & David Wickers (Oxford Illustrated Press).

Cycling in France, Susi Madron (George Philip).

Encyclopédie Pratique de la Chasse, Yves le Floc'h, Michel Durchon, Yves Ferrand (Hachette).

France by Bike, Karen & Terry Whitehill (Cordee).

Hounds of France, George Johnston (Spur).

Walking in France, Rob Hunter (Oxford Illustrated Press).

Walking Through France, Robin Neillands (Collins).

Miscellaneous

Atlas of Wine, Alice King (Hamlyn). Contains French recipes, regional maps and other useful information.

Factfinder, Ed. David Crystal (Penguin). Not specifically related to France, but some items of information are of general interest to the newcomer to France. The conversion tables from imperial to metric and acres to hectares are particularly useful.

French Vocabulary Handbook, Kate Dobson (Berlitz).

The Good Cellar Guide: How to Buy & Store Wine for Pleasure & Profit, John Thorn (Sidgwick & Jackson).

Life in a Postcard, Rosemary Bailey (Bantam).

Maison Therapy, Alastair Simpson (New Horizon).

The River Cottage Cookbook, Hugh Fearnley-Whittingstall (Harper Collins). Despite the title, this also contains a great deal on animal husbandry, gardening, fishing and shooting. Highly recommended.

Under the Sun, Caroline Conran (Pavilion). Essentially a book on French cooking, but it includes a personal account of a journey through France and explains much about rural French living: attitudes towards food, the history of certain ingredients, what to grow, the French names of most ingredients and everything else necessary to decipher restaurant menus. The photographs are stunning and evocative.

Magazines

The French are very keen on reading about their hobbies and interests, which is why the shelves of book shops and *bar/tabacs* are groaning with magazine titles. Just a few have been included in this list. All the UK magazines are available in France on subscription.

Poultry & Livestock

Country Smallholding, Exeter Airport Business Park, Clyst Honiton, Exeter EX5 2UL, UK (☎ 01392-888588). Monthly magazine. Contains articles on vegetable growing.

Fancy Fowl, The Publishing House, Station Road, Framlingham, Suffolk IP 9EE, UK (☎ 01728-622030). Monthly magazine covering all aspects of poultry keeping.

Farmer's Weekly, Quadrant House, The Quadrant, Sutton, Surrey SM2 5AS, UK (☎ 020-8652 4911). Weekly magazine mainly for British commercial farmers but occasionally including articles by 'amateurs' farming in France.

Smallholder, Hook House, Hook Road, Wimblington, March, Cambridgeshire PE15 0QL, UK (☎ 01354-741538). Monthly magazine. Contains articles on vegetable gardening, land management, machinery and organic farming.

Flower & Vegetable Gardening

Rustica l'Hebdo Jardin, 15–27 rue Moussorgski, 75895 Paris Cedex (☎ 01 53 26 33 00).

Living in France

Everything France, Brooklands Magazines Ltd, Medway House, Lower Road, Forest Row, East Sussex RH18 5HE, UK (☎ 01342-828700). Bi-monthly lifestyle magazine.

France Magazine, Archant House, Oriel Road, Cheltenham, Gloucestershire GL50 1BB, UK (☎ 01242-216050). Monthly lifestyle magazine.

French News, SARL Brussac, 225 route d'Angouleme, BP4042, 24004 Périgueux Cedex (☎ 05 53 06 84 40). Monthly newspaper covering all aspects of living in France.

French Property News, 6 Burgess Mews, London SW19 1UF, UK (☎ 020-8543 3113). Monthly magazine, mainly dealing with property buying but also covering French lifestyle.

Living France, Archant House, Oriel Road, Cheltenham, Gloucestershire GL50 1BB, UK (☎ 01242-216050). Monthly lifestyle/property magazine.

Normandie & South of England Magazine, 330 rue Valvire, BP414, 50004 Saint Lô (☎ 02 33 77 32 70). Published eight times a year, mainly written in French but with some English articles and translations.

Country Sports & Pursuits

Country Illustrated, Kent House, 14–17 Market Place, London W1W 8AJ, UK (☎ 020-7255 3330). Monthly magazine periodically including articles on hunting and shooting in France.

Countryman's Weekly, Yelverton, Devon, PL20 7PE, UK (☎ 01822-855372). Includes a regular column comparing rural and sporting life on either side of the Channel.

Le Chasseur de Petit Gibier, rue de Senuc, 08250 Vaux-les-Mourons (☎03 24 30 49 07). Quarterly magazine covering shotgun shooting, dog breeds, trapping, and wildlife habitat and management.

La Jaupitre, rue de la Vieille Forge, 35160 Monterfil (☎ 02 99 07 47 02). Covers all traditional rural sports and games.

Le Magazine du Piégeur, rue de Senuc, 08250 Vaux-les-Mourons (☎ 03 24 30 49 07). Quarterly magazine dealing mainly with the trapping of pests and providing information deriving from scientific research. Also has sections on dog breeds and management.

L'Officiel des Chiens de Chasse, 48 rue de Provence, 75009 Paris (☎ 01 45 26 75 01). Bi-monthly magazine for owners of sporting breeds of dog.

Vélo Magazine, 22 rue Boulanger, 75472 Paris Cedex 10 (☎ 01 55 56 70 54). Cycling magazine that specialises in road racing.

Appendix C: Useful Websites

Below is a list of general websites that might be of interest and aren't mentioned elsewhere in this book. Some of the expatriate websites are particularly useful when choosing a region to live in.

General Information

All About France (💻 www.all-about-france.com). General information about France.

All 4 France (💻 www.all4france.com). Information about living, working and buying property in France.

British Expatriates (💻 www.britishexpat.com). A website to keep British expatriates in touch.

Expat Exchange (💻 www.expatexchange.com). Supposedly the largest online community for English-speaking expatriates, providing a series of articles on relocation and also a question and answer facility through its expatriate network.

Family Life Abroad (💻 www.familylifeabroad.com). Much general information dealing with family life in other countries.

Francophiles (💻 www.francophiles.co.uk). Property in most areas.

French Discoveries (💻 www.frenchdiscoveries.net). Property in the north-west, including Brittany, Normandy, Poitou-Charentes and the Loire Valley.

French Embassy in the UK (💻 www.francealacarte.org.uk).

Pratique (💻 www.pratique.fr). General information about life in France.

Sinclair Overseas Property Network (💻 www.sinclair-frenchprops.com). Property in north-west, west and south-west France.

Country Sports & Pursuits

Association des Randonneurs de la Côte d'Opale (www.opalenews.com/fisches_assos). Association dealing with the requirements of hikers, ramblers and walkers.

Other sites dealing specifically with walking include:

- **www.balades-france.fr** – online magazine in French;
- **www.franceonfoot.com/links.html** – contains lots of useful links;
- **http://guidesnature.free.fr** – lists many nature walks throughout the country;
- **www.rando.net** – French rambling website;
- **www.randopale.com** – local walking clubs.

Fédération Française de Ball-trap et de Tir à Balle (www.fftb.asso.fr).

Fédération Gallèse des Jeux et Sports (www.jeuxbretons.org). Website devoted to the promotion of rural and traditional games and sports.

Animals & Poultry

Smallholder Bookshop (www.smallholderbooks.co.uk). Supplies English books on beekeeping, cows, DIY, goats, horses, organic produce, pigs, poultry, self-reliance and smallholdings. Also sells videos on bees, general farming, goats, horses, poultry, rabbits and sheep.

Other useful sites include:

- **www.agrisalon.com** – French/English website containing all kinds of information relating to livestock.

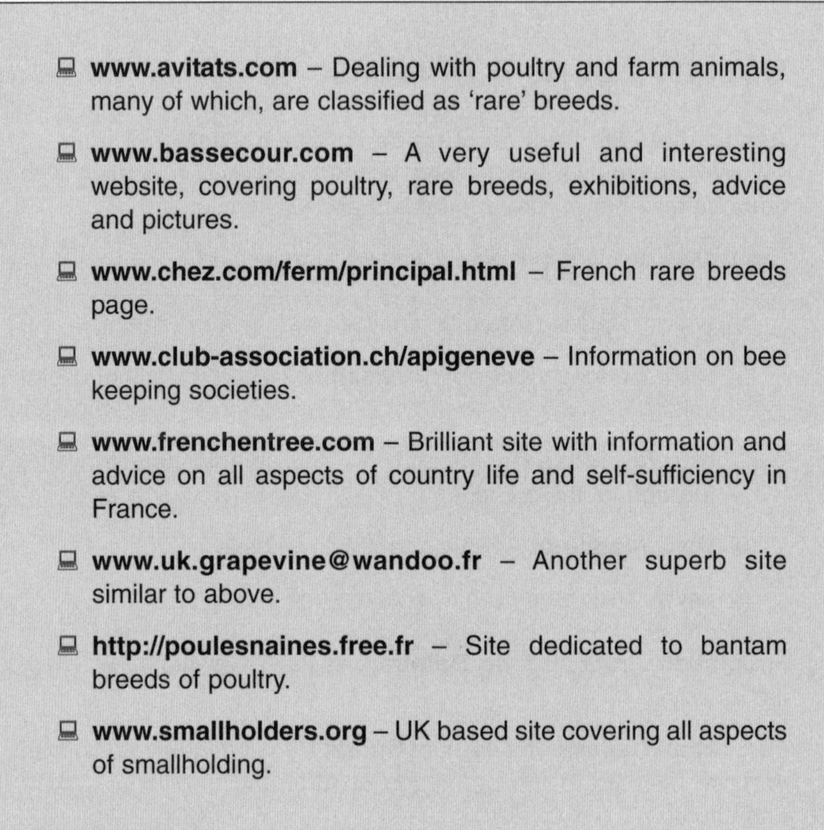

- **www.avitats.com** – Dealing with poultry and farm animals, many of which, are classified as 'rare' breeds.
- **www.bassecour.com** – A very useful and interesting website, covering poultry, rare breeds, exhibitions, advice and pictures.
- **www.chez.com/ferm/principal.html** – French rare breeds page.
- **www.club-association.ch/apigeneve** – Information on bee keeping societies.
- **www.frenchentree.com** – Brilliant site with information and advice on all aspects of country life and self-sufficiency in France.
- **www.uk.grapevine@wandoo.fr** – Another superb site similar to above.
- **http://poulesnaines.free.fr** – Site dedicated to bantam breeds of poultry.
- **www.smallholders.org** – UK based site covering all aspects of smallholding.

Gardening

Jardiland (www.jardiland.fr). A commercial company with garden centres throughout France. Known for supplying good quality plants, they also produce an excellent annual catalogue containing much useful information for the gardener.

Machinery & Equipment

Agriscape (http://fr.agriscape.com/societes/machinerie). Provides access to 30 sites offering various agricultural machinery and equipment.

BIMA (🖳 www.guideweb.agriculture.gouv.fr). The site of the magazine of the French Ministry of Agriculture and Fisheries, which acts as a portal to all kinds of information, including the sites of agricultural machinery and equipment manufacturers.

Jaulent Industrie (🖳 www.jaulent.com – available in 'English'). Manufacturer of agricultural equipment.

Second-hand machinery and equipment can be found on the following sites:

- 🖳 **www.agriaffaires.com**
- 🖳 **www.equipmentlocator.com/france/ag-fp**
- 🖳 **www.maison-koenig.com/ma.html**
- 🖳 **www.materiel-agricole.com** ('English' option)

Rural Living & Down-sizing

Useful sites include:

- 🖳 **www.acountrylife.com**
- 🖳 **www.downthelane.net**
- 🖳 **www.lifeshift.co.uk**
- 🖳 **www.proprietesrurales.com**
- 🖳 **www.safer.fr** – Contains essential information regarding the purchase of farming properties.
- 🖳 **www.yarnertrust.co.uk**

Appendix D: Weights & Measures

France uses the metric system of measurement. Those who are more familiar with the imperial system will find the tables on the following pages useful. Some comparisons are approximate, but are close enough for most everyday uses. In addition to the variety of measurement systems used, clothes sizes often vary considerably with the manufacturer (as we all know only too well). Try all clothes on before buying and don't be afraid to return something if, when you try it on at home, you decide it doesn't fit.

Women's Clothes

Continental	34	36	38	40	42	44	46	48	50	52
UK	8	10	12	14	16	18	20	22	24	26
US	6	8	10	12	14	16	18	20	22	24

Pullovers	Women's						Men's					
Continental	40	42	44	46	48	50	44	46	48	50	52	54
UK	34	36	38	40	42	44	34	36	38	40	42	44
US	34	36	38	40	42	44	sm	med		lar	xl	

Men's Shirts

Continental	36	37	38	39	40	41	42	43	44	46
UK/US	14	14	15	15	16	16	17	17	18	-

Men's Underwear

Continental	5	6	7	8	9	10
UK	34	36	38	40	42	44
US	sm	med		lar	xl	

Note: sm = small, med = medium, lar = large, xl = extra large

Children's Clothes

Continental	92	104	116	128	140	152
UK	16/18	20/22	24/26	28/30	32/34	36/38
US	2	4	6	8	10	12

Children's Shoes

Continental	18	19	20	21	22	23	24	25	26	27	28	29	30	31	32
UK/US	2	3	4	4	5	6	7	7	8	9	10	11	11	12	13

Continental	33	34	35	36	37	38
UK/US	1	2	2	3	4	5

Shoes (Women's and Men's)

Continental	35	36	37	37	38	39	40	41	42	42	43	44
UK	2	3	3	4	4	5	6	7	7	8	9	9
US	4	5	5	6	6	7	8	9	9	10	10	11

Weight

Imperial	**Metric**	**Metric**	**Imperial**
1oz	28.35g	1g	0.035oz
1lb*	454g	100g	3.5oz
1cwt	50.8kg	250g	9oz
1 ton	1,016kg	500g	18oz
2,205lb	1 tonne	1kg	2.2lb

Length

Imperial	**Metric**	**Metric**	**Imperial**
1in	2.54cm	1cm	0.39in
1ft	30.48cm	1m	3ft 3.25in
1yd	91.44cm	1km	0.62mi
1mi	1.6km	8km	5mi

Capacity

Imperial	**Metric**	**Metric**	**Imperial**
1 UK pint	0.57 litre	1 litre	1.75 UK pints
1 US pint	0.47 litre	1 litre	2.13 US pints
1 UK gallon	4.54 litres	1 litre	0.22 UK gallon
1 US gallon	3.78 litres	1 litre	0.26 US gallon

Note: An American 'cup' = around 250ml or 0.25 litre.

Area & Volume

Imperial	Metric	Metric	Imperial
1 sq. in	0.45 sq. cm	1 sq. cm	0.15 sq. in
1 sq. ft	0.09 sq. m	1 sq. m	10.76 sq. ft
1 sq. yd	0.84 sq. m	1 sq. m	1.2 sq. yds
1 acre	0.4 hectares	1 hectare	2.47 acres
1 sq. mile	2.56 sq. km	1 sq. km	0.39 sq. mile

Note: An *are* is one-hundredth of a hectare or $100m^2$.
A *stère* is a cubic metre of stacked wood, the net volume being between 0.55 and $0.8m^3$ depending on the size and length of the logs.

Temperature

°Celsius	°Fahrenheit	
0	32	(freezing point of water)
5	41	
10	50	
15	59	
20	68	
25	77	
30	86	
35	95	
40	104	
50	122	

Notes: The boiling point of water is 100°C / 212°F.

Normal body temperature (if you're alive and well) is 37°C / 98.4°F.

Temperature Conversion

Celsius to Fahrenheit: multiply by 9, divide by 5 and add 32. (For a quick and approximate conversion, double the Celsius temperature and add 30.)

Fahrenheit to Celsius: subtract 32, multiply by 5 and divide by 9. (For a quick and approximate conversion, subtract 30 from the Fahrenheit temperature and divide by 2.)

Oven Temperatures

Gas	Electric	
	°F	°C
-	225–250	110–120
1	275	140
2	300	150
3	325	160
4	350	180
5	375	190
6	400	200
7	425	220
8	450	230
9	475	240

Air Pressure

PSI	Bar
10	0.5
20	1.4
30	2
40	2.8

APPENDIX E: MAP

The map opposite shows the 22 regions and 96 departments of France (excluding overseas territories), which are listed below. Departments 91 to 95 come under the Ile-de-France region, which also includes Ville de Paris (75), Seine-et-Marne (77) and Yvelines (78), shown in detail opposite. The island of Corsica consists of two departments, 2A and 2B. The maps on the following pages show major airports and ports with cross-Channel ferry services, high-speed train (*TGV*) routes, and motorways and other major roads.

01 Ain
02 Aisne
2A Corse-du-Sud
2B Haute Corse
03 Allier
04 Alpes-de-Hte-Provence
05 Hautes-Alpes
06 Alpes-Maritimes
07 Ardèche
08 Ardennes
09 Ariège
10 Aube
11 Aude
12 Aveyron
13 Bouches-du-Rhône
14 Calvados
15 Cantal
16 Charente
17 Charente-Maritime
18 Cher
19 Corrèze
21 Côte-d'Or
22 Côte-d'Armor
23 Creuse
24 Dordogne
25 Doubs
26 Drôme
27 Eure
28 Eure-et-Loir
29 Finistère
30 Gard
31 Haute-Garonne
32 Gers
33 Gironde
34 Hérault
35 Ille-et-Vilaine
36 Indre
37 Indre-et-Loire
38 Isère
39 Jura
40 Landes
41 Loir-et-Cher
42 Loire
43 Haute-Loire
44 Loire-Atlantique
45 Loiret
46 Lot
47 Lot-et-Garonne
48 Lozère
49 Maine-et-Loire
50 Manche
51 Marne
52 Haute-Marne
53 Mayenne
54 Meurthe-et-Moselle
55 Meuse
56 Morbihan
57 Moselle
58 Nièvre
59 Nord
60 Oise
61 Orne
62 Pas-de-Calais
63 Puy-de-Dôme
64 Pyrénées-Atlantiques
65 Hautes-Pyrénées
66 Pyrénées-Orientales
67 Bas-Rhin
68 Haut-Rhin
69 Rhône
70 Haute-Saône
71 Saône-et-Loire
72 Sarthe
73 Savoie
74 Haute-Savoie
75 Paris
76 Seine-Maritime
77 Seine-et-Marne
78 Yvelines
79 Deux-Sèvres
80 Somme
81 Tarn
82 Tarn-et-Garonne
83 Var
84 Vaucluse
85 Vendée
86 Vienne
87 Haute-Vienne
88 Vosges
89 Yonne
90 Territoire de Belfort
91 Essonne
92 Hauts-de-Seine
93 Seine-Saint-Denis
94 Val-de-Marne
95 Val-d'Oise

REGIONS & DEPARTMENTS

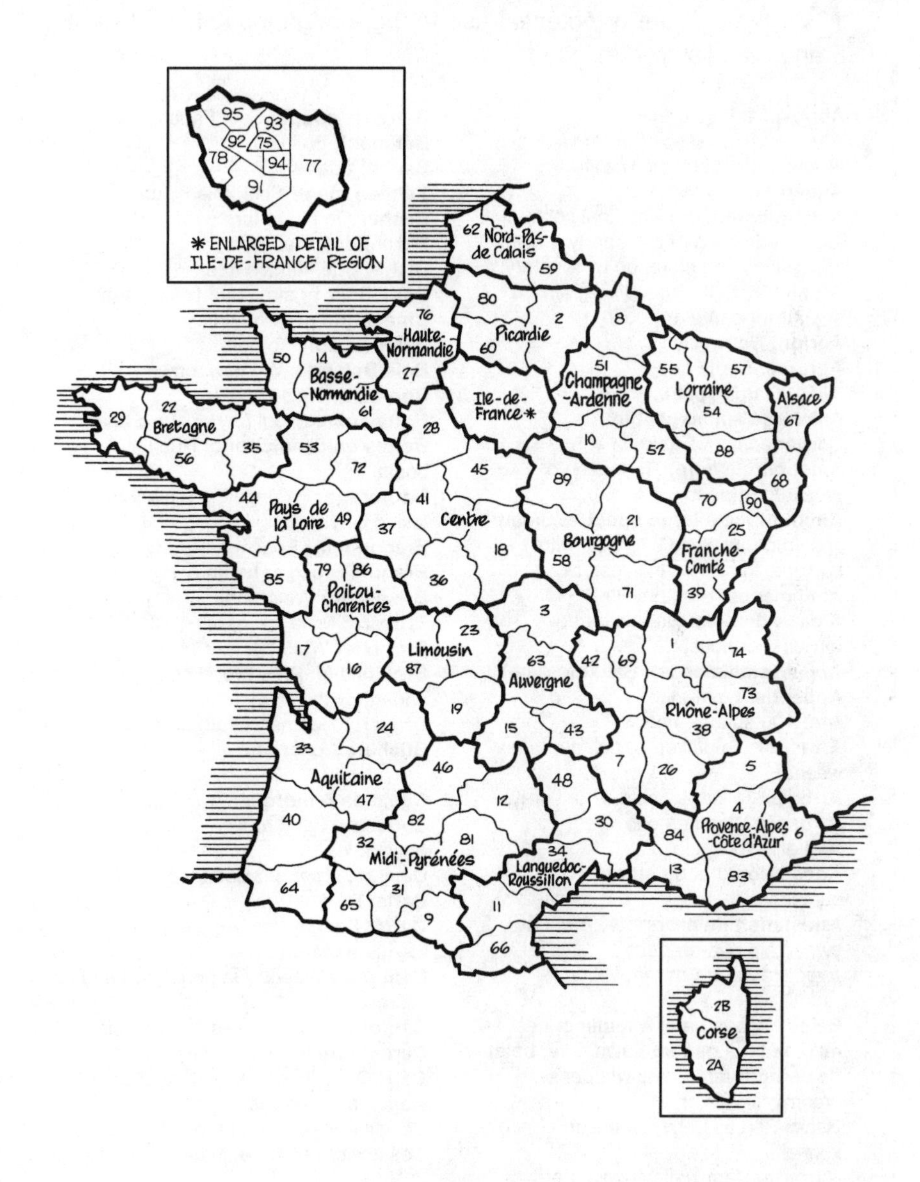

Appendix F: Glossary

A few names, terms and phrases not previously used or explained in the text but of potential use to the foreign inhabitant of rural France are listed here.

Abat-vent: Windbreak
Aire de vision de la faune: High seat or tower for observing wildlife.
Aquéreur: Buyer.
Acte authentique: The final contract for the purchase of a property drawn up, verified and stamped by a notary.
Agrainoir: Self-dispensing grain hopper for game or poultry.
Agrion: Damselfly.
Agrume: Citrus fruit.
Allée: Garden path.
Aménagé/aménageable: Converted/convertible.
Ameublir (la terre)**:** To loosen or break up (ground).
Antibiotique à large spectre: Broad-spectrum antibiotic – to deal with bacterial infections in livestock.
Antilimaces: Slug pellets.
À pans de bois: Half-timbered (building or house).
Appât (antilimaces): Bait (for slugs).
Appentis: Lean-to.
Are: 100 square metres.
Arracher: To pull up or pull out (e.g. weeds).
Arroser: To water, sprinkle or spray.
Arrosoir: Watering can.
Atelier: Workshop.
Attestation d'acquisition: Proof of purchase.
Attestation de propriété: Proof of ownership of a property.
Avec travaux: For renovation.

Balai: Broom; **balai à feuilles:** Leaf rake; **balai à gazon:** Lawn rake; **balai de cantonnier:** Roadsweeper's broom.
Banc: Bed used by hounds in kennels.
Barrage: Dam wall; sluice gate.
Barre de coupe: See 'Faucheuse'.
Bâtiment: Building.
Bêche: Spade.
Bêche tarière: Post-hole digger.
Bêcher: To dig or turn over (soil).
Bergerie: Sheep pen.
Biche: Doe, female deer.
Bief: 'Beat' or stretch of fishing river.
Binage (du sol): hoeing.
Biner (le sol): To hoe.
Bois/Boiserie: Wood/woodwork.
Bon état: Good condition.
Botteleuse: Small hay or straw baler.
Bottes en caoutchouc: Rubber boots.
Bouturage: Propagating a plant by taking cuttings.
Braconneur: Poacher.
Brande: Brush or heath.
Brise-vent: Windbreak.
Brocard: Male roe deer.
Brouette: Wheelbarrow.
Broussaille: Brushwood or undergrowth.
Bruyère: Heather; heath or moor.
Bûcher: Woodshed.

Câble de remorque: Tow rope.
Cadastre: Land registry/land registration.
Caisette à semis: Seed tray.
Carie: Dry rot.
Carré: Square (e.g. *un mètre carré* is a square metre).
Canon à effrayer: Gas-operated bird scarer.
Canton: Area occupied by gamebirds.
Centre foncier: Land office.
Cerf: Generic term for red deer or the stag of any species.
Cerisaie: Cherry orchard.
Cession: Transfer of lease.

Chantier: Builder's yard.
Charrançon: Weevil-like insect.
Charrue: Plough.
Chaume: Thatch (e.g. on roof).
Chaumière: Thatched cottage.
Chaux: Lime; **chaux agricole:** Agricultural lime; **chaux éteinte:** Slaked lime; **chaux vive:** Quicklime.
Chemin: Lane or unmade road.
Chevreuil: Roe deer.
Cimier : Group of deer.
Cisaille: Shears; **cisaille à gazon:** grass shears; **cisaille à haie:** hedge shears or clippers; **cisaille de jardin:** Garden shears.
Clôture électrique: Electric fencing.
Colombier: Pigeon house.
Combles: Loft; roof space.
Compromis de vente: Preliminary contract of sale for a property.
Conservateur des hypothèques: District land register.
Constructible: Land available for building.
Corps de bâtiments: A group of buildings.
Corvidés: General name for all members of the crow family.
Couche: Seedbed; **couche de multiplication:** Propagation bed.
Couper à ras du sol: To cut to ground level.
Cour: Yard or courtyard.
Cour de ferme: Farmyard.
Culture maraîchère: vegetable farming or growing.

Daim: Fallow deer.
Débroussailleuse: Brush cutter or strimmer.
Déchets végetaux: Vegetable waste.
Défricher: To clear land for cultivation or to bring land under cultivation.
Délabré: Dilapidated or tumbledown.
Demeure: Any dwelling, but usually a large house with extensive grounds.
Dépendance: Outbuilding.
Déplantoir: Garden trowel.
Dépôt de garantie: The deposit paid when buying or renting a property.
Déraciner: To dig up or uproot (a plant).
Digue: Any form of water barrier such as a dam.
Direction Départementale de l'Equipment (DDE): Departmental surveying, land planning and public works department.
Domaine: Stately home or country estate.
Douve: An open ditch between fields.
Droits de passage: Rights of way.

Ecurie: Stable.
Ecussonnoir: Budding knife.
Egaliser: To level (e.g. soil).
Elagage: Pruning, lopping or thinning (of trees and shrubs).
Elaguer: To prune, lop or thin.
Elevage: Breeding of livestock.
Embouchure: River mouth.
Emiettage: crumbling or breaking up.
Emietter: To crumble or break into pieces.
Enclos: Paddock or enclosure.
Epandeuse: Manure spreader.
Epoque de plantation: Planting season (for flowers, vegetables, shrubs and trees).
Etable: Cowshed.
Etang: Lake or pond.
Etat des lieux: Inventory of the contents and condition of a rented property.
Expert de bâtiment: Surveyor.
Expert géomètre: Land surveyor.

Faire le foin: To make hay.
Fauchage: Mowing of hay; cutting; reaping.
Faucher: To scythe; to mow.
Fauchet: Hay rake or billhook.
Faucheuse: Hay cutter.
Faucille: Sickle or hand scythe.
Faux: Scythe.
Ferme: Farm.
Fermette: Smallholding.
Floralies: Flower show or festival.
FNSAFER: Fédération Nationale des Société d'Aménagement Foncier et

d'Etablissement Rural.
Fosse à toutes eaux: A septic tank that filters all household wastewater before leaching it underground.
Four à pain: Bread oven or bakehouse.
Fourmilière: Ant's nest or anthill.
Fût: Bole (of tree).

Gâté: Rotten (e.g. fruit).
Garde-chasse: Gamekeeper.
Gentilhommière: Small manor house.
Germoir: Seed tray.
Gibier d'eau: General term for water fowl.
Grange: Barn.
Grainetier: Seed merchant.
Greffoir: Grafting knife.
Griffes: Claws (of animal).
Griffer: To rake (soil).
Grillage: Wire netting or mesh.
Grenier: Loft.
Groupe électrogène: Generator.
Gros oeuvre: Shell or structure of a building.

Hache: Axe.
Hâtiveau: Early producing fruit or vegetable.
Hameau: Hamlet.
Haut-siège: Seat accessed by ladder – usually in woodland and used to observe wildlife.
Herse: Harrow.
Hectare: 10,000 square metres or 2.471 acres.
Hormones de bouturage: Hormone rooting powder.
Hoyau: Mattock.
Huissier: An officer of the court who's roughly equivalent to a bailiff and serves writs and court orders and prepares statements of facts which are irrefutable in a court of law.

Insecticide polyvalent: Universal insecticide.
Irriguer: To irrigate.
Inventaire détaillé: Inventory of the contents and condition of a rented property.

Jardin de rapport: Market garden.
Jardinier: Gardener.
Jouissance: Possession or tenure.
Jouissance libre: Vacant possession.
Jumelles: Binoculars.

Labourage: Tilling or ploughing; general term for arable land.
Lentilles d'eau: Duckweed.
Levée: Embankment.
Libellule: Dragonfly.
Limace: Slug.
Locataire: Tenant.
Logis: Manor house.
Lucarne: Dormer window or skylight.
Louchet: Draining spade.
Lycée agricole: Agricultural college.

Maçon: Builder (e.g. bricklayer or stonemason).
Maison de campagne: House in the country.
Maison en carré: House built around a courtyard.
Maison de chasse: Hunting lodge (usually at the edge of a forest).
Maison paysanne: Farmhouse.
Maisonette: Cottage.
Maître: Title used when addressing a *notaire.*
Mandat de recherche: An agreement with an agent to find a property.
Mangeoire: Livestock feeder or manger.
Manutention (de terre): Working (ground).
Maraîcher: Vegetable grower.
Marais: Marsh or swamp.
Marécageux: Boggy or marshy.
Moisson: Harvest.
Monter en graine: To bolt or go to seed.
Motoculteur: Garden cultivator.
Motte (de terre): Clod (of earth).
Moulin: Mill.

Muer: To moult (in the case of birds), shed antlers (deer) or slough skin (reptiles).
Mugissement: Mooing or bellowing (of an animal).
Muguet: Properly the name for the lily-of-the-valley, but also used by rural people to describe a fungal disease affecting the crops of birds such as pigeons.
Mulot: Field mouse.
Mûr: Ripe.
Mûrier sauvage: Blackberry or bramble bush.
Museau: Muzzle or snout (of an animal).
Mutualité Sociale Agricole (MSA): French National Farmers' Union.

Nain: Dwarf type of a species.
Naseau: Nostril (of horse).
Noisette: Hazelnut.
Noisetier: Hazel tree.
Noix: Walnut.

Œil: Bud (of plant or tree).
Oléiculture: Olive growing.
Ortie brûlante: Stinging nettle.
Outillage: General equipment and tools.

Paille: Straw.
Pailler: To mulch.
Palissage: Training plants to climb up a wall or trellis by the use of wires and nails.
Parterre: Flower bed.
Pâture: General term for animal food.
Perce-oreille: Earwig.
Pic à tranche: Mattock.
Piège: Trap or snare.
Pioche: Two-pointed pickaxe.
Piquet: Stake or peg.
Plante frileuse: Plant sensitive to cold and frost.
Plateau: Hay cart.
Plate-bande: flower bed or border.
Préfecture: Administrative offices, usually in the capital town of a *département*.
Prieuré: Priory.
Produits du terroir: Food products from the surrounding area.
Portillon: Gate.
Poteau: Post.
Pulvérisateur: Sprayer.

Race: Breed or type (of domestic animal).
Rage: Rabies.
Rame: Thin stick (used for supporting peas and beans).
Ramener: To pick (fruit, etc.).
Râteau: Rake.
Râtelier: Hayrack (for feeding livestock).
Région: Administrative division, containing two or more *départements*.
Récolte: Harvesting or gathering of crops.
Remembrement des terres: Re-allocation or re-grouping of an area of land.
Remise: Shed or outhouse.
Remorque: Trailer.
Restaurer: To restore a building.
Retenue: Volume of water held back by a dam.
Rodonticide: Rat or mouse poison.
Rondballer: Large round baler.

Sable gras: Loamy sand.
Saignée: Drainage ditch.
Sarclage: Weeding.
Sarcler: To weed.
Sarcloir: Hoe.
Serpette: Pruning knife.
Serre: Greenhouse.
Service du cadastre: Land registry or surveyor's department.
Sentier: Footpath or trail.
Servitudes: Building regulations, rights of way or easements.
Siccateur à foin: Rack for drying small quantities of freshly-cut hay.
Sillonneur: Drill plough.
Sol: Soil or earth; **sol argileux:** Clay soil; **sol crayeux:** Chalky soil; **sol détrempé:** Waterlogged soil; **sol pierreux:** Stony soil; **sol**

sablonneux: Sandy soil; **sol tourbeux:** Peaty soil.
Souche: Stump or root bowl (of a tree).
Souricière: Mousetrap.

Taille-haies: Hedge cutter.
Taxe d'habitation: Property tax based on occupancy, not ownership, of a property.
Taxe foncière: Property tax levied on owners. The tax is split into two amounts: one for the building (*taxe foncière bâtie*) and a smaller one for the land (*taxe foncière non bâtie*).
Terrain: Land.
Terrain à bâtir: Building land (usually seen as 'for sale').
Terrautage: Composting.
Terre émiettée: Garden soil raked down to a fine tilth.
Terreautage: To spread compost over the ground.
Titre de propriété: Title deeds.
Tondeuse: Lawn mower; **tondeuse autoportée :** Sit-on mower; **tondeuse mécanique:** Push mower; **tondeuse sur coussin d'air:** Hover mower.
Tondre le gazon: To mow the lawn.
Tontine: Webbing or sacking protecting roots of tree during transportation.
Tout à l'égout: Mains drainage system.
Tracteur: Tractor.
Tremper: To soak or drench (e.g. root ball of tree before planting).
Trompe de chasse: Hunting horn.
Tronc d'arbre: Tree trunk.
Troupeau: Flock (e.g. sheep).
Tuteur: Plant stake or prop.

Valeur cadastrale: Assessment of a property's value for land tax purposes.
Valeur vénale: Market value.
Vanne: Sluice gate (on river, canal or pond).
Vaporisateur: Sprayer.
Vendange: Grape harvest.
Vendanger: To harvest grapes.
Vermifuge: Wormer.
Verger: Orchard.
Vivace: Perennial or long-living.
Volière: Enclosed pen used for breeding and releasing game birds.
Volis: Windbreak.
VTT (vélo tout terrain): Mountain bike.

INDEX

A

B

C

D

E

F

G

M

N

O

P

R

S

Other Survival Books

The Alien's Guides: *The Alien's Guides to Britain* and *France* will help you to appreciate the peculiarities (in both senses) of the British and French.

The Best Places to Buy a Home in France/Spain: The most comprehensive homebuying guides to France and Spain, containing detailed profiles of the most popular regions for home-buying.

Buying, Selling and Letting Property: The most comprehensive and up-to-date source of information on buying, selling and letting property in the UK.

Earning Money From Your Home: Essential guides to earning income from property in France and Spain, including short- and long-term letting.

Foreigners in France/Spain: Triumphs & Disasters: Real-life experiences of people who have emigrated to France and Spain, recounted in their own words.

Lifelines: Essential guides to life in specific regions of France and Spain. See order form for a list of current titles in the series.

Making a Living: Essential guides to self-employment and starting a business in France and Spain.

Renovating & Maintaining Your French Home: The ultimate guide to renovating and maintaining your dream home in France.

Retiring Abroad: The most comprehensive source of practical information available about retiring to a foreign country.

Shooting Caterpillars in Spain: The compelling story of two innocents abroad in the depths of Andalusia in the late '80s; their experiences will have you in tears of laughter as they lurch from one disaster to another.

Surprised by France: Even after living there for ten years, Donald Carroll finds plenty of surprises in the Hexagon.

Broaden your horizons with Survival Books!

Order your copies today by phone, fax, post or email from: Survival Books, PO Box 3780, YEOVIL, BA21 5WX, United Kingdom (☎/🖷 +44 (0)1935-700060, ✉ sales@survivalbooks.net, 💻 www.survivalbooks.net).

Qty.	Title	Price (incl. p&p)			Total
		UK	Europe	World	
	The Alien's Guide to Britain	£6.95	£8.95	£12.45	
	The Alien's Guide to France	£6.95	£8.95	£12.45	
	The Best Places to Buy a Home in France	£13.95	£15.95	£19.45	
	The Best Places to Buy a Home in Spain	£13.95	£15.95	£19.45	
	Buying a Home Abroad	£13.95	£15.95	£19.45	
	Buying a Home in Australia & NZ	£13.95	£15.95	£19.45	
	Buying a Home in Cyprus	£13.95	£15.95	£19.45	
	Buying a Home in Florida	£13.95	£15.95	£19.45	
	Buying a Home in France	£13.95	£15.95	£19.45	
	Buying a Home in Greece	£13.95	£15.95	£19.45	
	Buying a Home in Ireland	£11.95	£13.95	£17.45	
	Buying a Home in Italy	£13.95	£15.95	£19.45	
	Buying a Home in Portugal	£13.95	£15.95	£19.45	
	Buying a Home in South Africa	£13.95	£15.95	£19.45	
	Buying a Home in Spain	£13.95	£15.95	£19.45	
	Buying, Letting & Selling Property	£11.95	£13.95	£17.45	
	Earning Money From Your French Home	£13.95	£13.95	£17.45	
	Earning Money From Your Spanish Home	£13.95	£15.95	£19.45	
	Foreigners in France: Triumphs & Disasters	£11.95	£15.95	£19.45	
	Foreigners in Spain: Triumphs & Disasters	£11.95	£13.95	£17.45	
	Costa Blanca Lifeline	£11.95	£13.95	£17.45	
	Costa del Sol Lifeline	£11.95	£13.95	£17.45	
	Dordogne/Lot Lifeline	£11.95	£13.95	£17.45	
	Normandy Lifeline	£11.95	£13.95	£17.45	
	Poitou-Charentes Lifeline	£11.95	£13.95	£17.45	
	Provence-Côte d'Azur Lifeline	£11.95	£13.95	£17.45	
	Living & Working Abroad	£14.95	£16.95	£20.45	
	Living & Working in America	£16.95	£18.95	£22.45	
	Living & Working in Australia	£16.95	£18.95	£22.45	
	Living & Working in Britain	£16.95	£18.95	£22.45	
	Living & Working in Canada	£16.95	£18.95	£22.45	
	Living & Working in the European Union	£16.95	£18.95	£22.45	
	Living & Working in the Far East	£16.95	£18.95	£22.45	
	Total carried forward (see over)				

ORDER FORM

Qty.	Title	UK	Europe	World	Total
		Total brought forward			
		Price (incl. p&p)			
	Living & Working in France	£16.95	£18.95	£22.45	
	Living & Working in Germany	£16.95	£18.95	£22.45	
	L&W in the Gulf States & Saudi Arabia	£16.95	£18.95	£22.45	
	L&W in Holland, Belgium & Luxembourg	£14.95	£16.95	£20.45	
	Living & Working in Ireland	£14.95	£16.95	£20.45	
	Living & Working in Italy	£16.95	£18.95	£22.45	
	Living & Working in London	£13.95	£15.95	£19.45	
	Living & Working in New Zealand	£16.95	£18.95	£22.45	
	Living & Working in Spain	£16.95	£18.95	£22.45	
	Living & Working in Switzerland	£16.95	£18.95	£22.45	
	Making a Living in France	£13.95	£15.95	£19.45	
	Making a Living in Spain	£13.95	£15.95	£19.45	
	Renovating & Maintaining Your French Home	£16.95	£18.95	£22.45	
	Retiring Abroad	£14.95	£16.95	£20.45	
	Shooting Caterpillars in Spain	£9.95	£11.95	£15.45	
	Surprised by France	£11.95	£13.95	£17.45	
				Grand Total	

Order your copies today by phone, fax, post or email from: Survival Books, PO Box 3780, YEOVIL, BA21 5WX, United Kingdom (☎/🖷 +44 (0)1935-700060, ✉ sales@survivalbooks.net, 🖳 www.survivalbooks.net). If you aren't entirely satisfied, simply return them to us within 14 days for a full and unconditional refund.

I enclose a cheque for the grand total/Please charge my Amex/Delta/Maestro (Switch)/MasterCard/Visa card as follows. (delete as applicable)

Card No. _ _ _ _ _ _ _ _ _ _ _ _ _ _ _ _ Security Code* _ _ _

Expiry date ________ Issue number (Maestro/Switch only) ________

Signature ________________ Tel. No. ________________

NAME ______________________________

ADDRESS ______________________________

____

* The security code is the last three digits on the signature strip.